IN THE FLOOD™

FAWKES
LOUGHRIDGE
MAUER

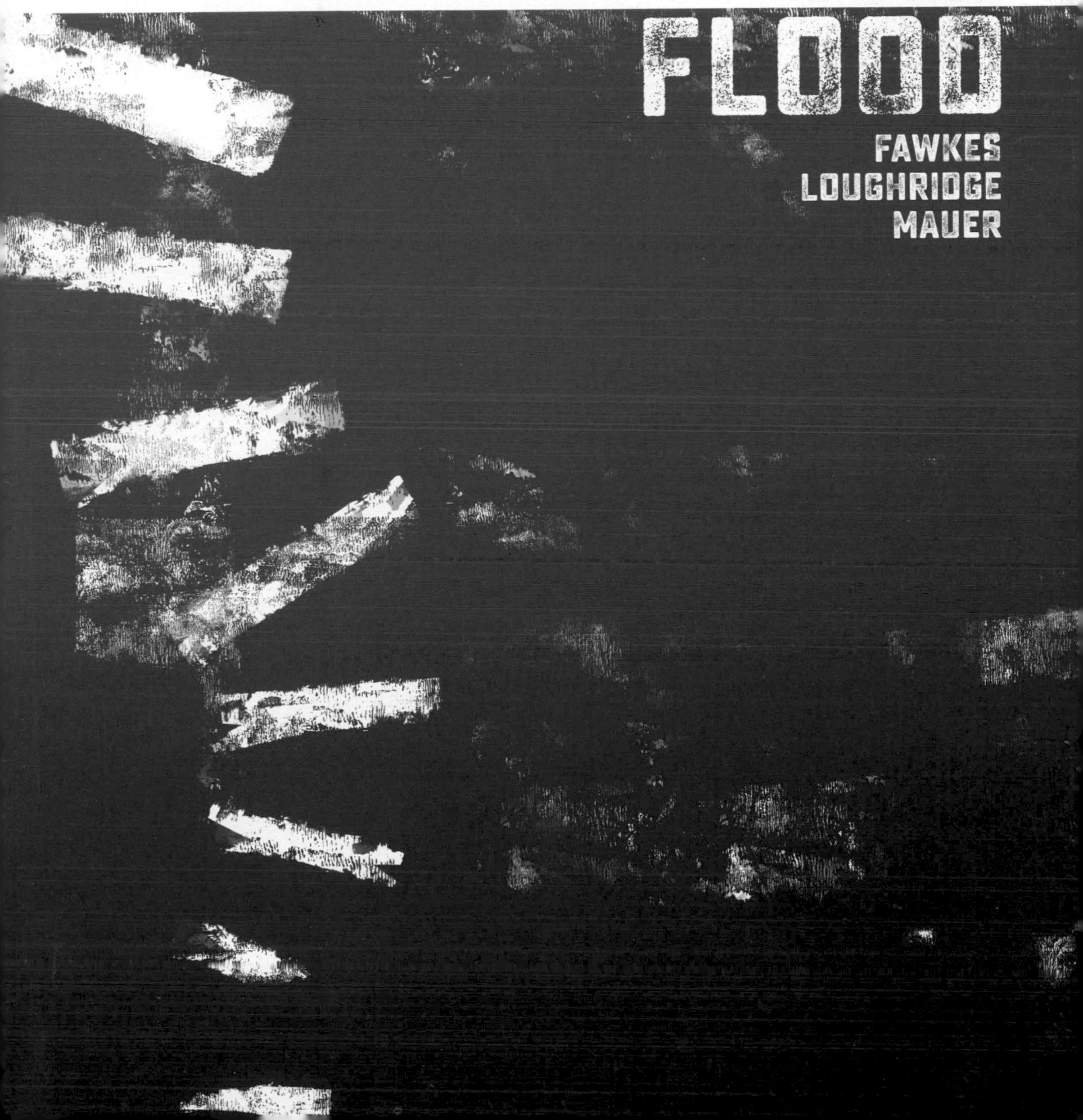

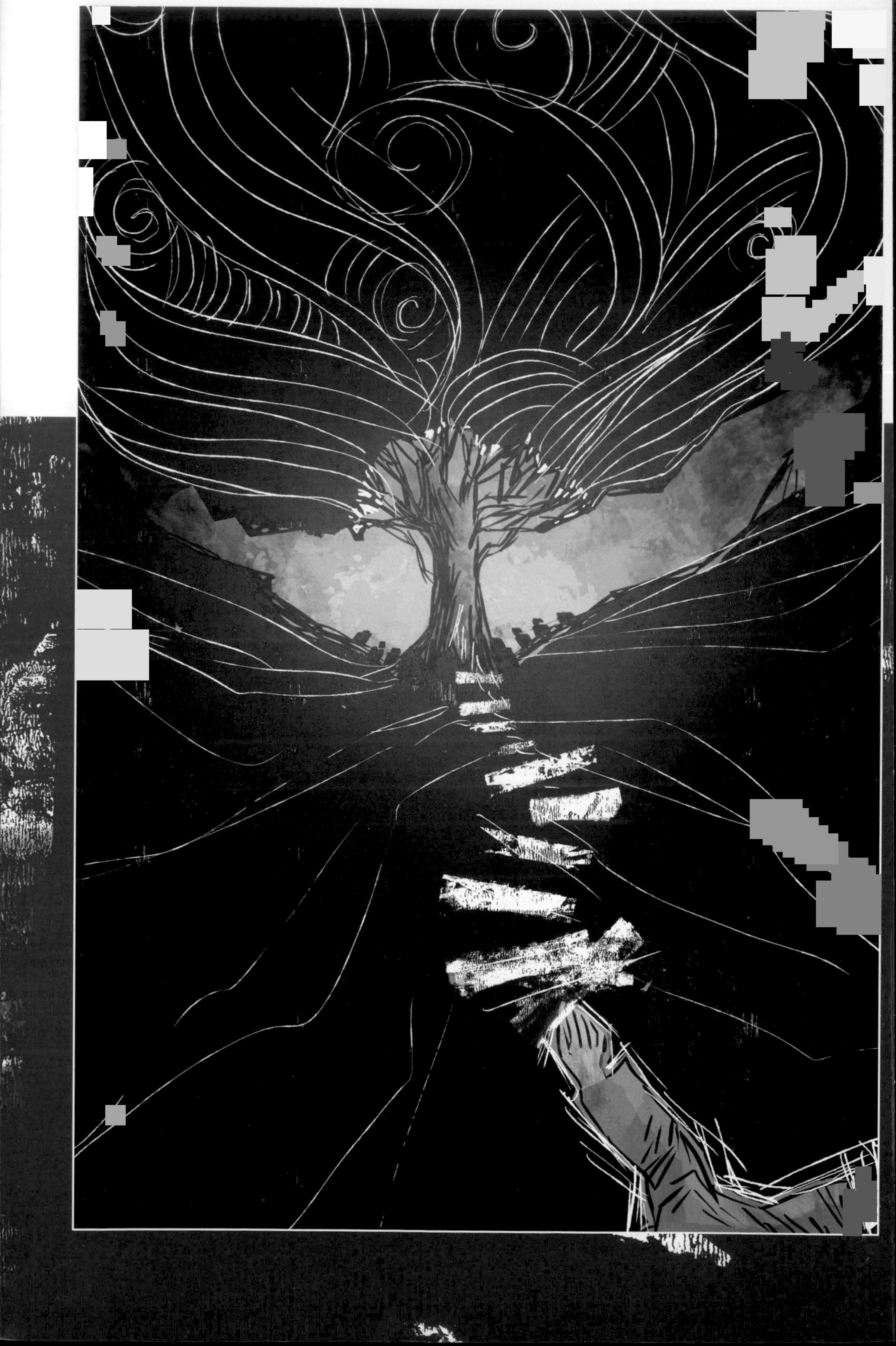

IN THE FLOOD

WRITER & ARTIST
RAY FAWKES

COLORIST
LEE LOUGHRIDGE

LETTERER &
ORIGINAL BOOK DESIGNER
THOMAS MAUER

CREATED BY
RAY FAWKES

DARK HORSE BOOKS

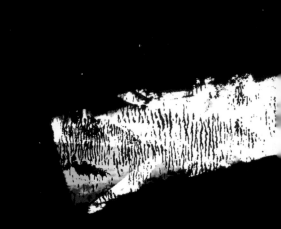

DARK HORSE TEAM

PRESIDENT AND PUBLISHER
MIKE RICHARDSON

EDITOR
DANIEL CHABON

ASSISTANT EDITORS
CHUCK HOWITT
KONNER KNUDSEN

DESIGNER
KATHLEEN BARNETT

DIGITAL ART TECHNICIAN
JASON RICKERD

SPECIAL THANKS TO:
DAVID STEINBERGER
CHIP MOSHER
BRYCE GOLD

NEIL HANKERSON EXECUTIVE VICE PRESIDENT / TOM WEDDLE CHIEF FINANCIAL OFFICER / DALE LAFOUNTAIN CHIEF INFORMATION OFFICER / TIM WIESCH VICE PRESIDENT OF LICENSING / MATT PARKINSON VICE PRESIDENT OF MARKETING / VANESSA TODD-HOLMES VICE PRESIDENT OF PRODUCTION AND SCHEDULING / MARK BERNARDI VICE PRESIDENT OF BOOK TRADE AND DIGITAL SALES / RANDY LAHRMAN VICE PRESIDENT OF PRODUCT DEVELOPMENT / KEN LIZZI GENERAL COUNSEL / DAVE MARSHALL EDITOR IN CHIEF / DAVEY ESTRADA EDITORIAL DIRECTOR / CHRIS WARNER SENIOR BOOKS EDITOR / CARY GRAZZINI DIRECTOR OF SPECIALTY PROJECTS / LIA RIBACCHI ART DIRECTOR / MATT DRYER DIRECTOR OF DIGITAL ART AND PREPRESS / MICHAEL GOMBOS SENIOR DIRECTOR OF LICENSED PUBLICATIONS / KARI YADRO DIRECTOR OF CUSTOM PROGRAMS / KARI TORSON DIRECTOR OF INTERNATIONAL LICENSING

PUBLISHED BY DARK HORSE BOOKS
A DIVISION OF DARK HORSE COMICS LLC
10956 SE MAIN STREET
MILWAUKIE, OR 97222

FIRST EDITION: MARCH 2022

TRADE PAPERBACK ISBN: 978-1-50672-469-0

10 9 8 7 6 5 4 3 2 1

PRINTED IN CHINA

COMIC SHOP LOCATOR SERVICE: COMICSHOPLOCATOR.COM

CHAPTER 1

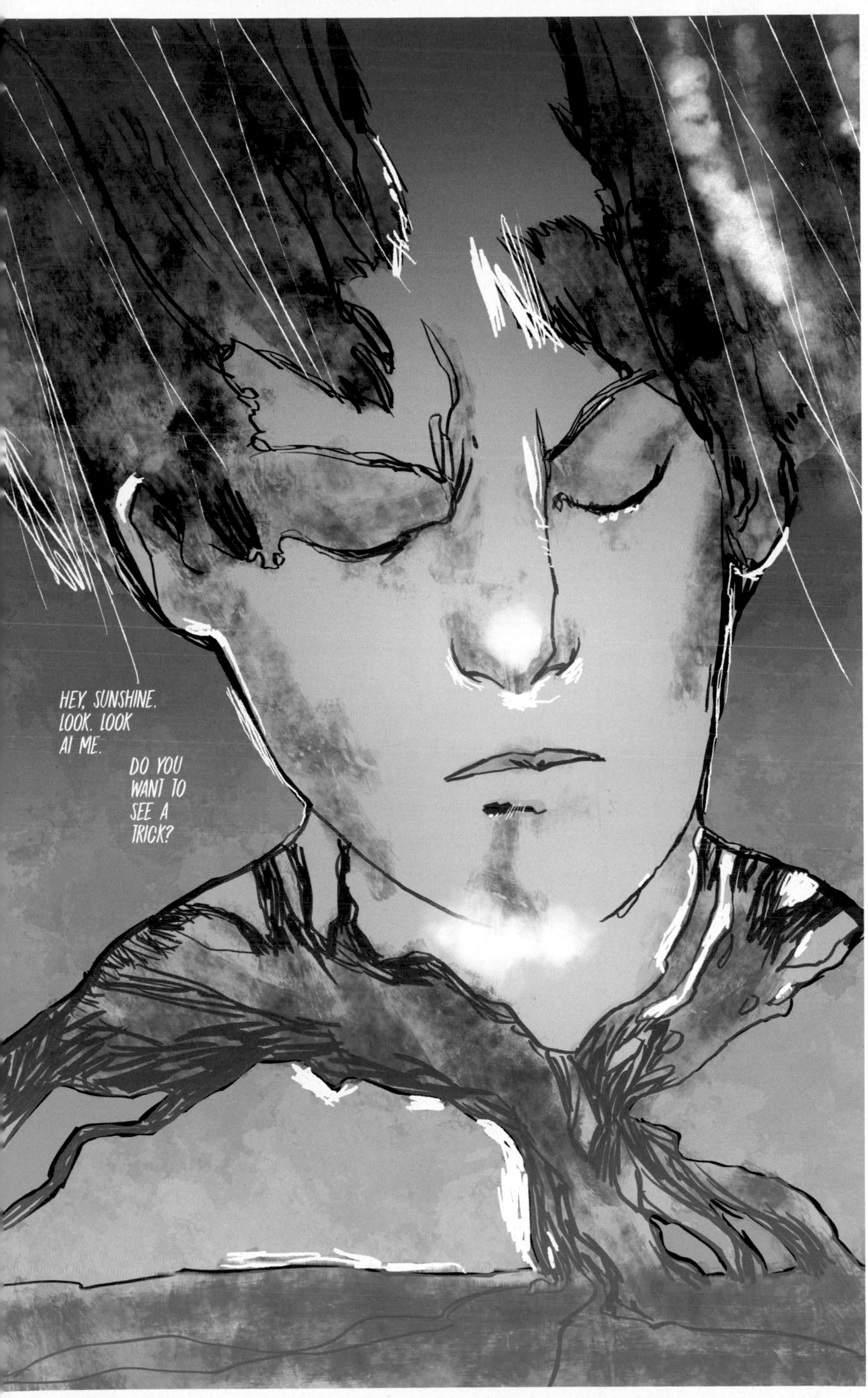
HEY, SUNSHINE. LOOK. LOOK AT ME.
DO YOU WANT TO SEE A TRICK?

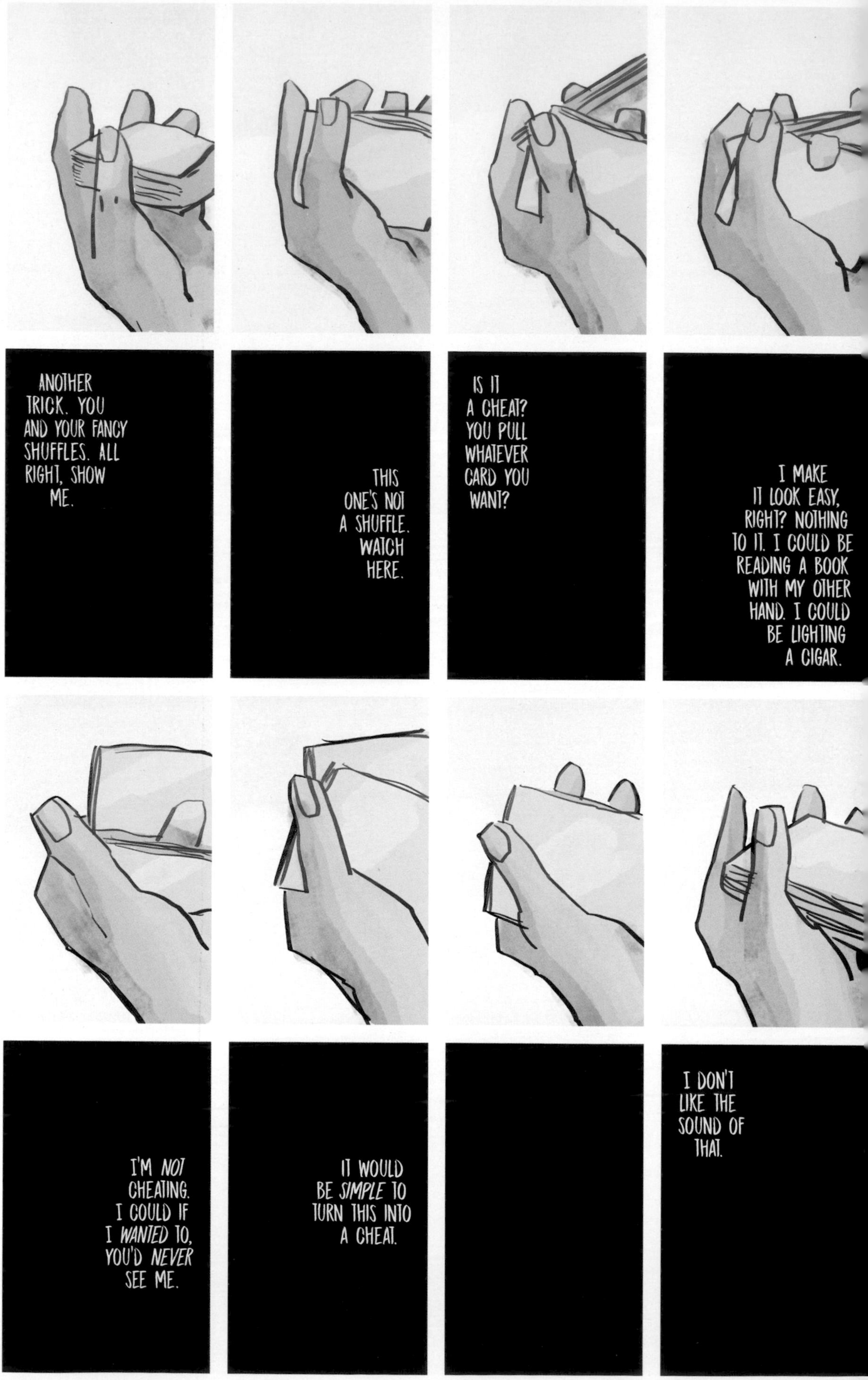
ANOTHER TRICK. YOU AND YOUR FANCY SHUFFLES. ALL RIGHT, SHOW ME.
THIS ONE'S NOT A SHUFFLE. WATCH HERE.
IS IT A CHEAT? YOU PULL WHATEVER CARD YOU WANT?
I MAKE IT LOOK EASY, RIGHT? NOTHING TO IT. I COULD BE READING A BOOK WITH MY OTHER HAND. I COULD BE LIGHTING A CIGAR.
I'M *NOT* CHEATING. I COULD IF I *WANTED* TO, YOU'D *NEVER* SEE ME.
IT WOULD BE *SIMPLE* TO TURN THIS INTO A CHEAT.
I DON'T LIKE THE SOUND OF THAT.

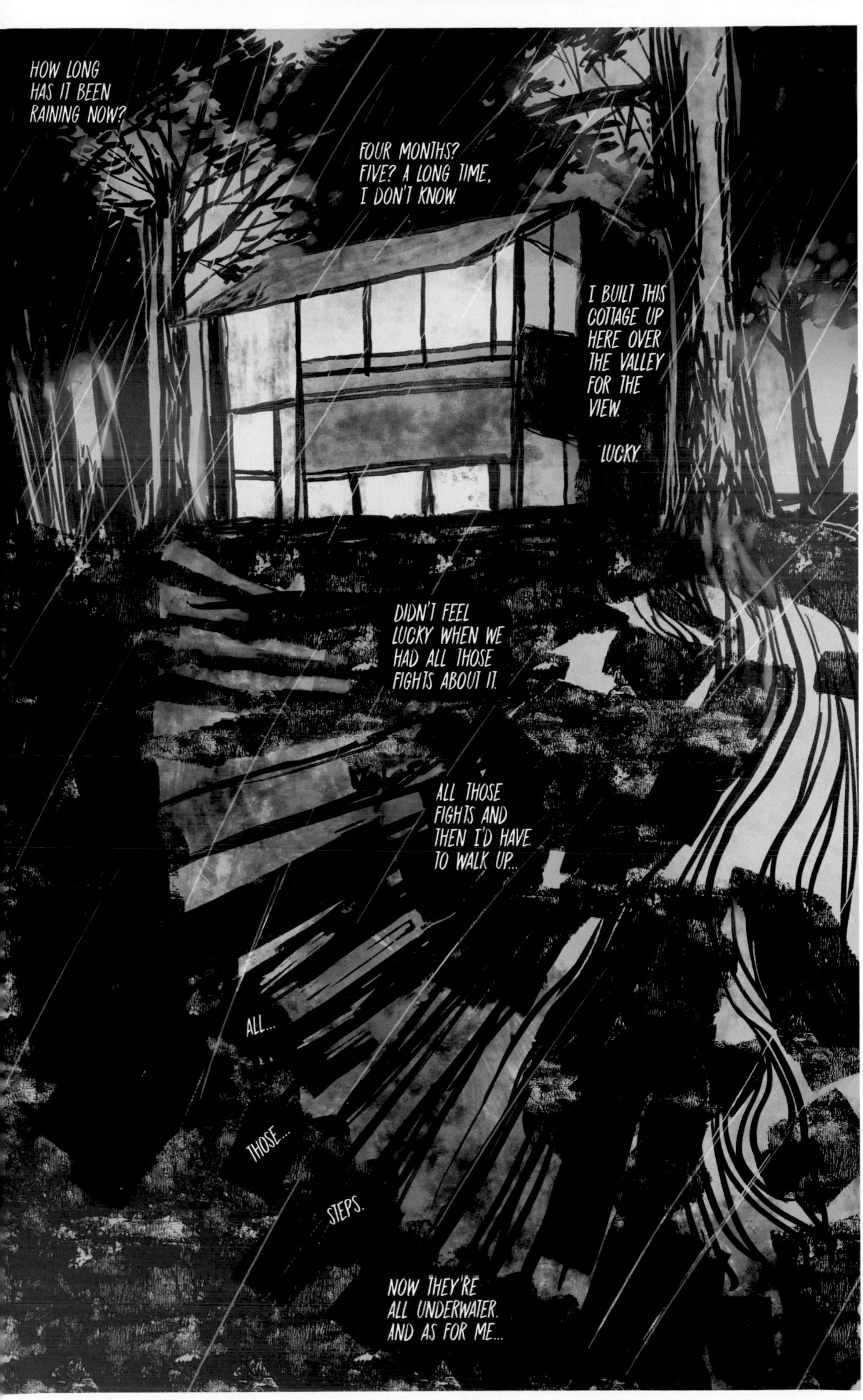
HOW LONG HAS IT BEEN RAINING NOW?
FOUR MONTHS? FIVE? A LONG TIME, I DON'T KNOW.
I BUILT THIS COTTAGE UP HERE OVER THE VALLEY FOR THE VIEW.
LUCKY.
DIDN'T FEEL LUCKY WHEN WE HAD ALL THOSE FIGHTS ABOUT IT.
ALL THOSE FIGHTS AND THEN I'D HAVE TO WALK UP...
ALL...
THOSE...
STEPS.
NOW THEY'RE ALL UNDERWATER. AND AS FOR ME...

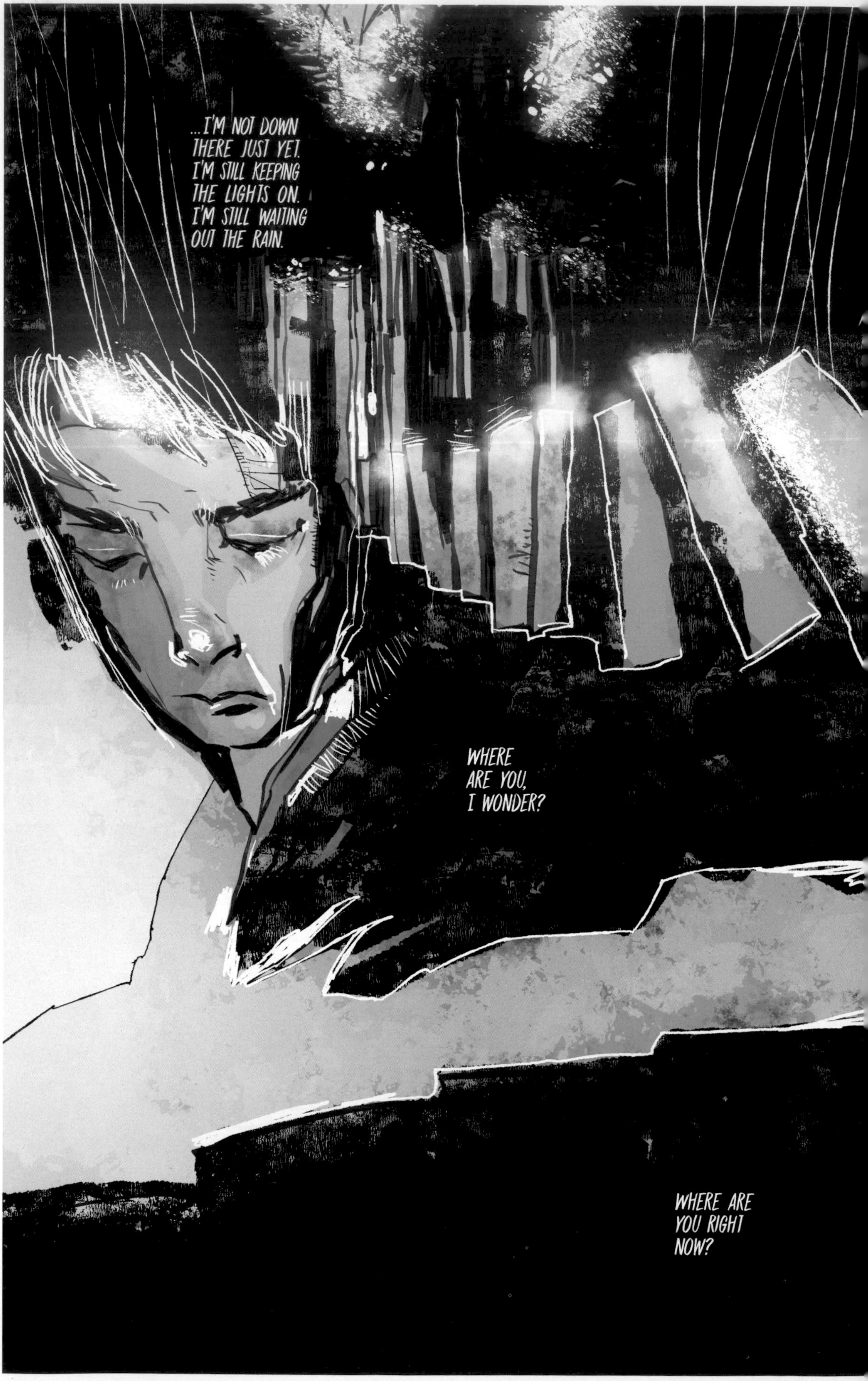
...I'M NOT DOWN THERE JUST YET. I'M STILL KEEPING THE LIGHTS ON. I'M STILL WAITING OUT THE RAIN.
WHERE ARE YOU, I WONDER?
WHERE ARE YOU RIGHT NOW?

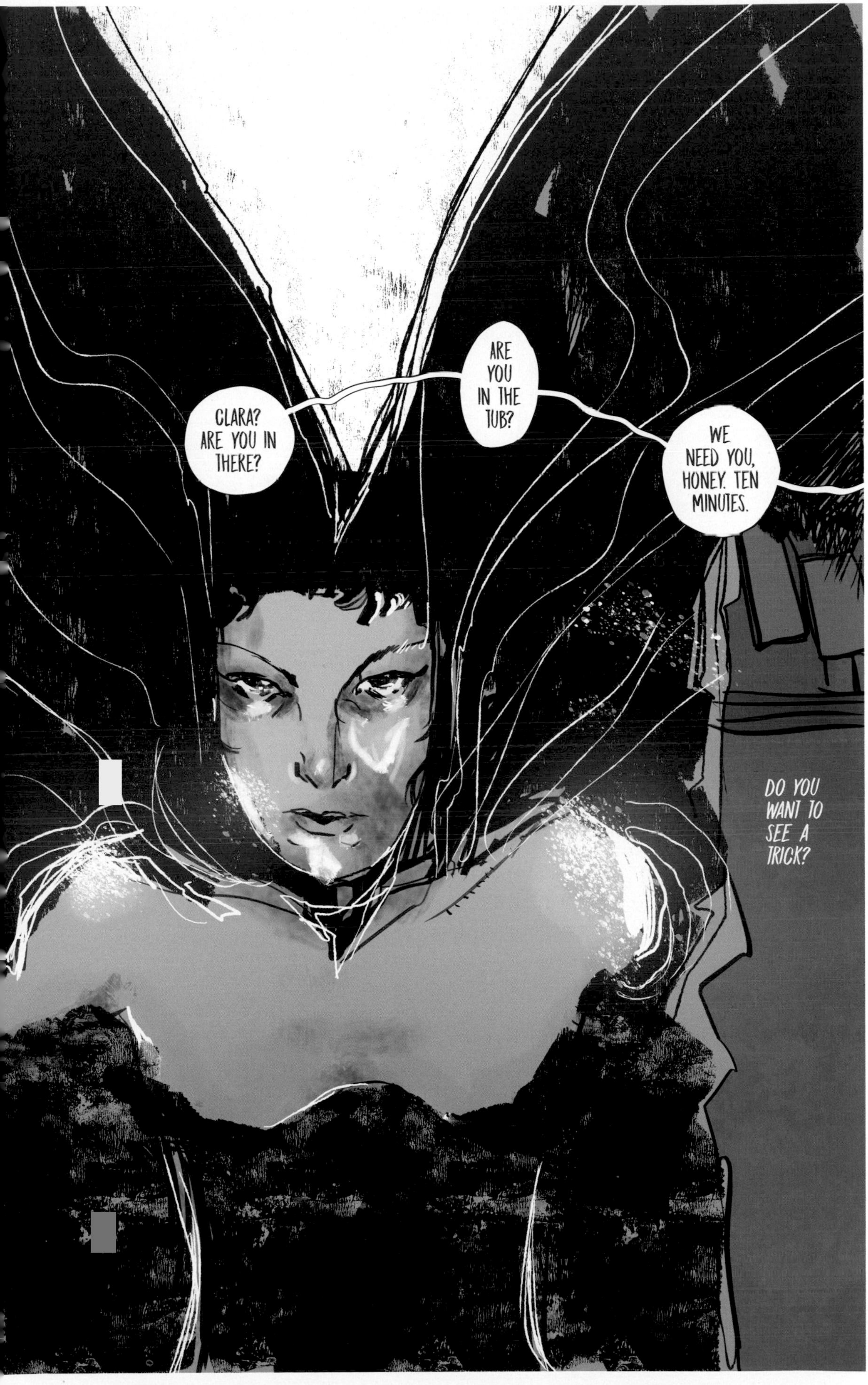
CLARA? ARE YOU IN THERE?
ARE YOU IN THE TUB?
WE NEED YOU, HONEY. TEN MINUTES.
DO YOU WANT TO SEE A TRICK?

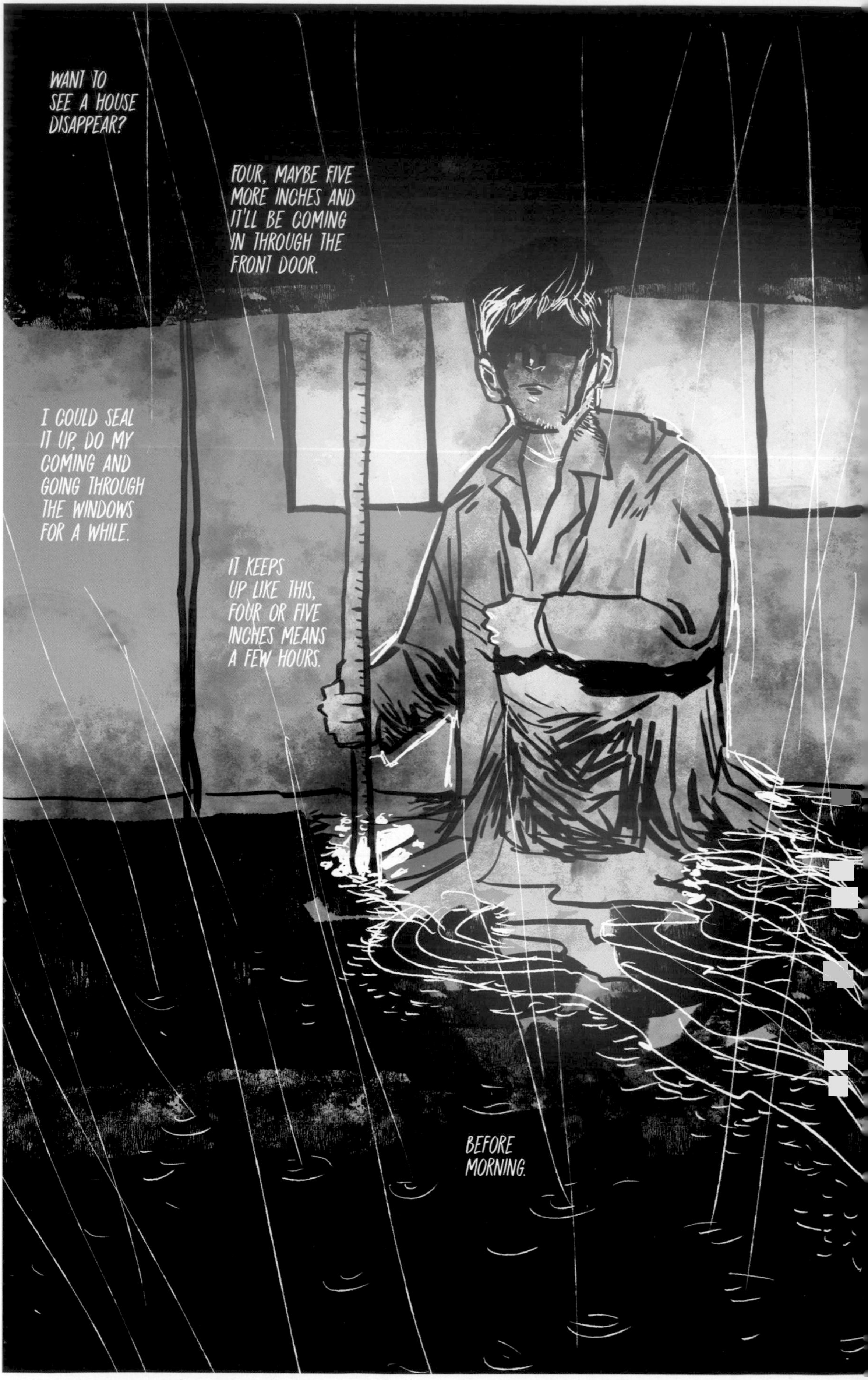
WANT TO SEE A HOUSE DISAPPEAR?
FOUR, MAYBE FIVE MORE INCHES AND IT'LL BE COMING IN THROUGH THE FRONT DOOR.
I COULD SEAL IT UP, DO MY COMING AND GOING THROUGH THE WINDOWS FOR A WHILE.
IT KEEPS UP LIKE THIS, FOUR OR FIVE INCHES MEANS A FEW HOURS.
BEFORE MORNING.

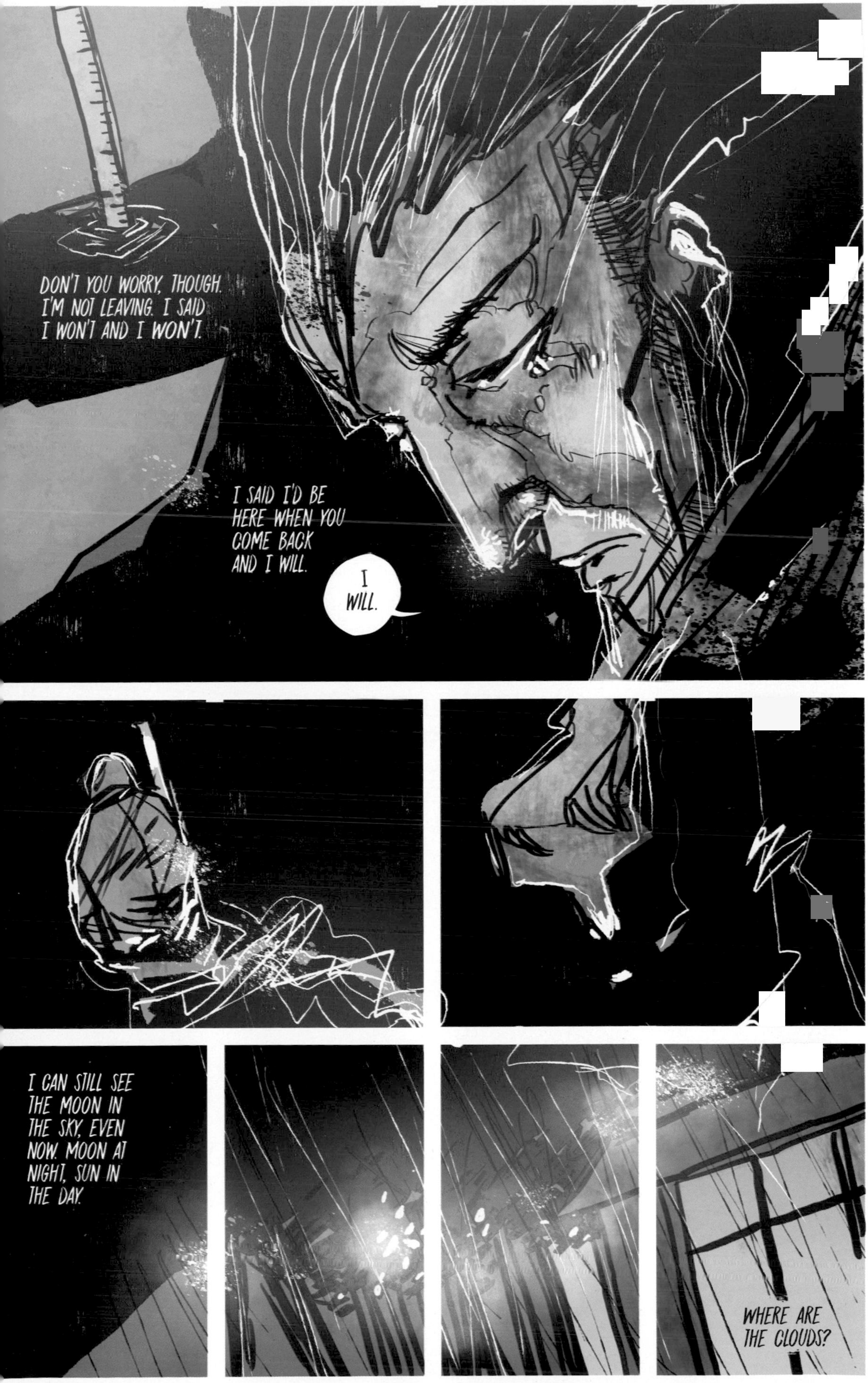

DON'T YOU WORRY, THOUGH. I'M NOT LEAVING. I SAID I WON'T AND I WON'T.
I SAID I'D BE HERE WHEN YOU COME BACK AND I WILL.
I WILL.
I CAN STILL SEE THE MOON IN THE SKY, EVEN NOW. MOON AT NIGHT, SUN IN THE DAY.
WHERE ARE THE CLOUDS?

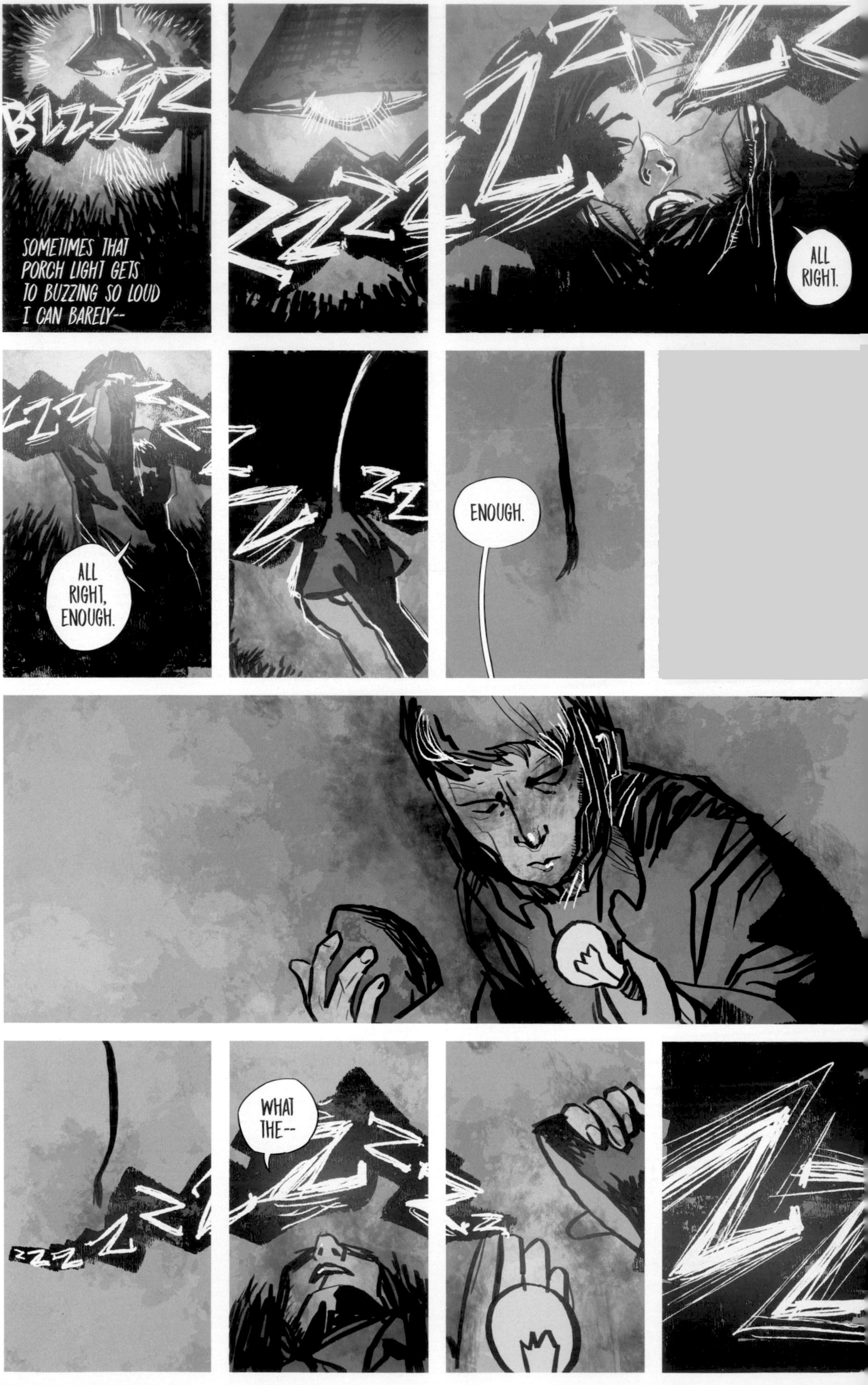
BZZZZZ
SOMETIMES THAT PORCH LIGHT GETS TO BUZZING SO LOUD I CAN BARELY--
ALL RIGHT.
ALL RIGHT, ENOUGH.
ENOUGH.
WHAT THE--

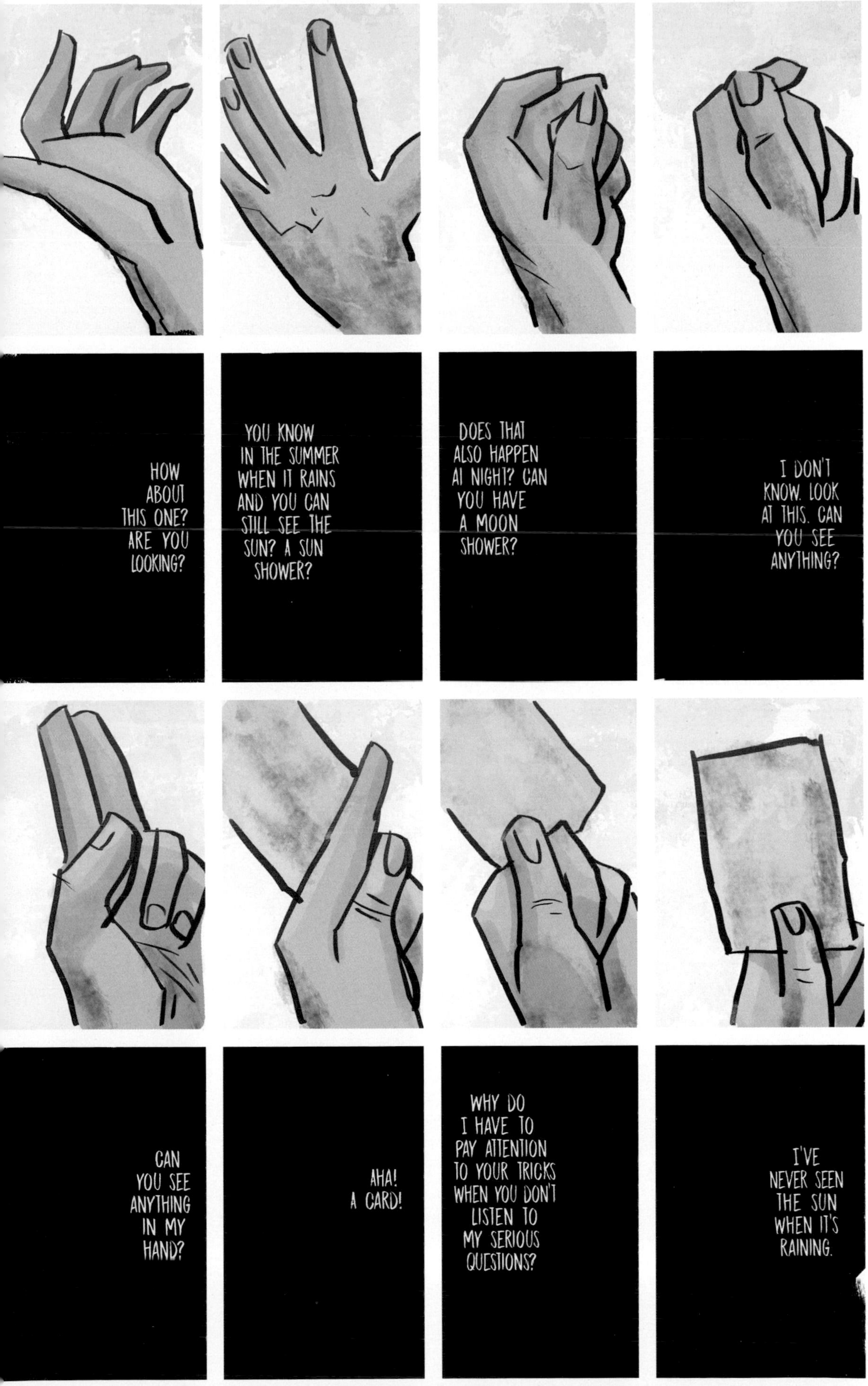
HOW ABOUT THIS ONE? ARE YOU LOOKING?
YOU KNOW IN THE SUMMER WHEN IT RAINS AND YOU CAN STILL SEE THE SUN? A SUN SHOWER?
DOES THAT ALSO HAPPEN AT NIGHT? CAN YOU HAVE A MOON SHOWER?
I DON'T KNOW. LOOK AT THIS. CAN YOU SEE ANYTHING?
CAN YOU SEE ANYTHING IN MY HAND?
AHA! A CARD!
WHY DO I HAVE TO PAY ATTENTION TO YOUR TRICKS WHEN YOU DON'T LISTEN TO MY SERIOUS QUESTIONS?
I'VE NEVER SEEN THE SUN WHEN IT'S RAINING.

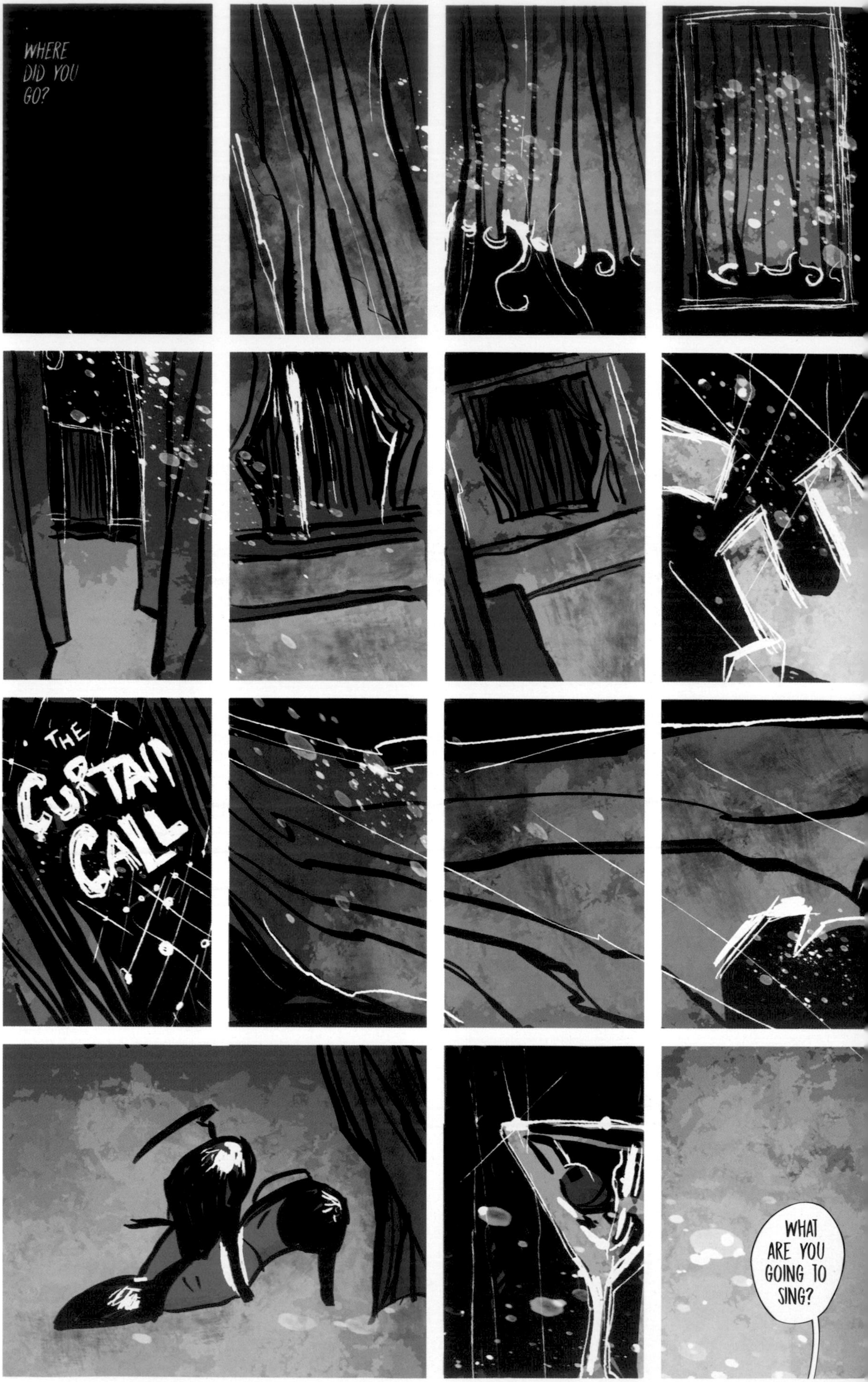
WHERE DID YOU GO?
THE CURTAIN CALL
WHAT ARE YOU GOING TO SING?

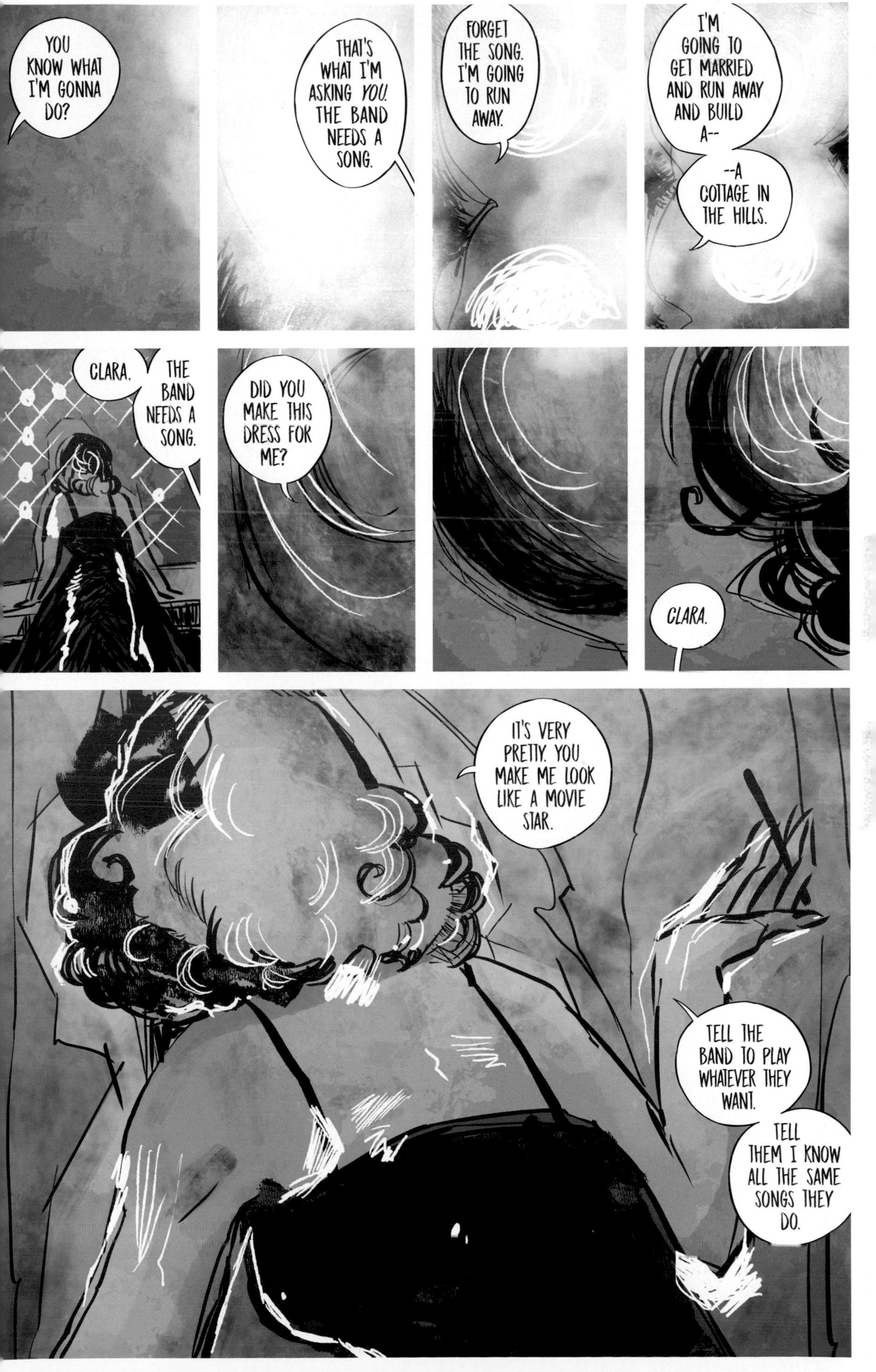
YOU KNOW WHAT I'M GONNA DO?
THAT'S WHAT I'M ASKING *YOU*. THE BAND NEEDS A SONG.
FORGET THE SONG. I'M GOING TO RUN AWAY.
I'M GOING TO GET MARRIED AND RUN AWAY AND BUILD A--
--A COTTAGE IN THE HILLS.
CLARA.
THE BAND NEEDS A SONG.
DID YOU MAKE THIS DRESS FOR ME?
CLARA.
IT'S VERY PRETTY. YOU MAKE ME LOOK LIKE A MOVIE STAR.
TELL THE BAND TO PLAY WHATEVER THEY WANT.
TELL THEM I KNOW ALL THE SAME SONGS THEY DO.

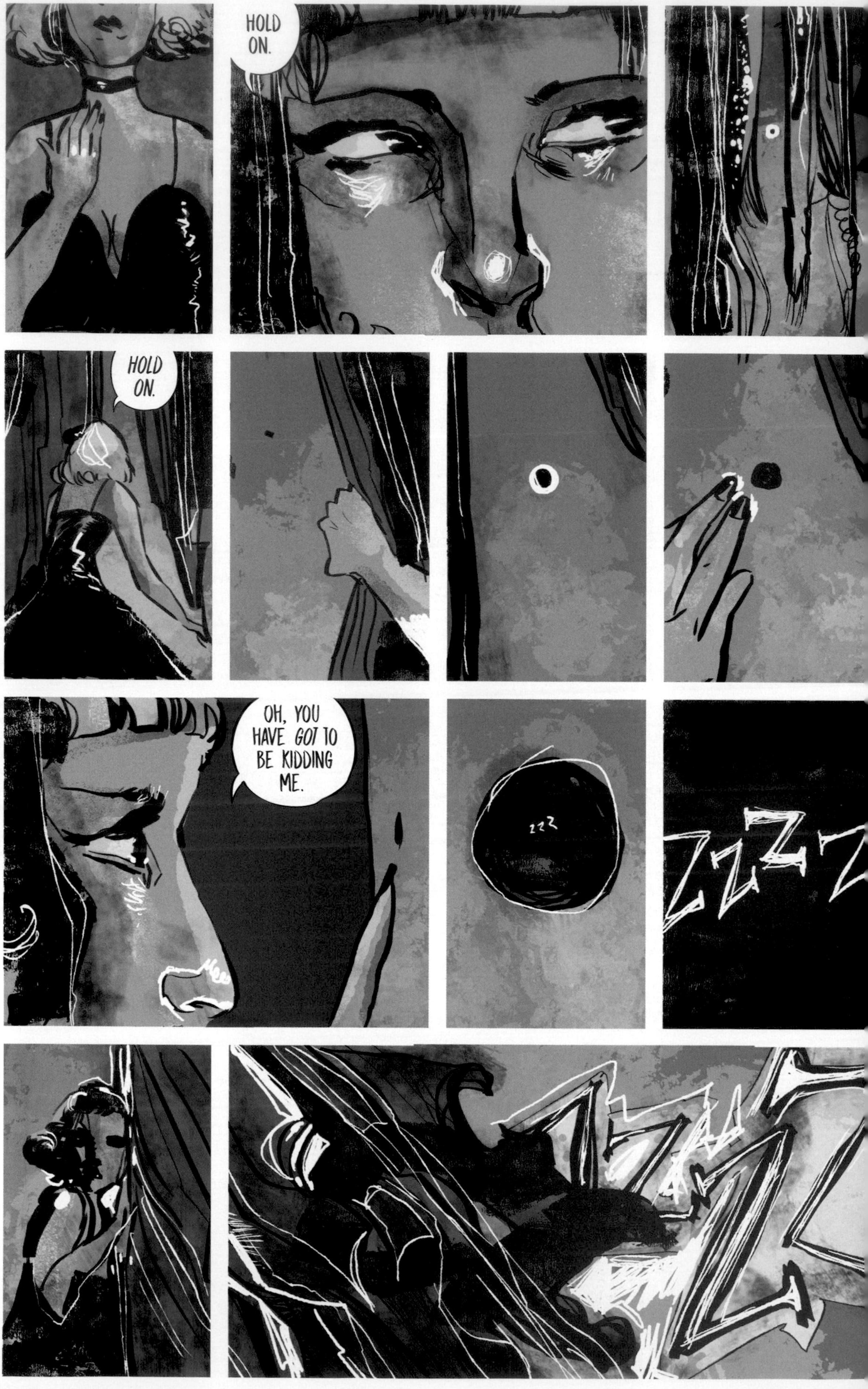
HOLD ON.
HOLD ON.
OH, YOU HAVE *GOT* TO BE KIDDING ME.
ZZZ
ZZZZ

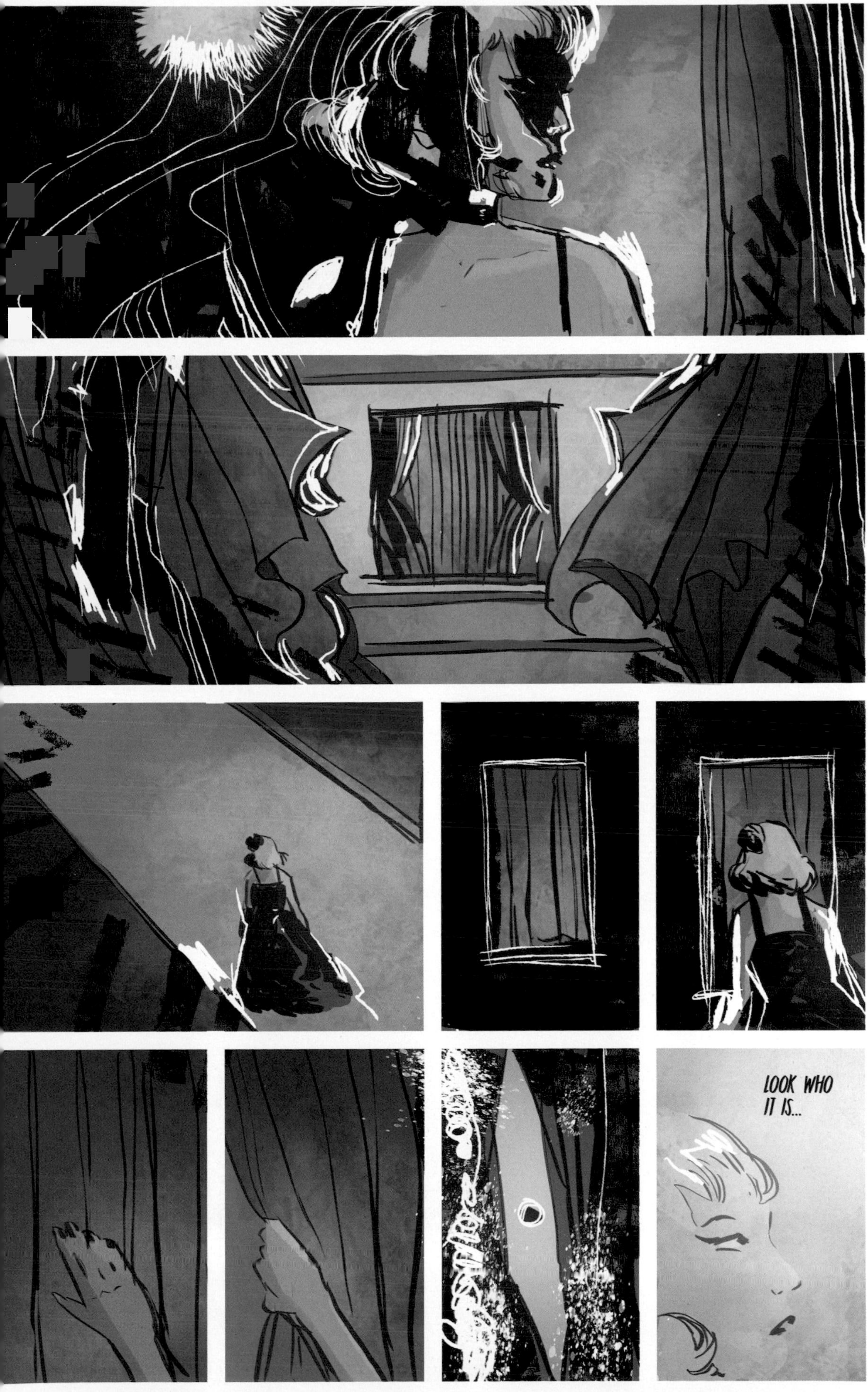
LOOK WHO IT IS...

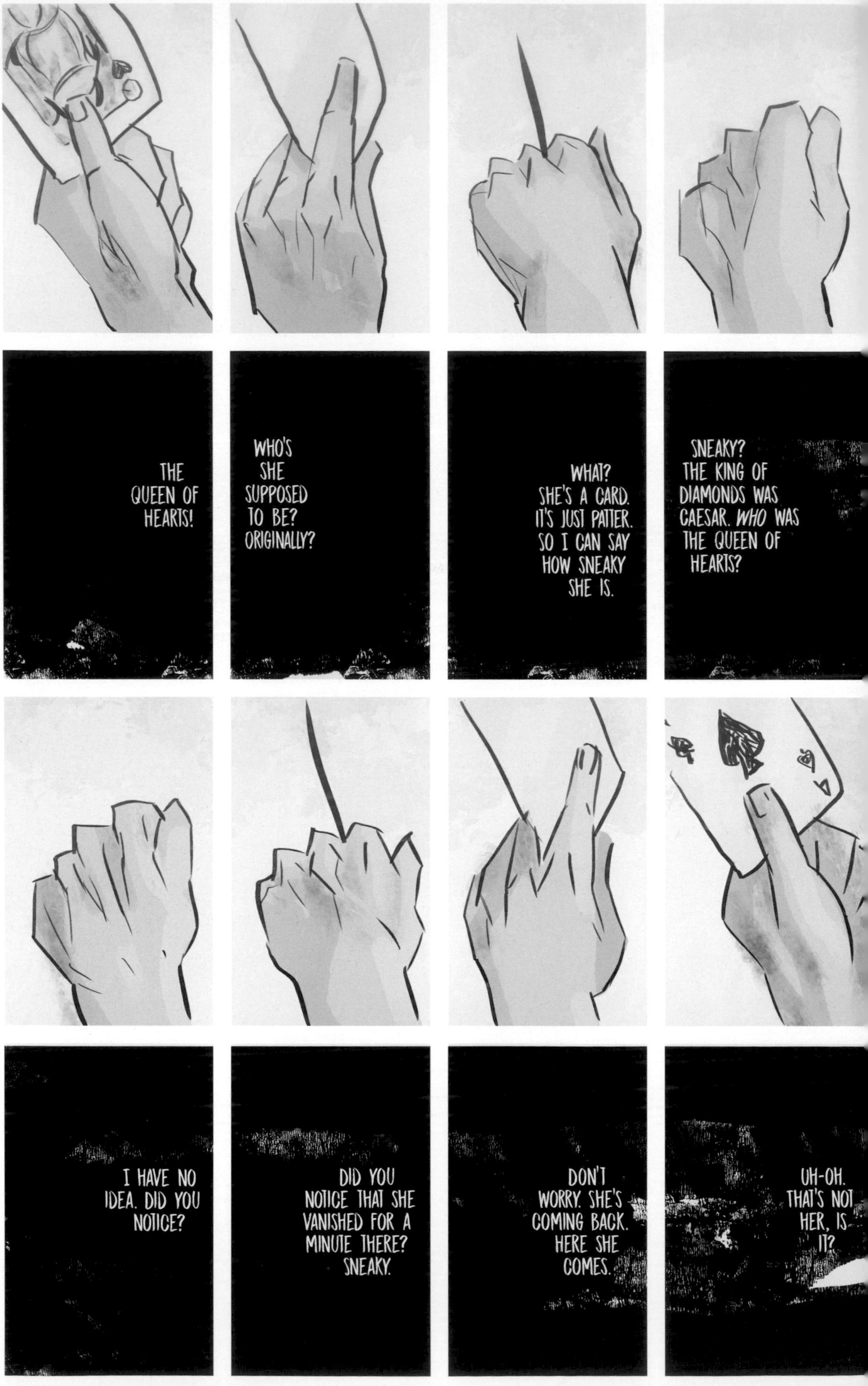
THE QUEEN OF HEARTS!
WHO'S SHE SUPPOSED TO BE? ORIGINALLY?
WHAT? SHE'S A CARD. IT'S JUST PATTER. SO I CAN SAY HOW SNEAKY SHE IS.
SNEAKY? THE KING OF DIAMONDS WAS CAESAR. *WHO* WAS THE QUEEN OF HEARTS?
I HAVE NO IDEA. DID YOU NOTICE?
DID YOU NOTICE THAT SHE VANISHED FOR A MINUTE THERE? SNEAKY.
DON'T WORRY. SHE'S COMING BACK. HERE SHE COMES.
UH-OH. THAT'S NOT HER, IS IT?

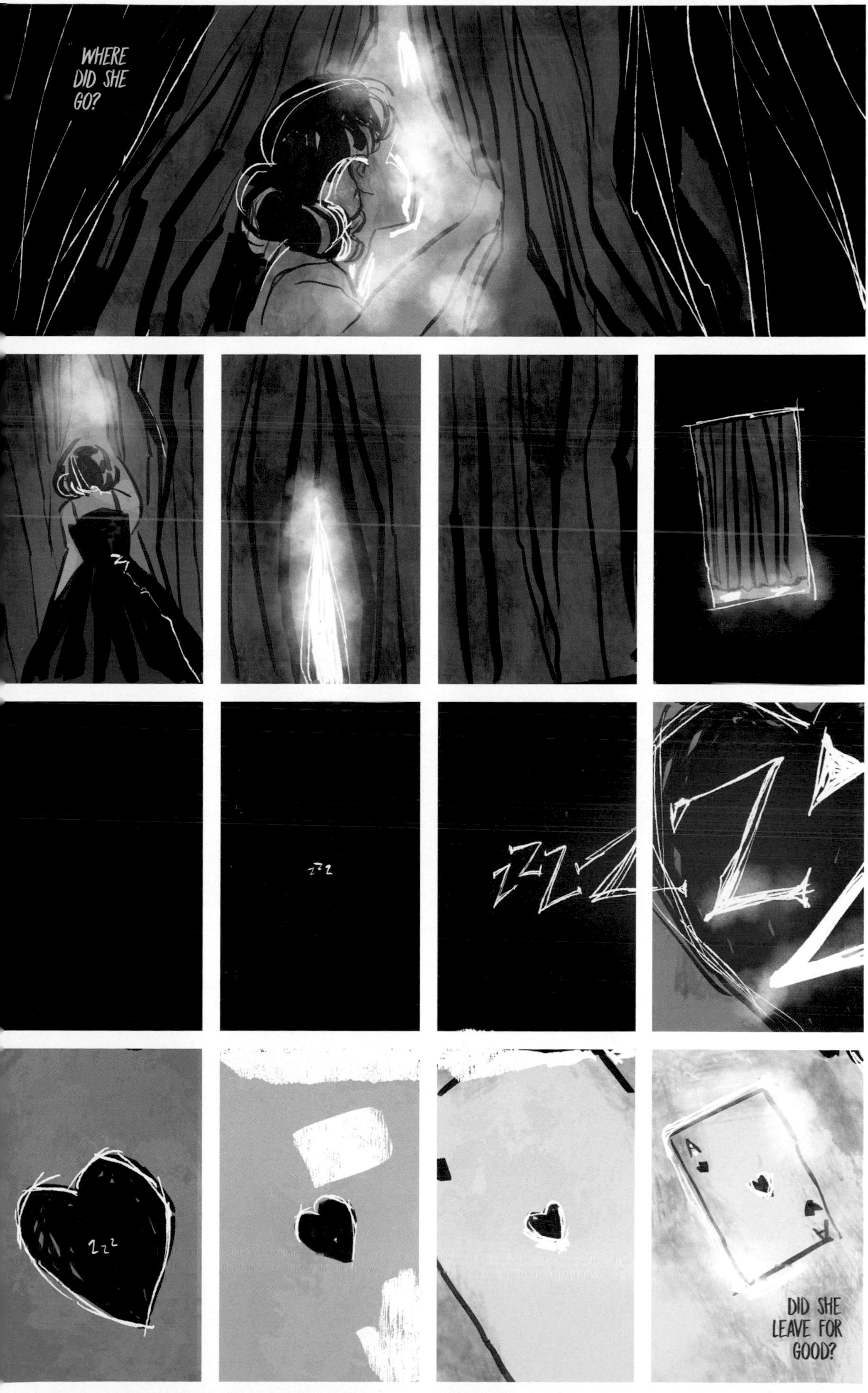
WHERE DID SHE GO?
DID SHE LEAVE FOR GOOD?

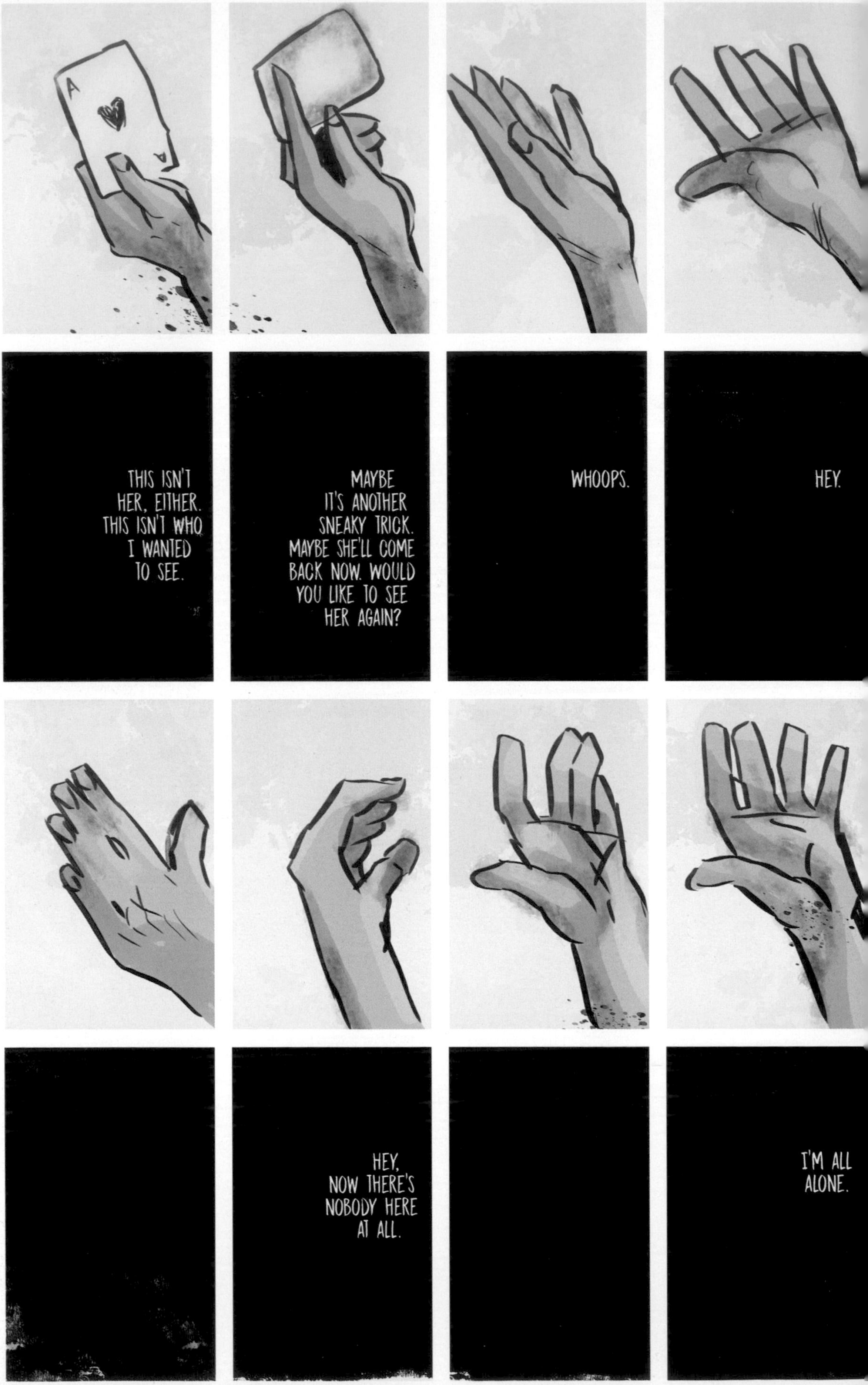
THIS ISN'T HER, EITHER. THIS ISN'T WHO I WANTED TO SEE.
MAYBE IT'S ANOTHER SNEAKY TRICK. MAYBE SHE'LL COME BACK NOW. WOULD YOU LIKE TO SEE HER AGAIN?
WHOOPS.
HEY.
HEY, NOW THERE'S NOBODY HERE AT ALL.
I'M ALL ALONE.

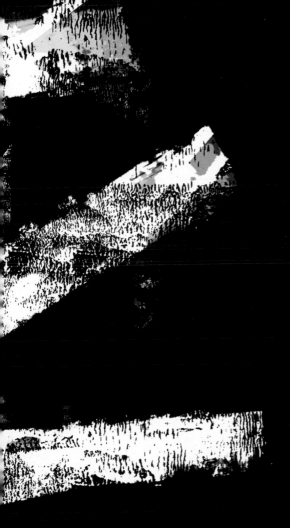

CHAPTER 2

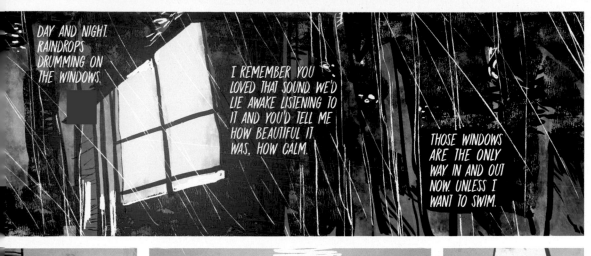

DAY AND NIGHT. RAINDROPS DRUMMING ON THE WINDOWS.

I REMEMBER YOU LOVED THAT SOUND. WE'D LIE AWAKE LISTENING TO IT AND YOU'D TELL ME HOW BEAUTIFUL IT WAS, HOW CALM.

THOSE WINDOWS ARE THE ONLY WAY IN AND OUT NOW. UNLESS I WANT TO SWIM.

I KNOW YOU'LL FIND YOUR WAY BACK.

I KNOW IT.

I USED TO TELL YOU RIDDLES.

I USED TO SHOW YOU TRICKS. YOU'D PRETEND TO BE ANNOYED BUT I'D SEE YOU SMILE.

YOU CAN'T SEE ME, BUT I'M PRECIOUS TO YOU.

YOU CAN KILL ME WITHOUT DOING ANYTHING AT ALL.

WHAT AM I?

I DON'T NEED A DRINK. I DON'T NEED ANYTHING. I JUST NEED YOU.

I CAN WAIT.

ZZZ

MAYBE.

MAYBE JUST A LITTLE DRINK TO WARM UP.

THAT SOUND...

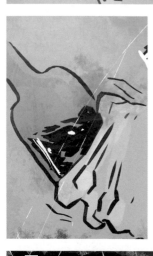

WHAT'S MAKING THAT SOUND?

SOMEBODY'S HERE.

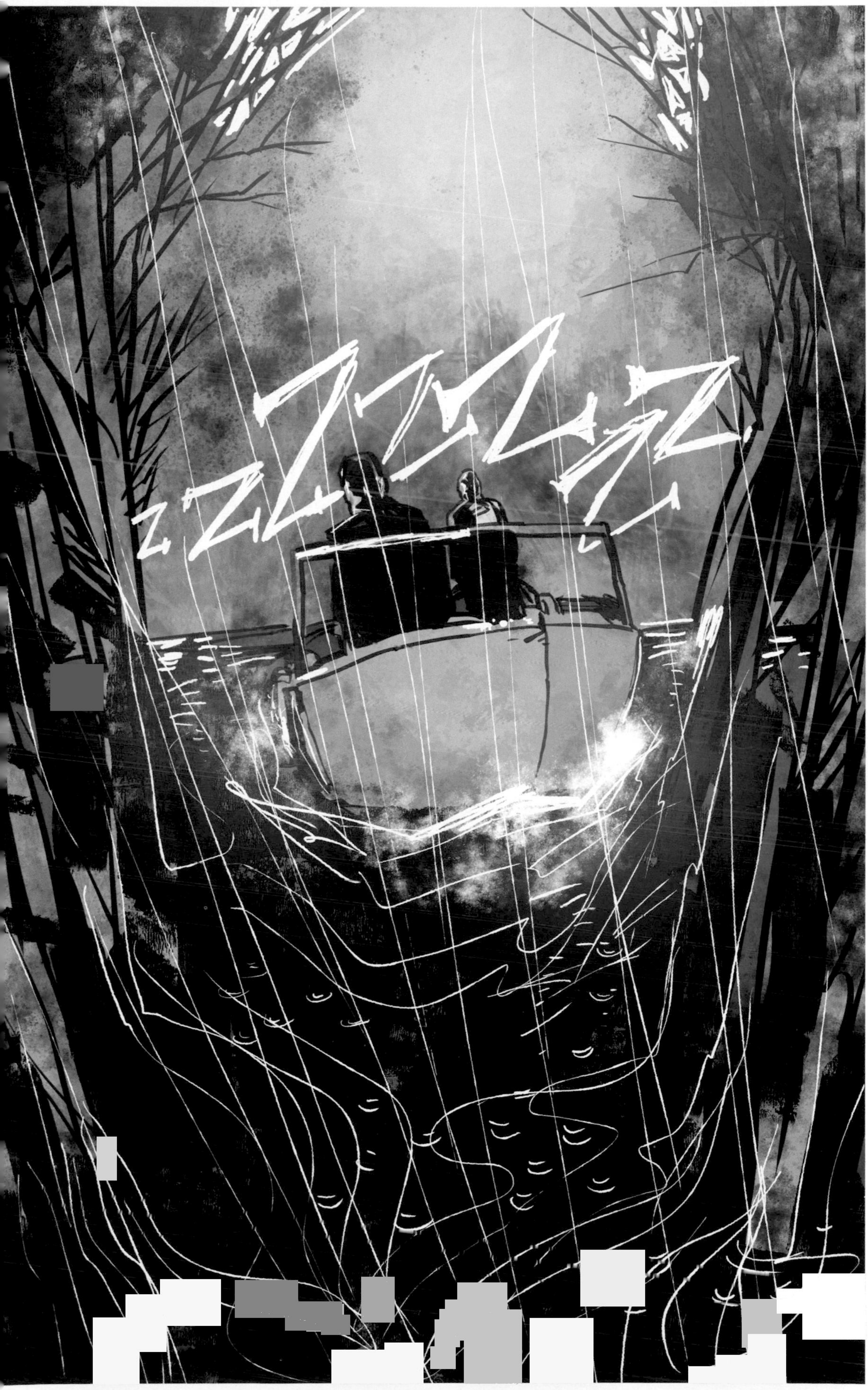

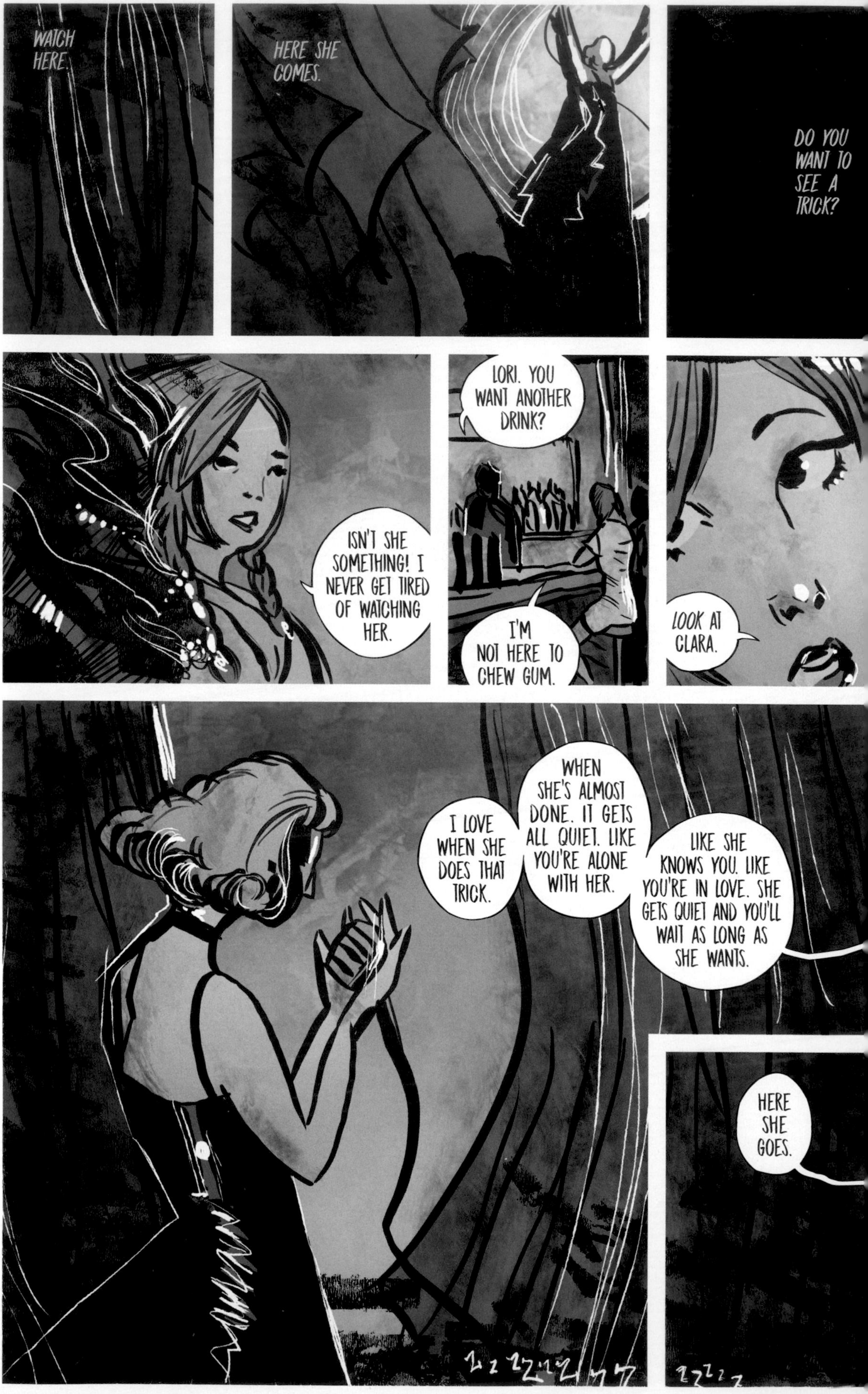
WATCH HERE.
HERE SHE COMES.
DO YOU WANT TO SEE A TRICK?
ISN'T SHE SOMETHING! I NEVER GET TIRED OF WATCHING HER.
LORI. YOU WANT ANOTHER DRINK?
I'M NOT HERE TO CHEW GUM.
LOOK AT CLARA.
I LOVE WHEN SHE DOES THAT TRICK.
WHEN SHE'S ALMOST DONE. IT GETS ALL QUIET. LIKE YOU'RE ALONE WITH HER.
LIKE SHE KNOWS YOU. LIKE YOU'RE IN LOVE. SHE GETS QUIET AND YOU'LL WAIT AS LONG AS SHE WANTS.
HERE SHE GOES.

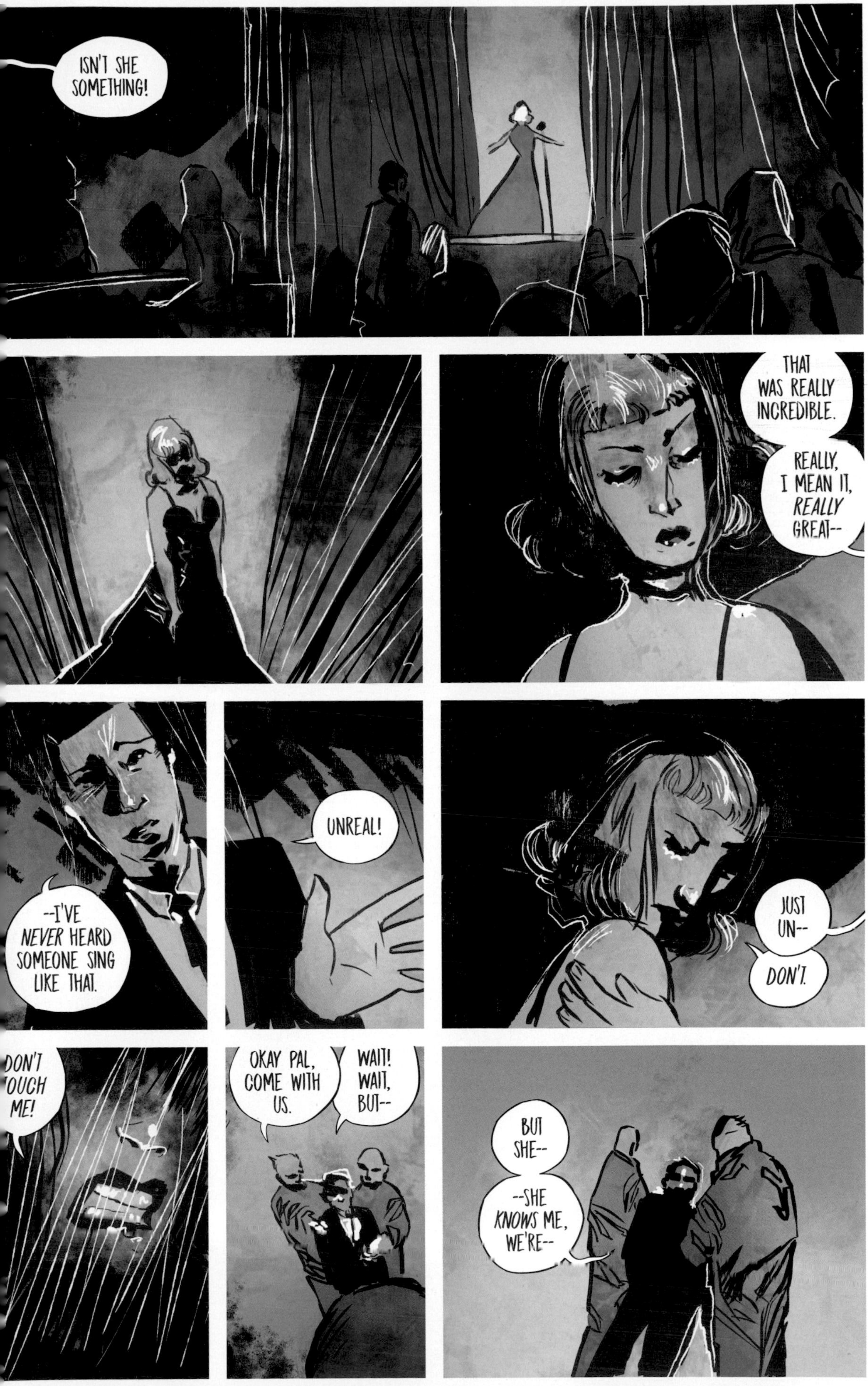
ISN'T SHE SOMETHING!
THAT WAS REALLY INCREDIBLE.
REALLY, I MEAN IT, *REALLY* GREAT--
--I'VE *NEVER* HEARD SOMEONE SING LIKE THAT.
UNREAL!
JUST UN--
DON'T.
DON'T TOUCH ME!
OKAY PAL, COME WITH US.
WAIT! WAIT, BUT--
BUT SHE--
--SHE *KNOWS* ME, WE'RE--

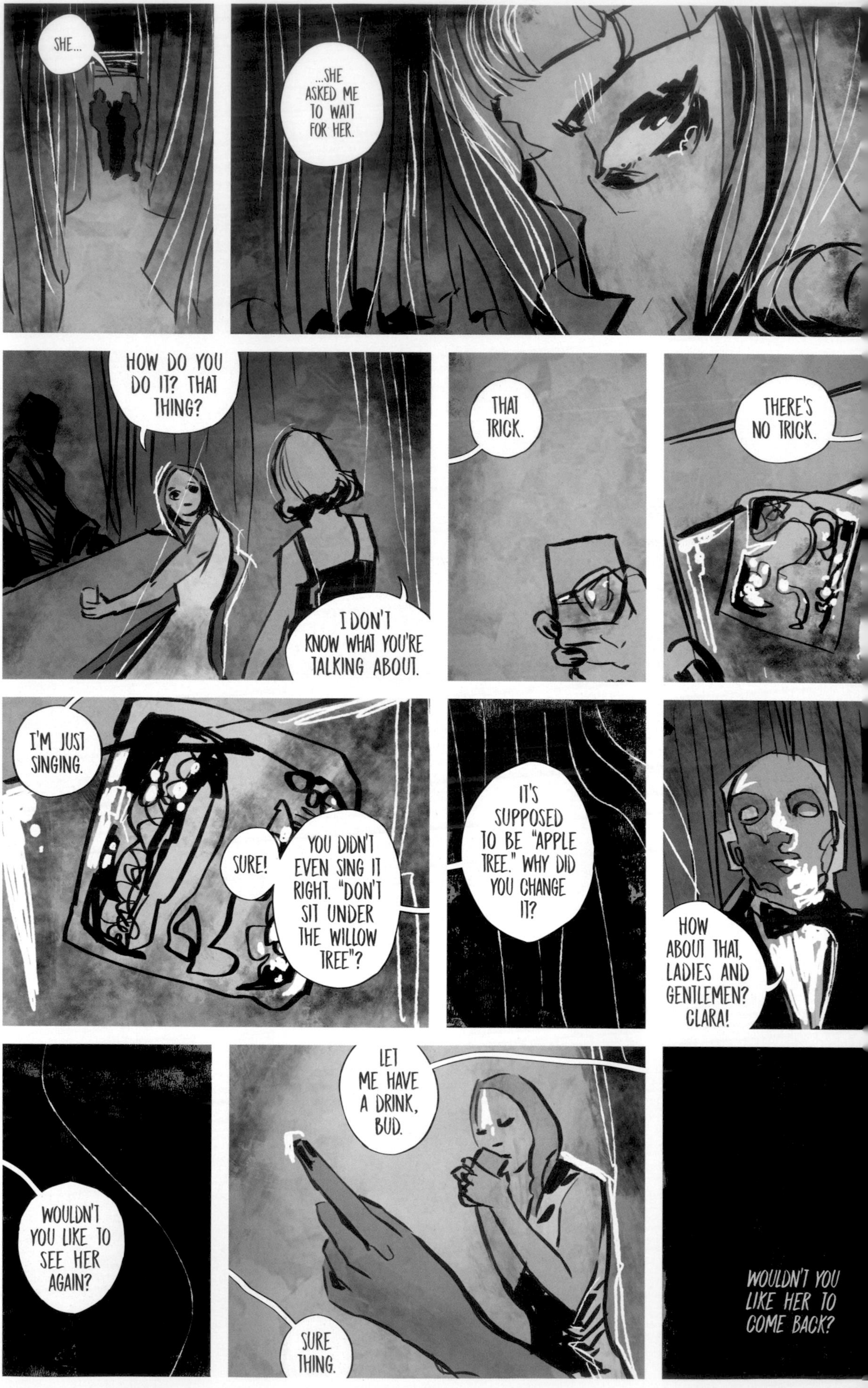
SHE...
...SHE ASKED ME TO WAIT FOR HER.
HOW DO YOU DO IT? THAT THING?
I DON'T KNOW WHAT YOU'RE TALKING ABOUT.
THAT TRICK.
THERE'S NO TRICK.
I'M JUST SINGING.
SURE!
YOU DIDN'T EVEN SING IT RIGHT. "DON'T SIT UNDER THE WILLOW TREE"?
IT'S SUPPOSED TO BE "APPLE TREE." WHY DID YOU CHANGE IT?
HOW ABOUT THAT, LADIES AND GENTLEMEN? CLARA!
WOULDN'T YOU LIKE TO SEE HER AGAIN?
LET ME HAVE A DRINK, BUD.
SURE THING.
WOULDN'T YOU LIKE HER TO COME BACK?

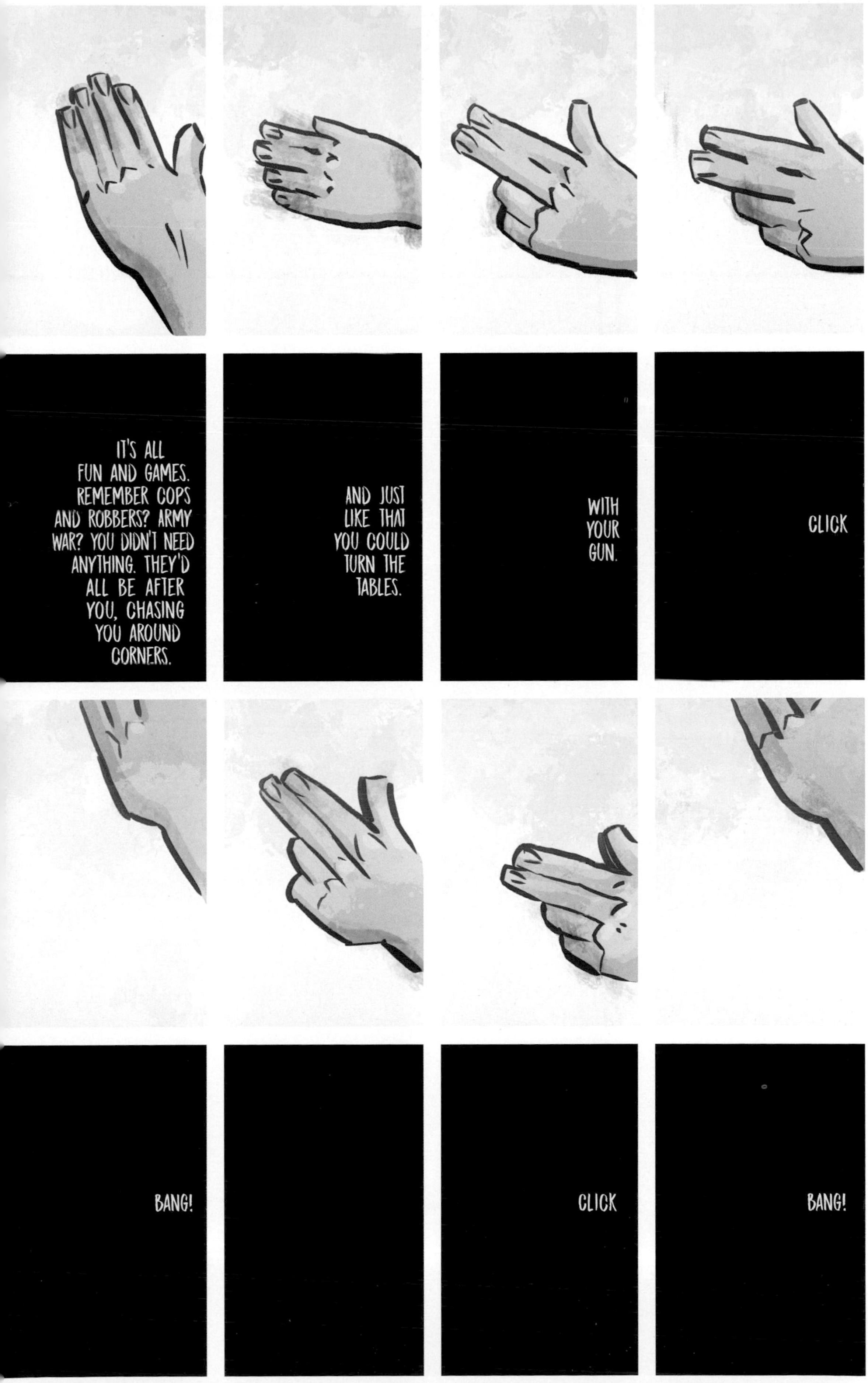
IT'S ALL FUN AND GAMES. REMEMBER COPS AND ROBBERS? ARMY WAR? YOU DIDN'T NEED ANYTHING. THEY'D ALL BE AFTER YOU, CHASING YOU AROUND CORNERS.
AND JUST LIKE THAT YOU COULD TURN THE TABLES.
WITH YOUR GUN.
CLICK
BANG!
CLICK
BANG!

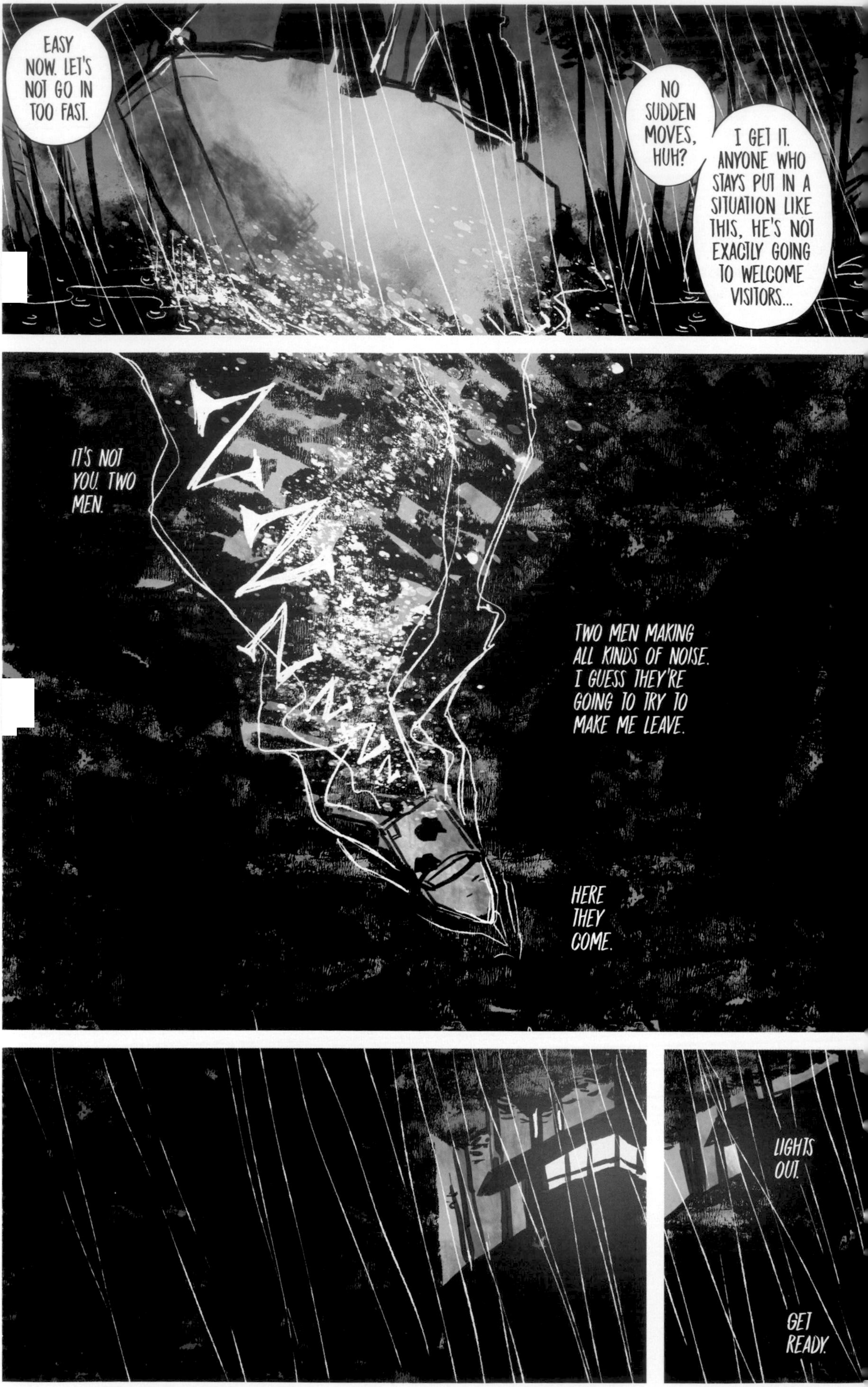
EASY NOW. LET'S NOT GO IN TOO FAST.
NO SUDDEN MOVES, HUH?
I GET IT. ANYONE WHO STAYS PUT IN A SITUATION LIKE THIS, HE'S NOT EXACTLY GOING TO WELCOME VISITORS...
IT'S NOT YOU. TWO MEN.
TWO MEN MAKING ALL KINDS OF NOISE. I GUESS THEY'RE GOING TO TRY TO MAKE ME LEAVE.
HERE THEY COME.
LIGHTS OUT.
GET READY.

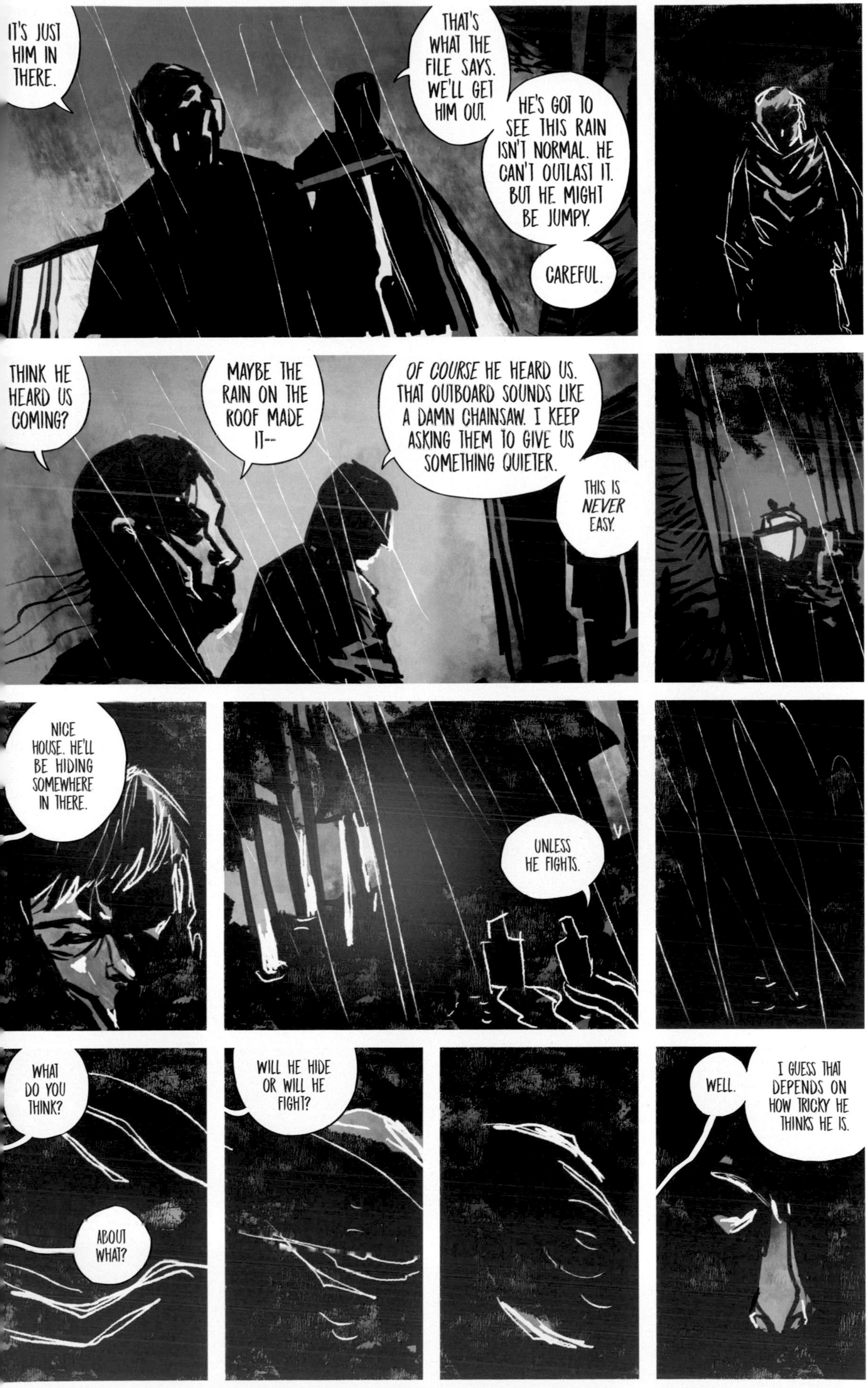
IT'S JUST HIM IN THERE.
THAT'S WHAT THE FILE SAYS. WE'LL GET HIM OUT.
HE'S GOT TO SEE THIS RAIN ISN'T NORMAL. HE CAN'T OUTLAST IT. BUT HE MIGHT BE JUMPY.
CAREFUL.
THINK HE HEARD US COMING?
MAYBE THE RAIN ON THE ROOF MADE IT--
OF COURSE HE HEARD US. THAT OUTBOARD SOUNDS LIKE A DAMN CHAINSAW. I KEEP ASKING THEM TO GIVE US SOMETHING QUIETER.
THIS IS *NEVER* EASY.
NICE HOUSE. HE'LL BE HIDING SOMEWHERE IN THERE.
UNLESS HE FIGHTS.
WHAT DO YOU THINK?
ABOUT WHAT?
WILL HE HIDE OR WILL HE FIGHT?
WELL.
I GUESS THAT DEPENDS ON HOW TRICKY HE THINKS HE IS.

HERE'S A SHOT FOR YOU.

DID I ORDER THIS?

SAME AS ALWAYS, CLARA.

NNGH

YOU, TOO, *HUH?* I GET THE SHAKES EVERY TIME I SING.

SOMETIMES FOR HOURS. I FIGURED I'D GET USED TO IT BUT I NEVER DID.

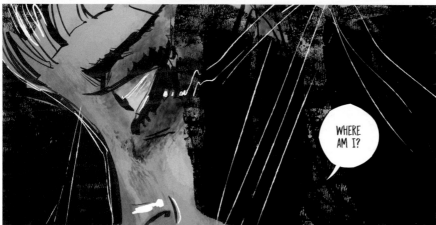

WHERE AM I?

HUH?

DID YOU SAY SOMETHING?

YOU AND YOUR FANCY SHUFFLES.

ALL RIGHT, SHOW ME.

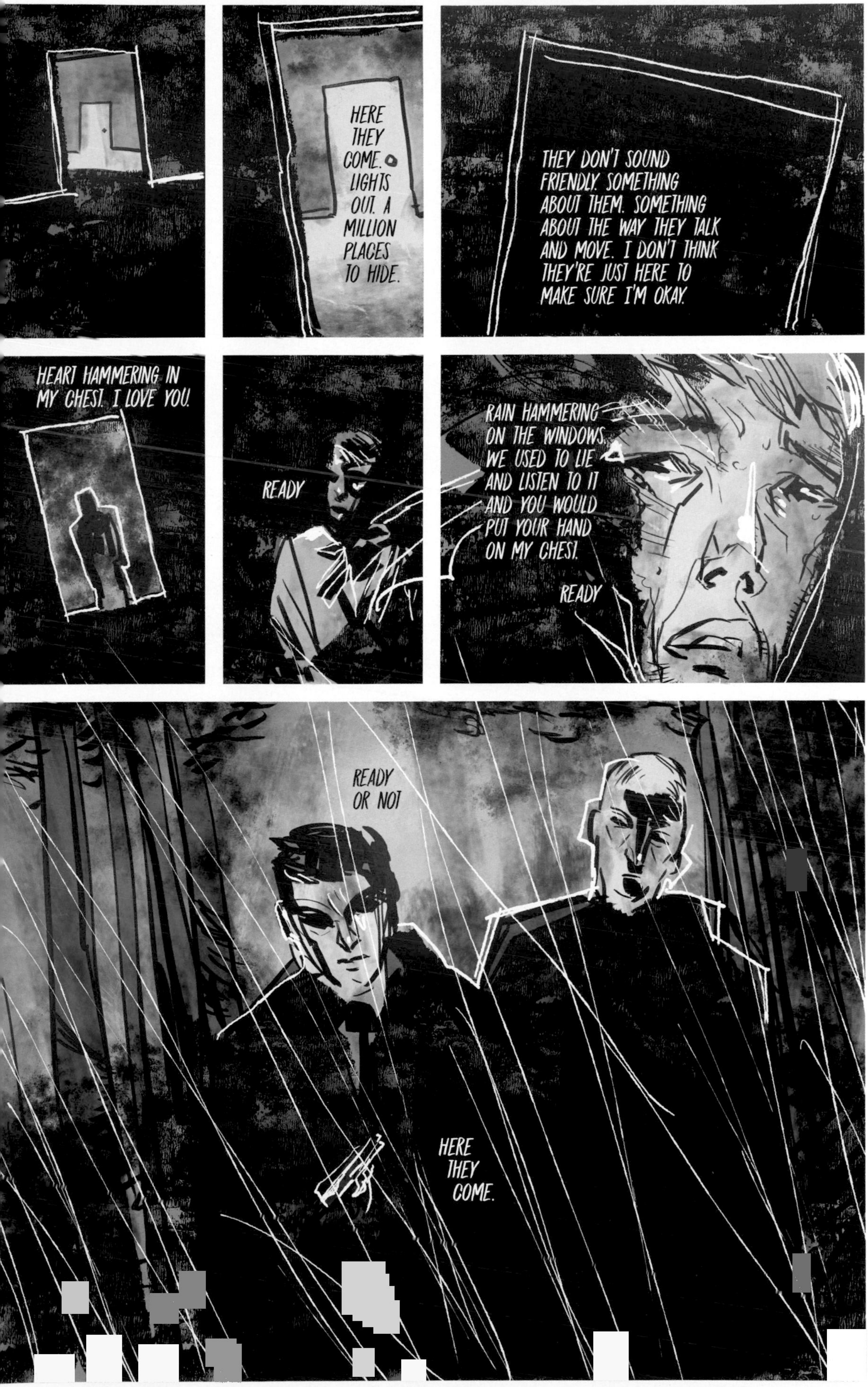
HERE THEY COME. LIGHTS OUT. A MILLION PLACES TO HIDE.
THEY DON'T SOUND FRIENDLY. SOMETHING ABOUT THEM. SOMETHING ABOUT THE WAY THEY TALK AND MOVE. I DON'T THINK THEY'RE JUST HERE TO MAKE SURE I'M OKAY.
HEART HAMMERING IN MY CHEST. I LOVE YOU.
READY
RAIN HAMMERING ON THE WINDOWS. WE USED TO LIE AND LISTEN TO IT AND YOU WOULD PUT YOUR HAND ON MY CHEST.
READY
READY OR NOT
HERE THEY COME.

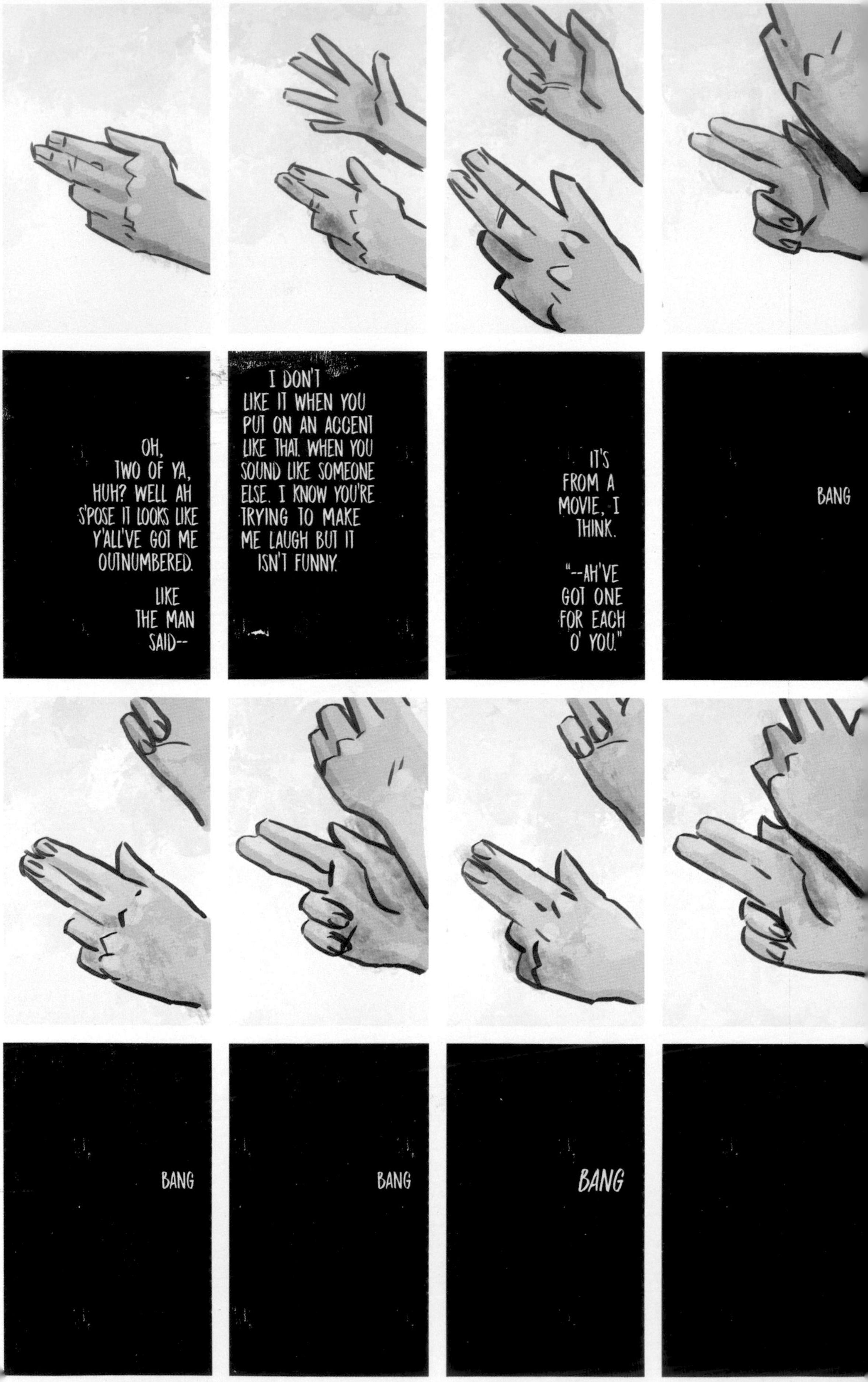
OH, TWO OF YA, HUH? WELL AH S'POSE IT LOOKS LIKE Y'ALL'VE GOT ME OUTNUMBERED.
LIKE THE MAN SAID--
I DON'T LIKE IT WHEN YOU PUT ON AN ACCENT LIKE THAT. WHEN YOU SOUND LIKE SOMEONE ELSE. I KNOW YOU'RE TRYING TO MAKE ME LAUGH BUT IT ISN'T FUNNY.
IT'S FROM A MOVIE, I THINK.
"--AH'VE GOT ONE FOR EACH O' YOU."
BANG
BANG
BANG
BANG

BANG!!!

THE WATER CREPT UP OVER THE ROOTS OF THE WILLOW TREE.

IT LOOKED LIKE IT WAS JUST COMING UP OUT OF THE GROUND.

BEFORE THE RAIN.

THERE WAS A STRONG WIND. YOU SMILED AND MADE A JOKE ABOUT "THE WIZARD OF OZ."

THE DRAPES WERE BLOWING AND I WENT TO CLOSE THE WINDOW.

I LOOKED DOWN INTO THE VALLEY AND THE WATER WAS COMING UP OUT OF THE GROUND.

AND THEN THE RAIN CAME.

AND IT DIDN'T STOP.

IT JUST KEPT ON COMING.

DID YOU WANT ANOTHER SHOT?

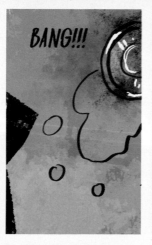

BANG!!!

FROM THE GROUND BELOW AND THE SKY ABOVE.

FOR DAYS AND DAYS.

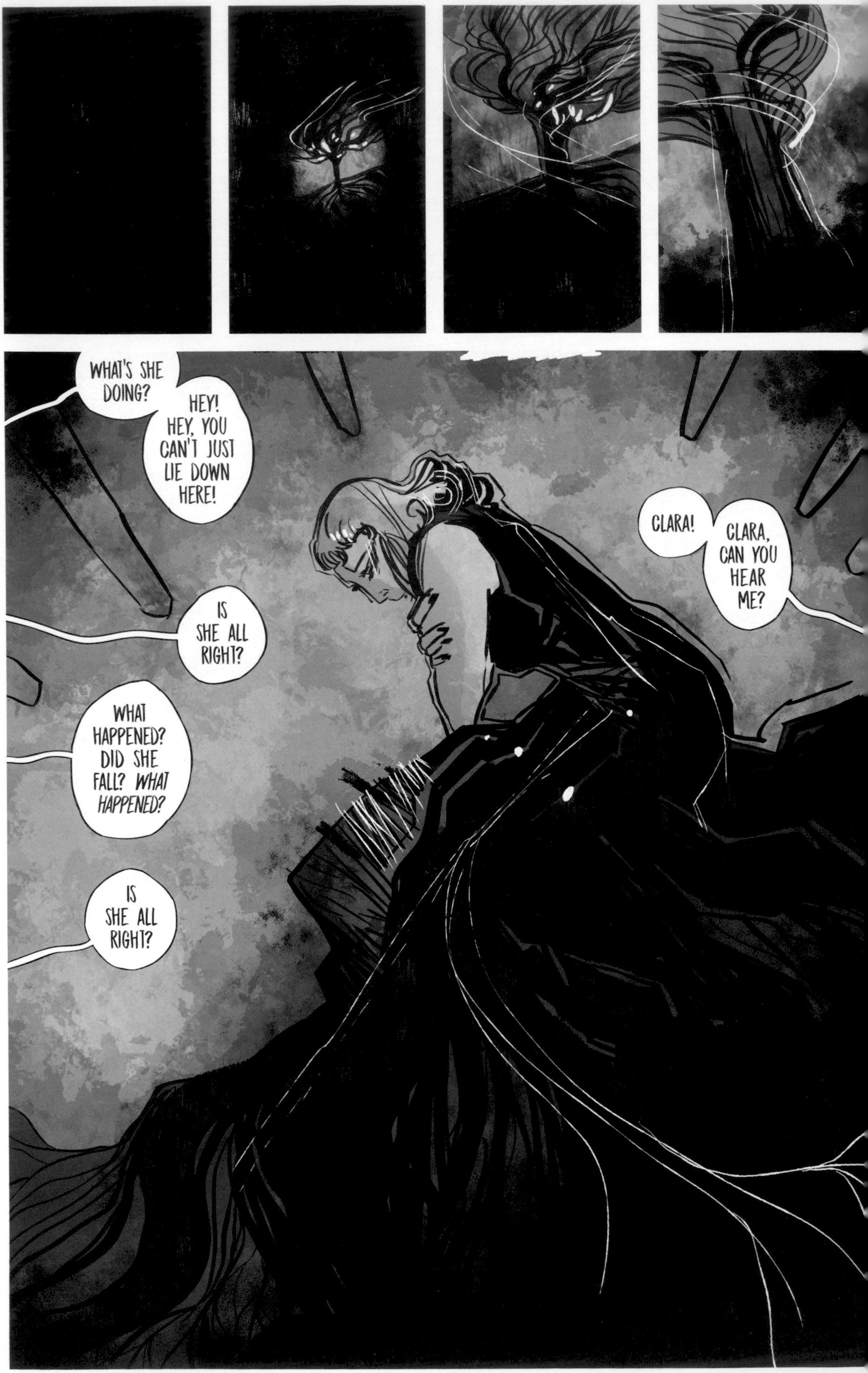
WHAT'S SHE DOING?
HEY! HEY, YOU CAN'T JUST LIE DOWN HERE!
CLARA!
CLARA, CAN YOU HEAR ME?
IS SHE ALL RIGHT?
WHAT HAPPENED? DID SHE FALL? WHAT HAPPENED?
IS SHE ALL RIGHT?

I PULLED
A BOOK OFF
THE SHELF.

I REMEMBER
WE'D JUST BEEN
FIGHTING.

YOU
WOULDN'T
PUT DOWN
THOSE CARDS.

THERE
WAS A
PHOTO.

I
DIDN'T
FEEL
RIGHT
LOOKING
AT IT.

IT MADE
ME FEEL...

A PHOTO
OF A MAN
WITH BEES.

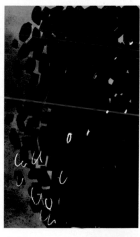

WHAT--

WHAT THE
FUCK--

HEY! HEY,
YOU'RE DRIPPING
ALL OVER THE
CARPET! HEY!

OH,
HELL.

I JUST CAME
IN FROM THE
RAIN...OR...I'M
ABOUT TO...

OH,
HELL.

DID SOMEBODY
ELSE JUST COME IN
HERE? ANOTHER GUY
LIKE ME?

DAMN.
IT'S NEVER
EASY.

DON'T COME
IN HERE DRIPPING
LIKE THAT!

IT MADE
ME FEEL...

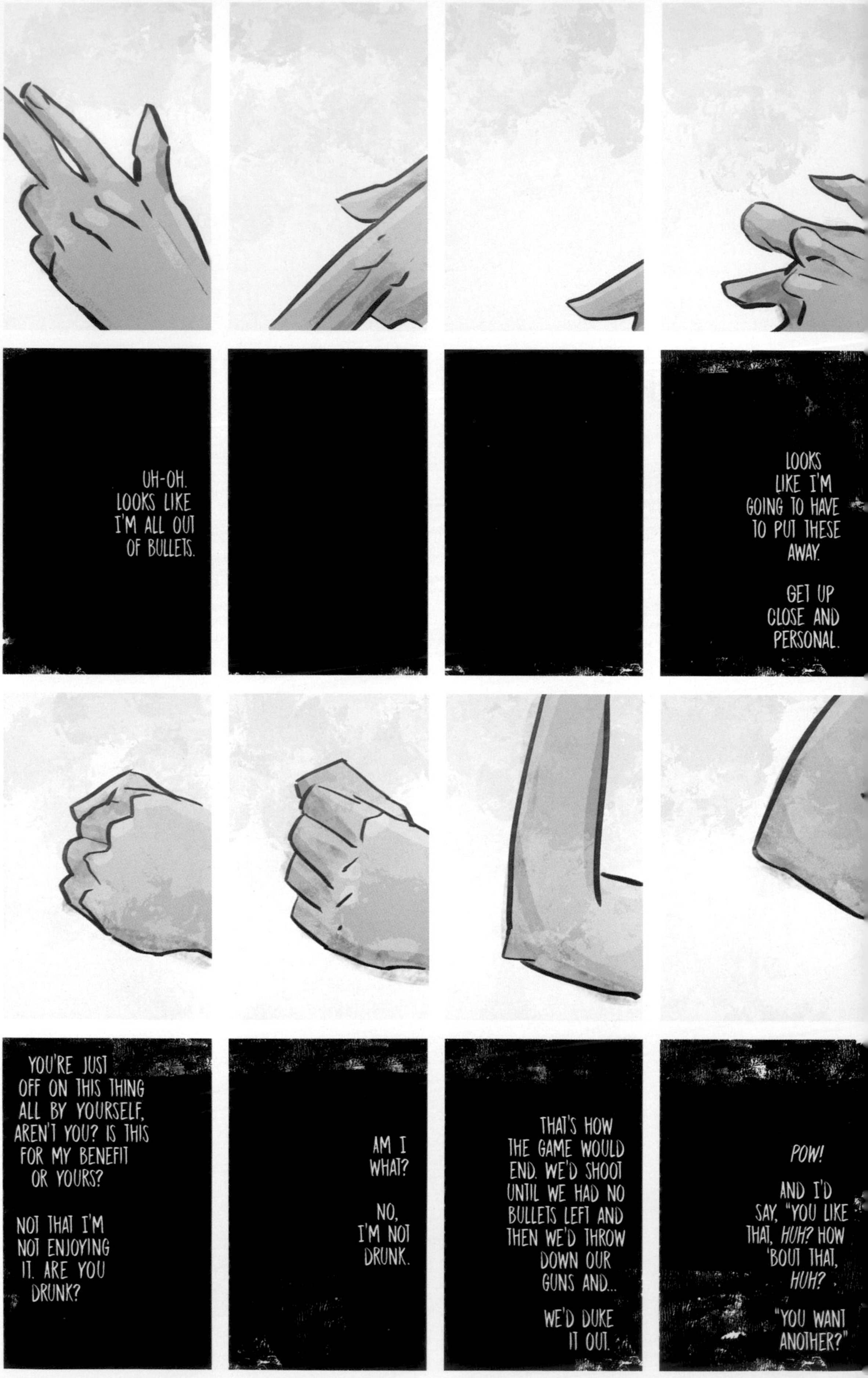
UH-OH. LOOKS LIKE I'M ALL OUT OF BULLETS.
LOOKS LIKE I'M GOING TO HAVE TO PUT THESE AWAY.
GET UP CLOSE AND PERSONAL.
YOU'RE JUST OFF ON THIS THING ALL BY YOURSELF, AREN'T YOU? IS THIS FOR MY BENEFIT OR YOURS?
NOT THAT I'M NOT ENJOYING IT. ARE YOU DRUNK?
AM I WHAT?
NO, I'M NOT DRUNK.
THAT'S HOW THE GAME WOULD END. WE'D SHOOT UNTIL WE HAD NO BULLETS LEFT AND THEN WE'D THROW DOWN OUR GUNS AND...
WE'D DUKE IT OUT.
POW!
AND I'D SAY, "YOU LIKE THAT, *HUH?* HOW 'BOUT THAT, *HUH?*
"YOU WANT ANOTHER?"

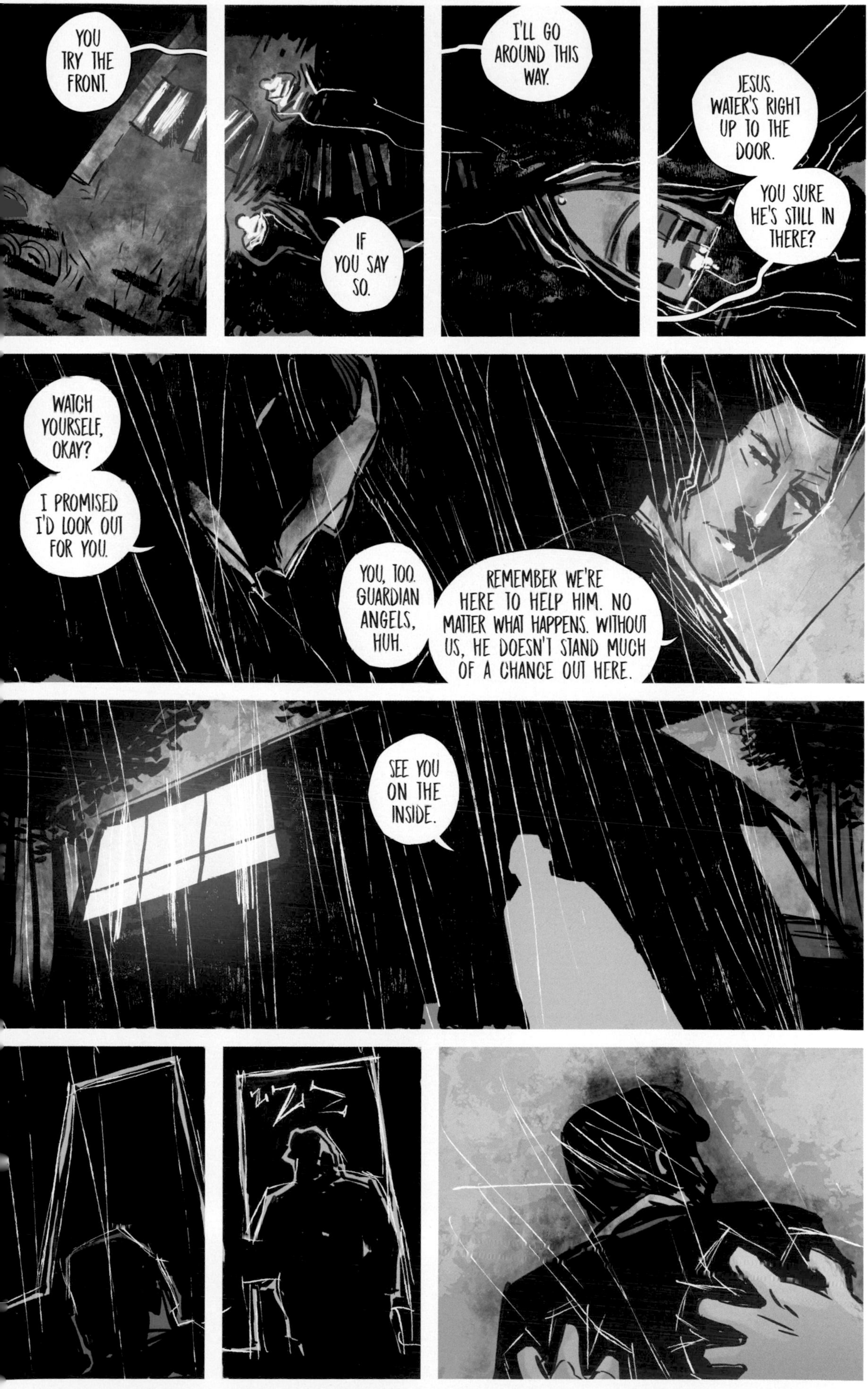
YOU TRY THE FRONT.
IF YOU SAY SO.
I'LL GO AROUND THIS WAY.
JESUS. WATER'S RIGHT UP TO THE DOOR.
YOU SURE HE'S STILL IN THERE?
WATCH YOURSELF, OKAY?
I PROMISED I'D LOOK OUT FOR YOU.
YOU, TOO. GUARDIAN ANGELS, HUH.
REMEMBER WE'RE HERE TO HELP HIM. NO MATTER WHAT HAPPENS. WITHOUT US, HE DOESN'T STAND MUCH OF A CHANCE OUT HERE.
SEE YOU ON THE INSIDE.

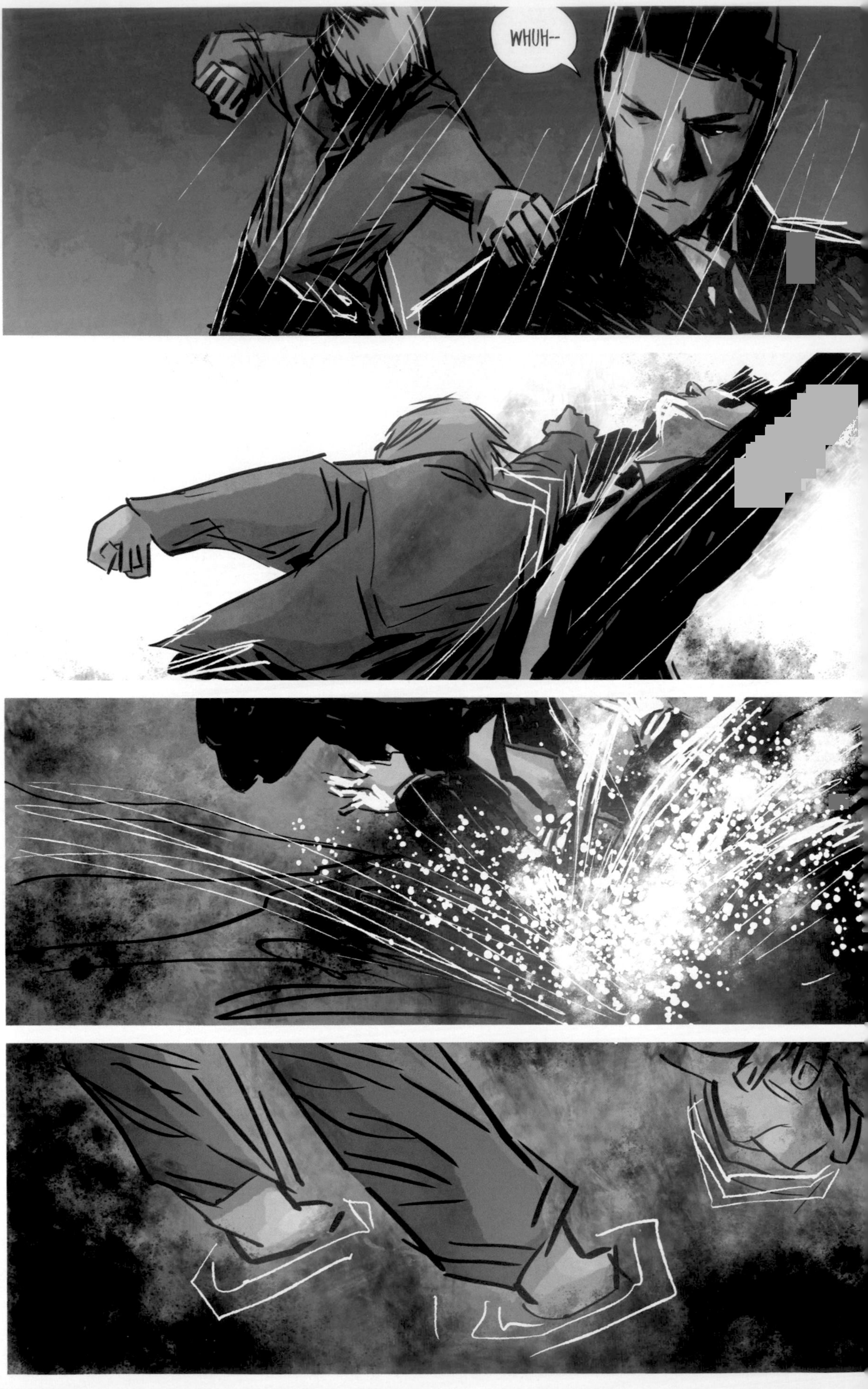
WHUH--

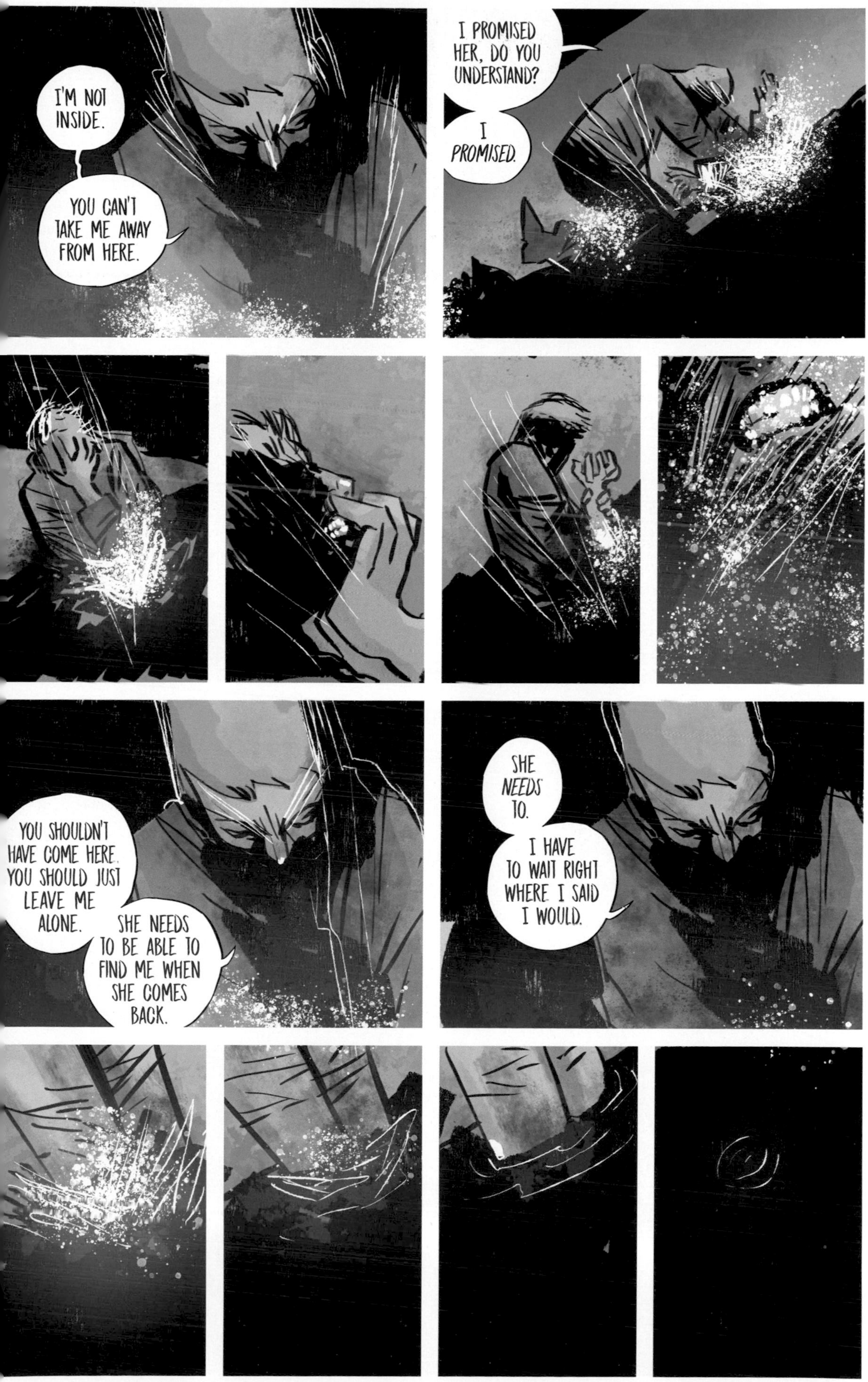
I'M NOT INSIDE.
YOU CAN'T TAKE ME AWAY FROM HERE.
I PROMISED HER, DO YOU UNDERSTAND?
I PROMISED.
YOU SHOULDN'T HAVE COME HERE. YOU SHOULD JUST LEAVE ME ALONE.
SHE NEEDS TO BE ABLE TO FIND ME WHEN SHE COMES BACK.
SHE NEEDS TO.
I HAVE TO WAIT RIGHT WHERE I SAID I WOULD.

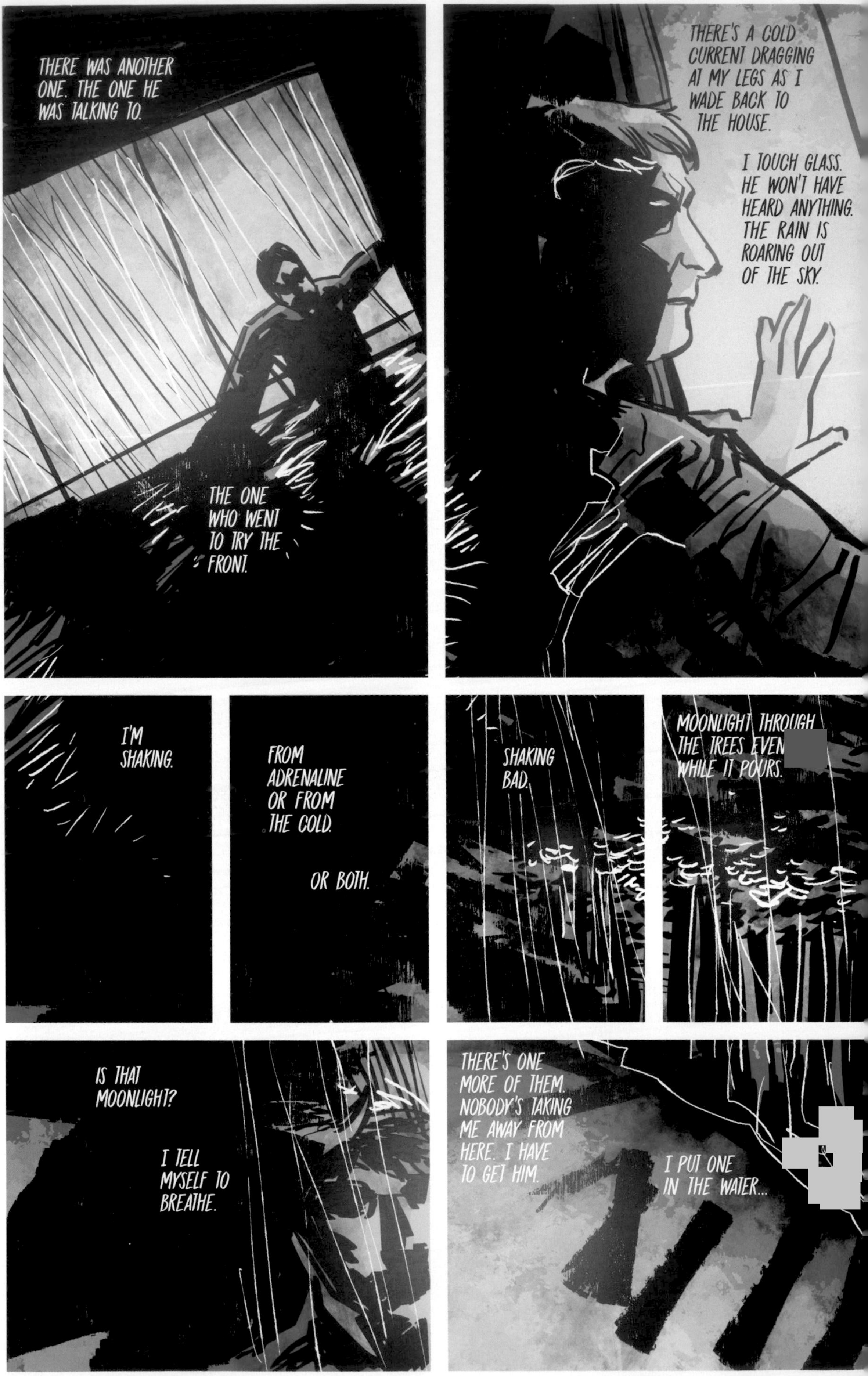

THERE WAS ANOTHER ONE. THE ONE HE WAS TALKING TO.
THE ONE WHO WENT TO TRY THE FRONT.
THERE'S A COLD CURRENT DRAGGING AT MY LEGS AS I WADE BACK TO THE HOUSE.
I TOUCH GLASS. HE WON'T HAVE HEARD ANYTHING. THE RAIN IS ROARING OUT OF THE SKY.
I'M SHAKING.
FROM ADRENALINE OR FROM THE COLD.
OR BOTH.
SHAKING BAD.
MOONLIGHT THROUGH THE TREES EVEN WHILE IT POURS.
IS THAT MOONLIGHT?
I TELL MYSELF TO BREATHE.
THERE'S ONE MORE OF THEM. NOBODY'S TAKING ME AWAY FROM HERE. I HAVE TO GET HIM.
I PUT ONE IN THE WATER...

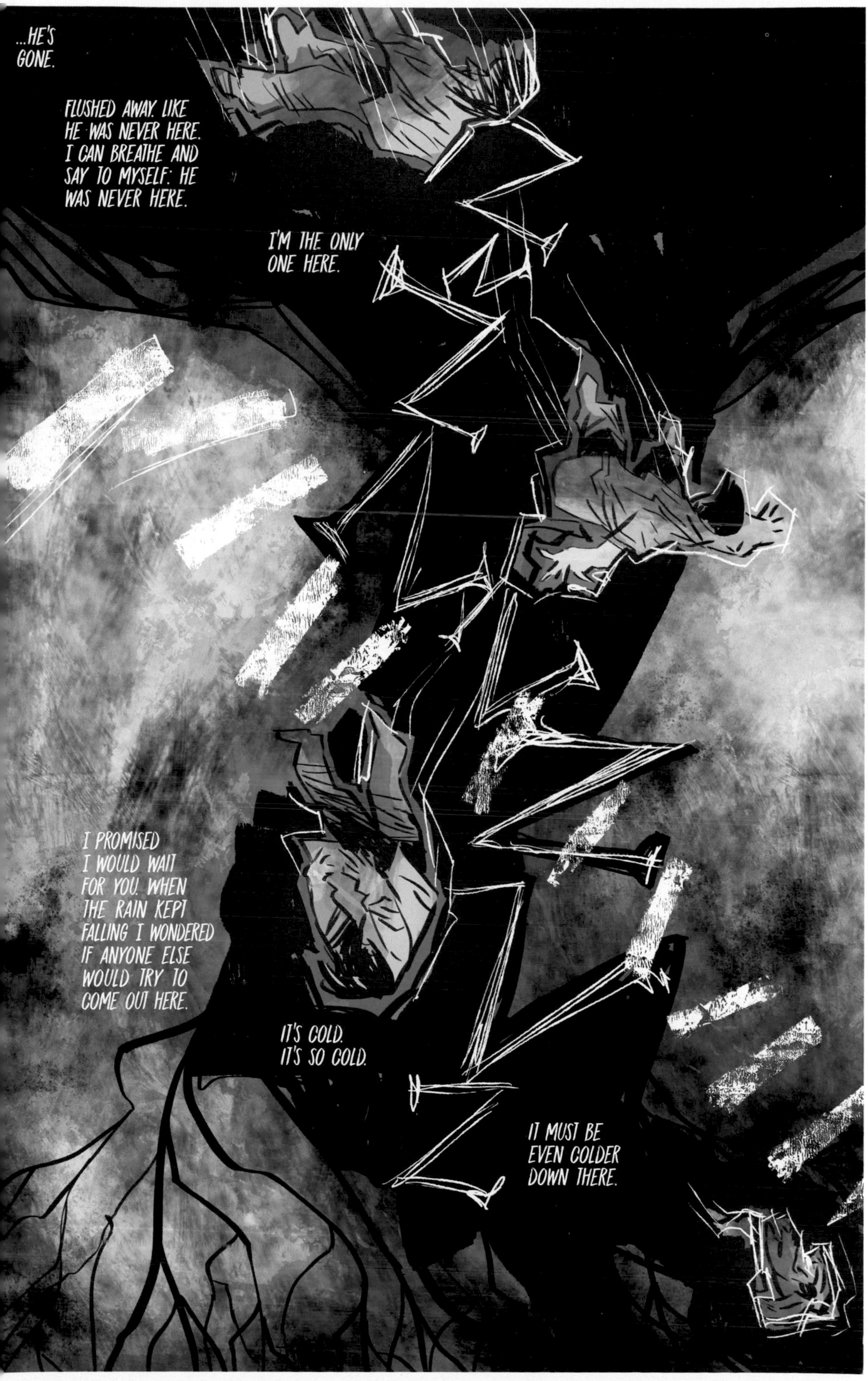
...HE'S GONE.
FLUSHED AWAY. LIKE HE WAS NEVER HERE. I CAN BREATHE AND SAY TO MYSELF: HE WAS NEVER HERE.
I'M THE ONLY ONE HERE.
I PROMISED I WOULD WAIT FOR YOU. WHEN THE RAIN KEPT FALLING I WONDERED IF ANYONE ELSE WOULD TRY TO COME OUT HERE.
IT'S COLD. IT'S SO COLD.
IT MUST BE EVEN COLDER DOWN THERE.

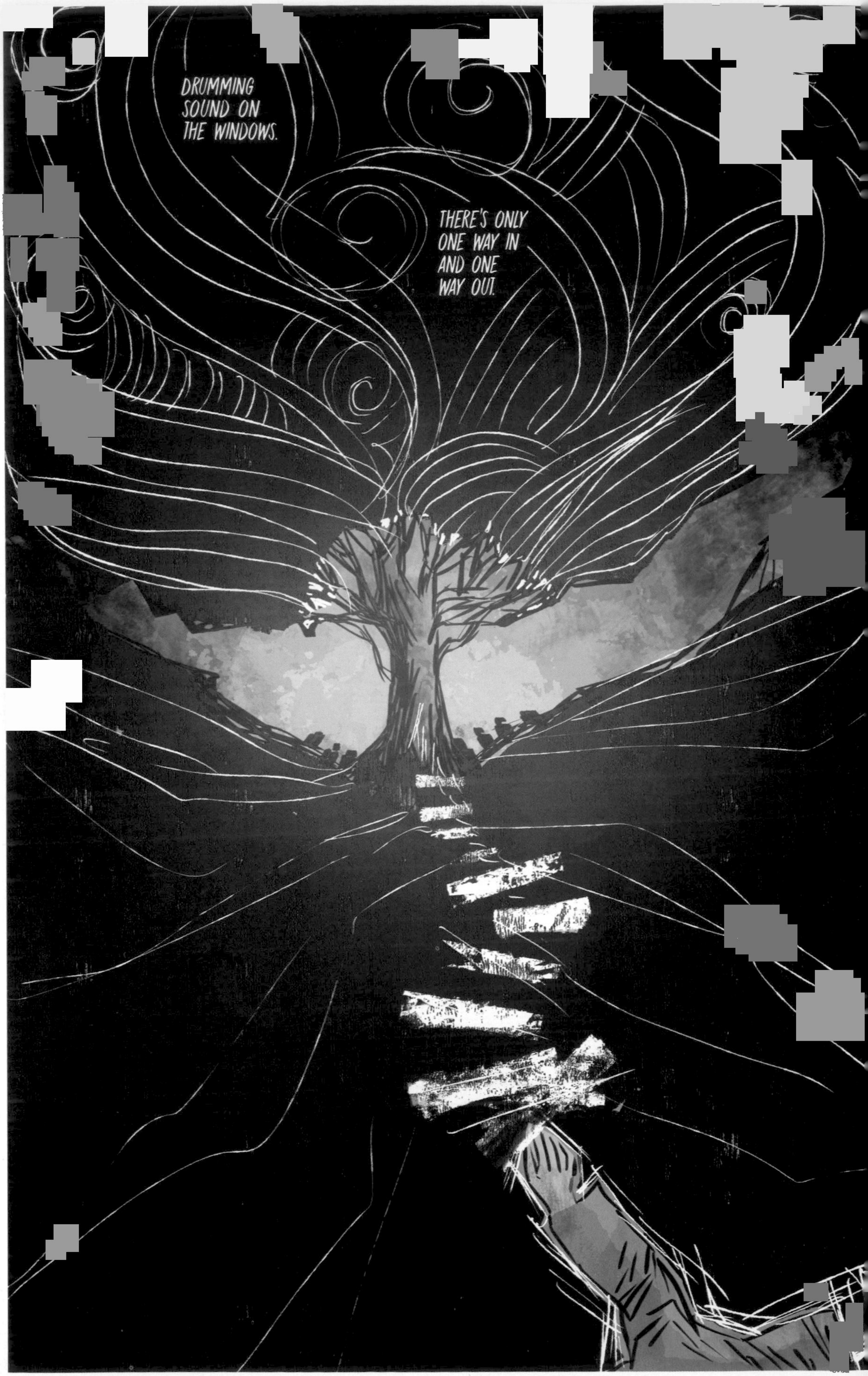
DRUMMING SOUND ON THE WINDOWS.
THERE'S ONLY ONE WAY IN AND ONE WAY OUT.

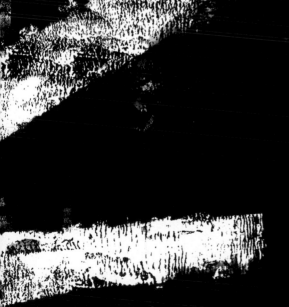

CHAPTER 3

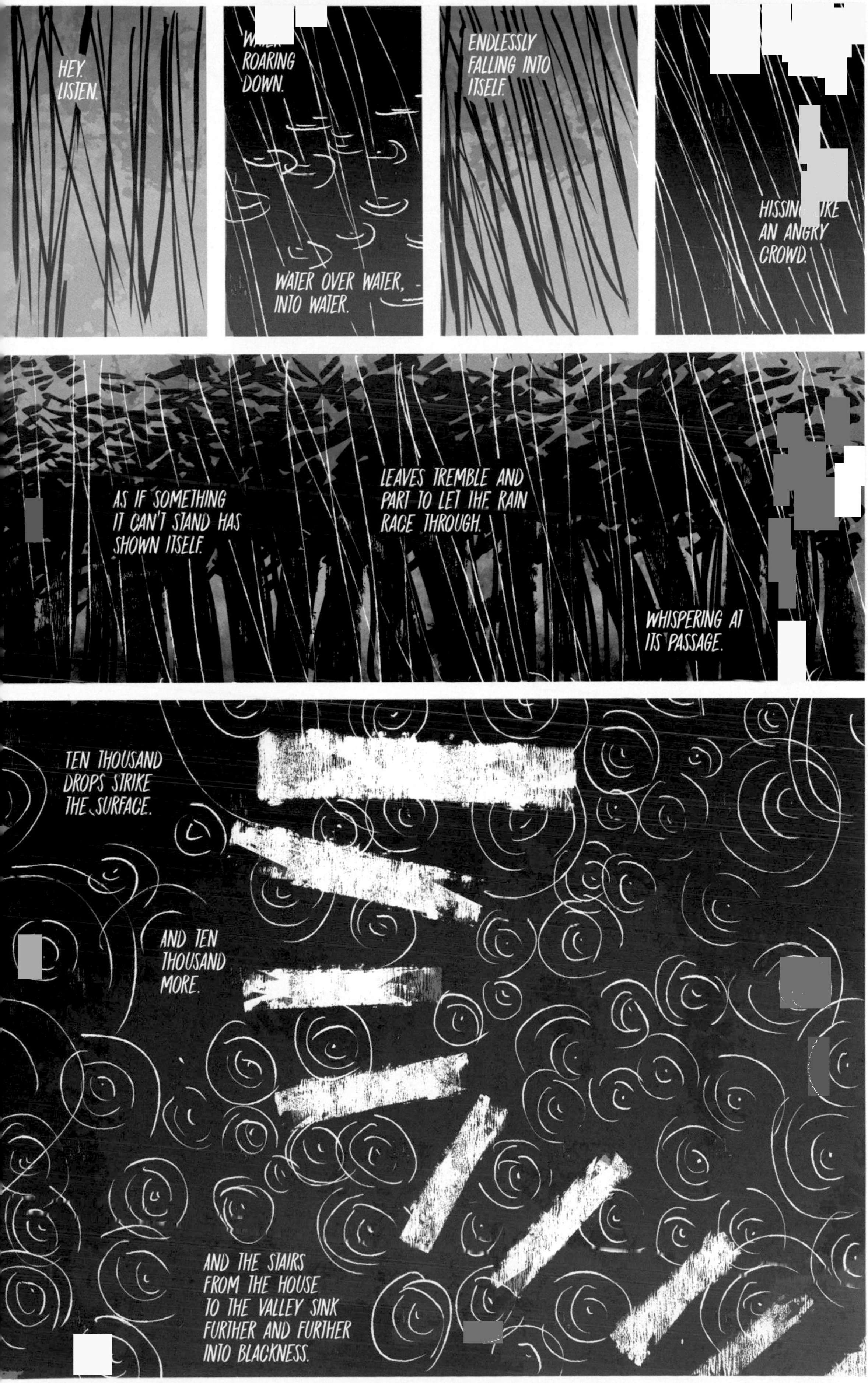
HEY. LISTEN.
ROARING DOWN.
WATER OVER WATER, INTO WATER.
ENDLESSLY FALLING INTO ITSELF.
AN ANGRY CROWD.
AS IF SOMETHING IT CAN'T STAND HAS SHOWN ITSELF.
LEAVES TREMBLE AND PART TO LET THE RAIN RACE THROUGH.
WHISPERING AT ITS PASSAGE.
TEN THOUSAND DROPS STRIKE THE SURFACE.
AND TEN THOUSAND MORE.
AND THE STAIRS FROM THE HOUSE TO THE VALLEY SINK FURTHER AND FURTHER INTO BLACKNESS.

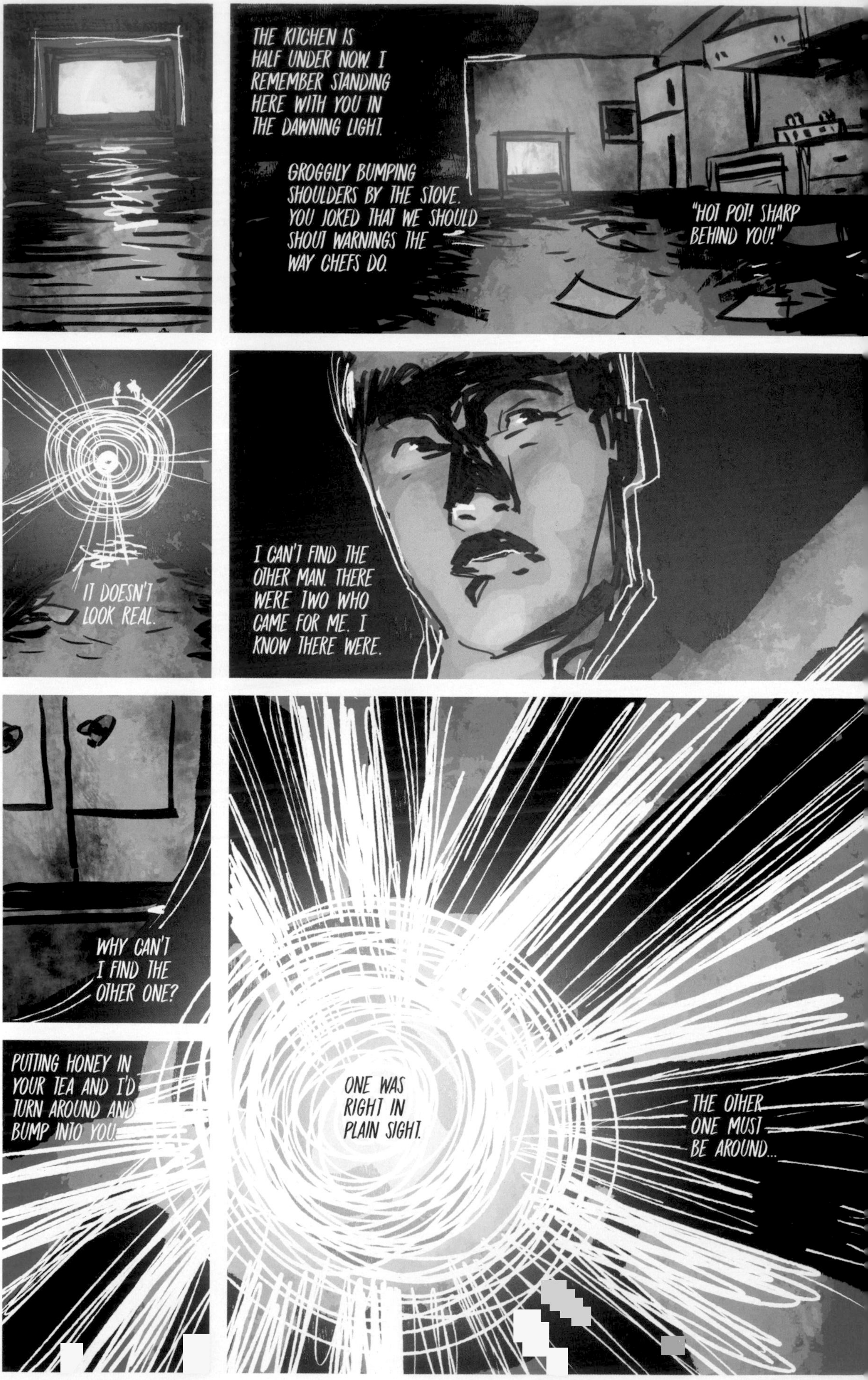
THE KITCHEN IS HALF UNDER NOW. I REMEMBER STANDING HERE WITH YOU IN THE DAWNING LIGHT.
GROGGILY BUMPING SHOULDERS BY THE STOVE. YOU JOKED THAT WE SHOULD SHOUT WARNINGS THE WAY CHEFS DO.
"HOT POT! SHARP BEHIND YOU!"
IT DOESN'T LOOK REAL.
I CAN'T FIND THE OTHER MAN. THERE WERE TWO WHO CAME FOR ME. I KNOW THERE WERE.
WHY CAN'T I FIND THE OTHER ONE?
PUTTING HONEY IN YOUR TEA AND I'D TURN AROUND AND BUMP INTO YOU.
ONE WAS RIGHT IN PLAIN SIGHT.
THE OTHER ONE MUST BE AROUND...

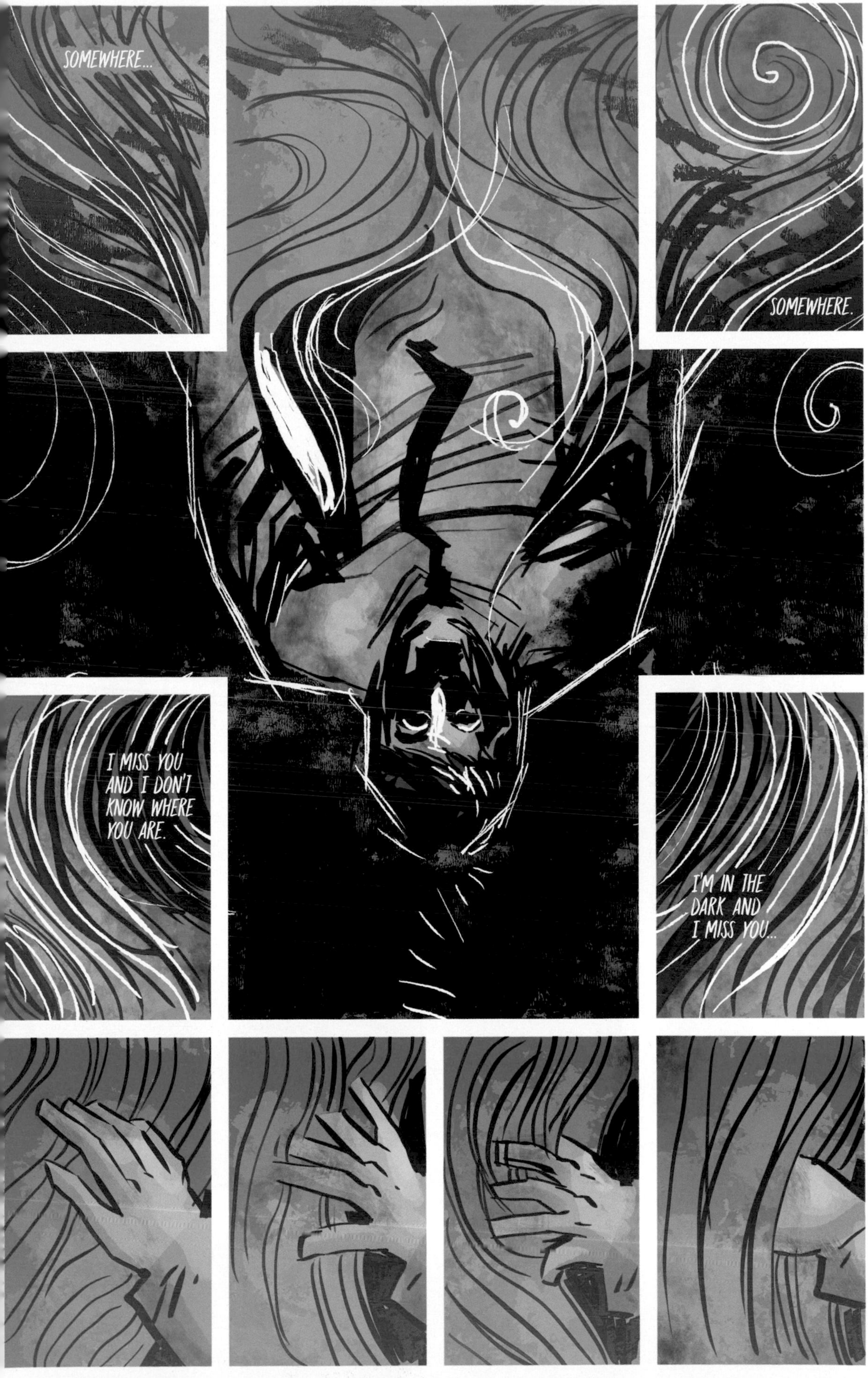
SOMEWHERE...
SOMEWHERE.
I MISS YOU AND I DON'T KNOW WHERE YOU ARE.
I'M IN THE DARK AND I MISS YOU...

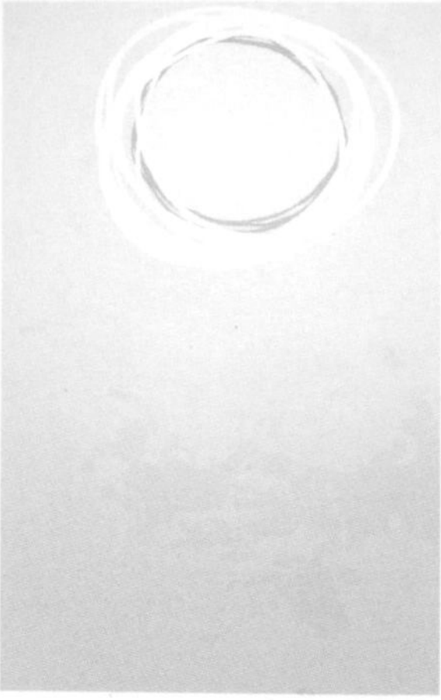

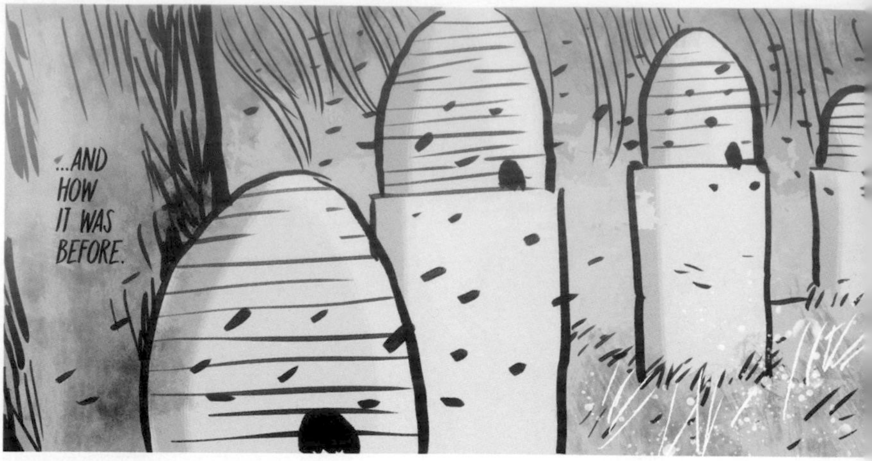
...AND HOW IT WAS BEFORE.

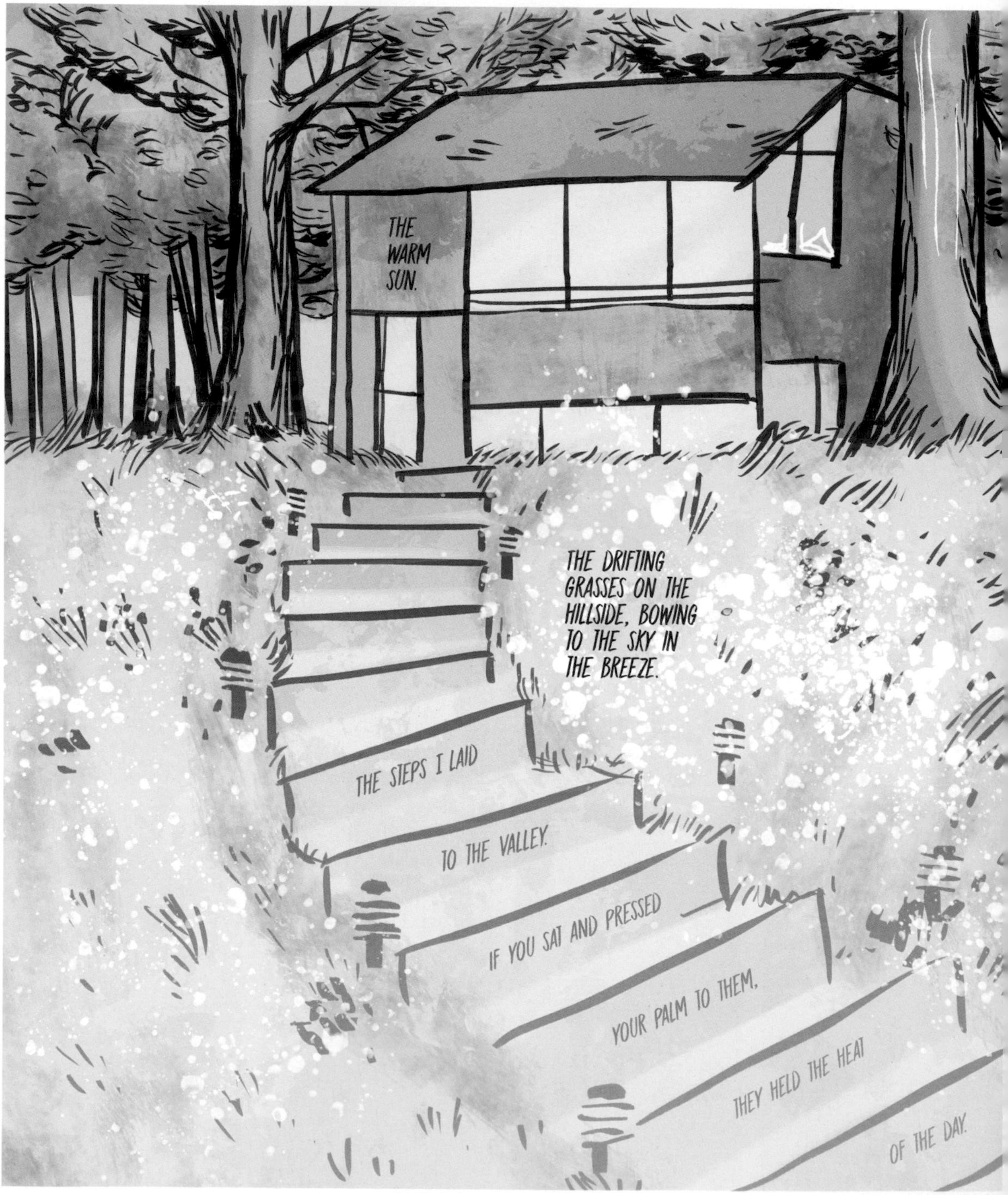
THE WARM SUN.
THE DRIFTING GRASSES ON THE HILLSIDE, BOWING TO THE SKY IN THE BREEZE.
THE STEPS I LAID
TO THE VALLEY.
IF YOU SAT AND PRESSED
YOUR PALM TO THEM,
THEY HELD THE HEAT
OF THE DAY.

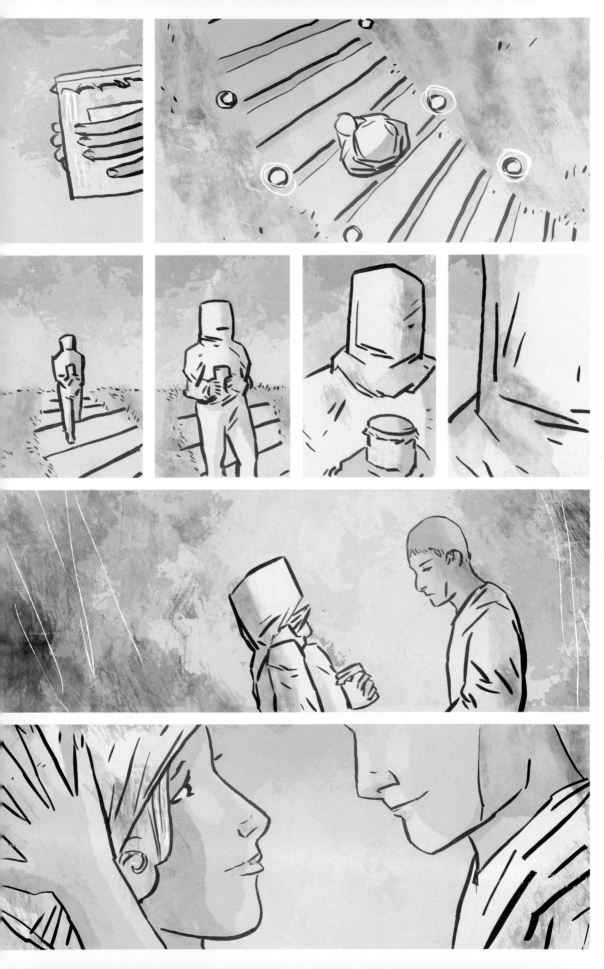

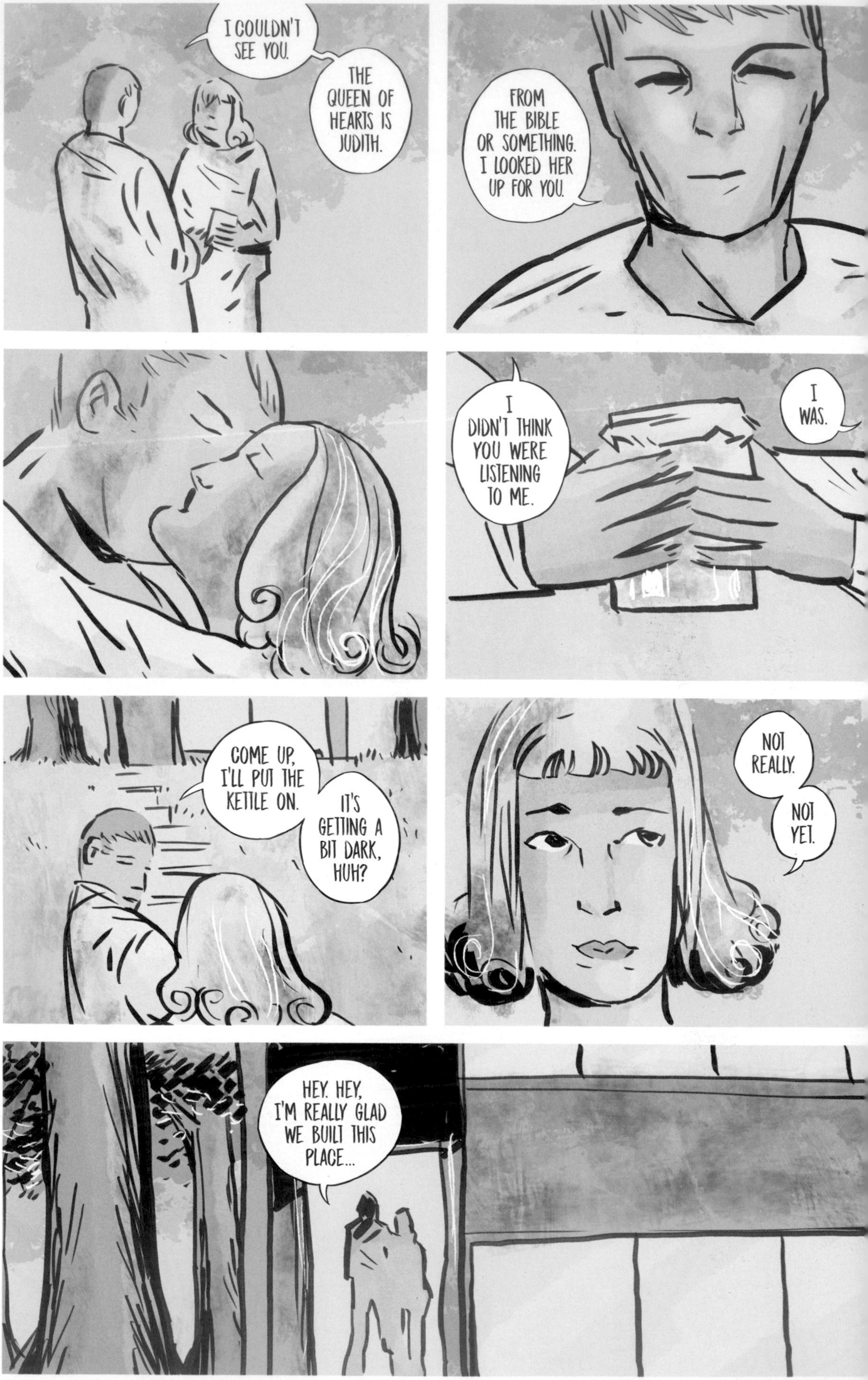
I COULDN'T SEE YOU.
THE QUEEN OF HEARTS IS JUDITH.
FROM THE BIBLE OR SOMETHING. I LOOKED HER UP FOR YOU.
I DIDN'T THINK YOU WERE LISTENING TO ME.
I WAS.
COME UP, I'LL PUT THE KETTLE ON.
IT'S GETTING A BIT DARK, HUH?
NOT REALLY.
NOT YET.
HEY. HEY, I'M REALLY GLAD WE BUILT THIS PLACE...

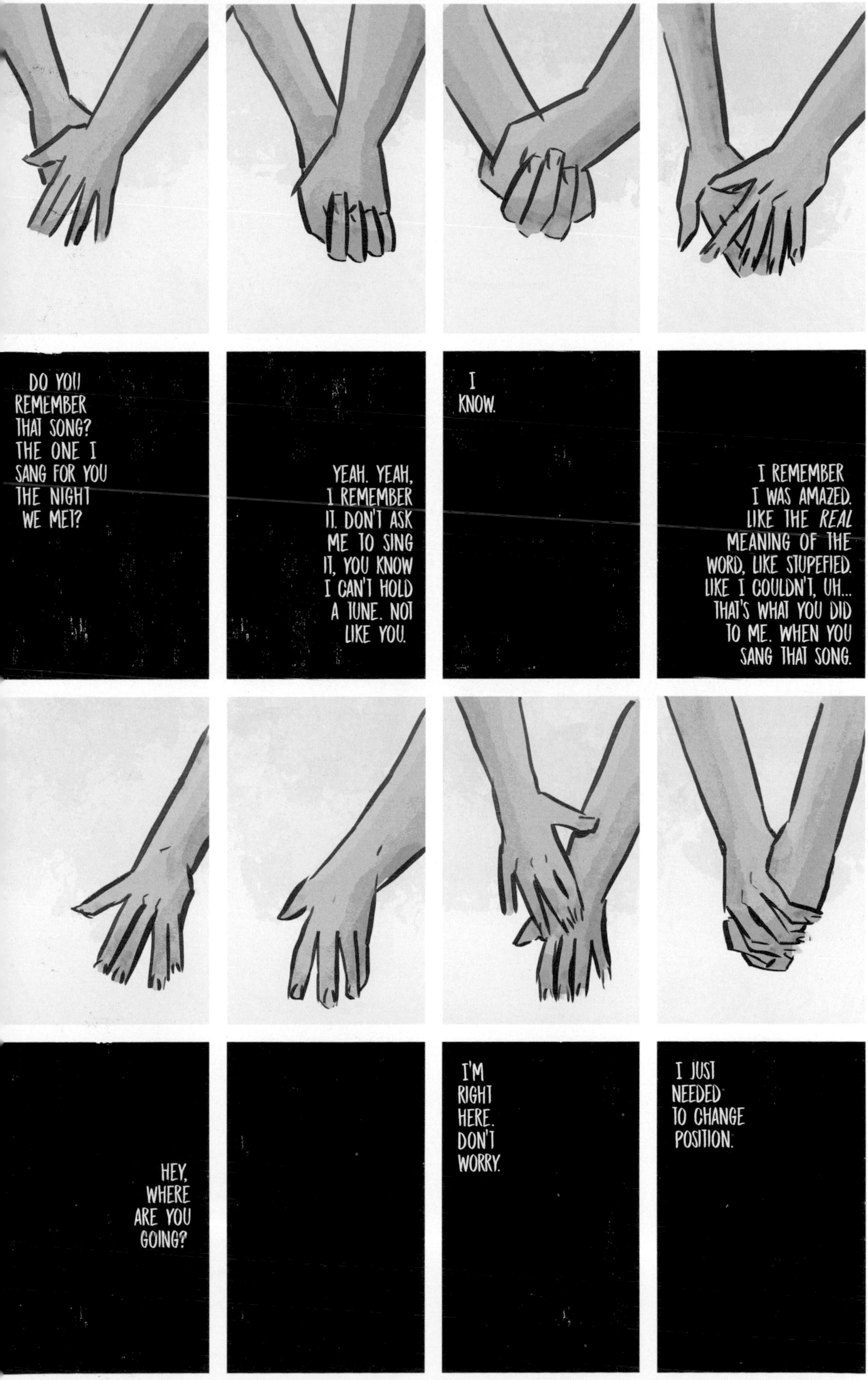
DO YOU REMEMBER THAT SONG? THE ONE I SANG FOR YOU THE NIGHT WE MET?
YEAH. YEAH, I REMEMBER IT. DON'T ASK ME TO SING IT, YOU KNOW I CAN'T HOLD A TUNE. NOT LIKE YOU.
I KNOW.
I REMEMBER I WAS AMAZED. LIKE THE *REAL* MEANING OF THE WORD, LIKE STUPEFIED. LIKE I COULDN'T, UH... THAT'S WHAT YOU DID TO ME. WHEN YOU SANG THAT SONG.
HEY, WHERE ARE YOU GOING?
I'M RIGHT HERE. DON'T WORRY.
I JUST NEEDED TO CHANGE POSITION.

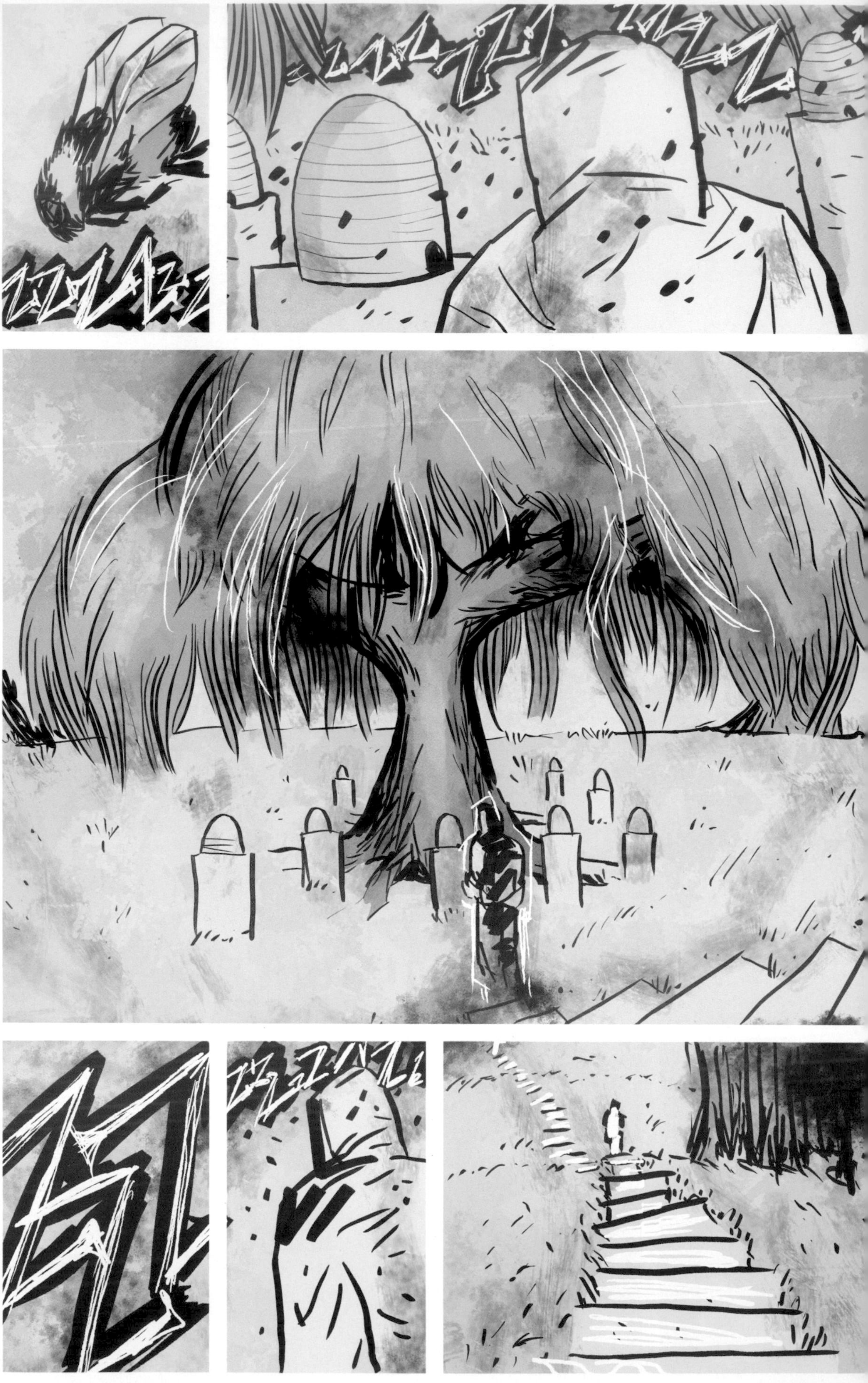

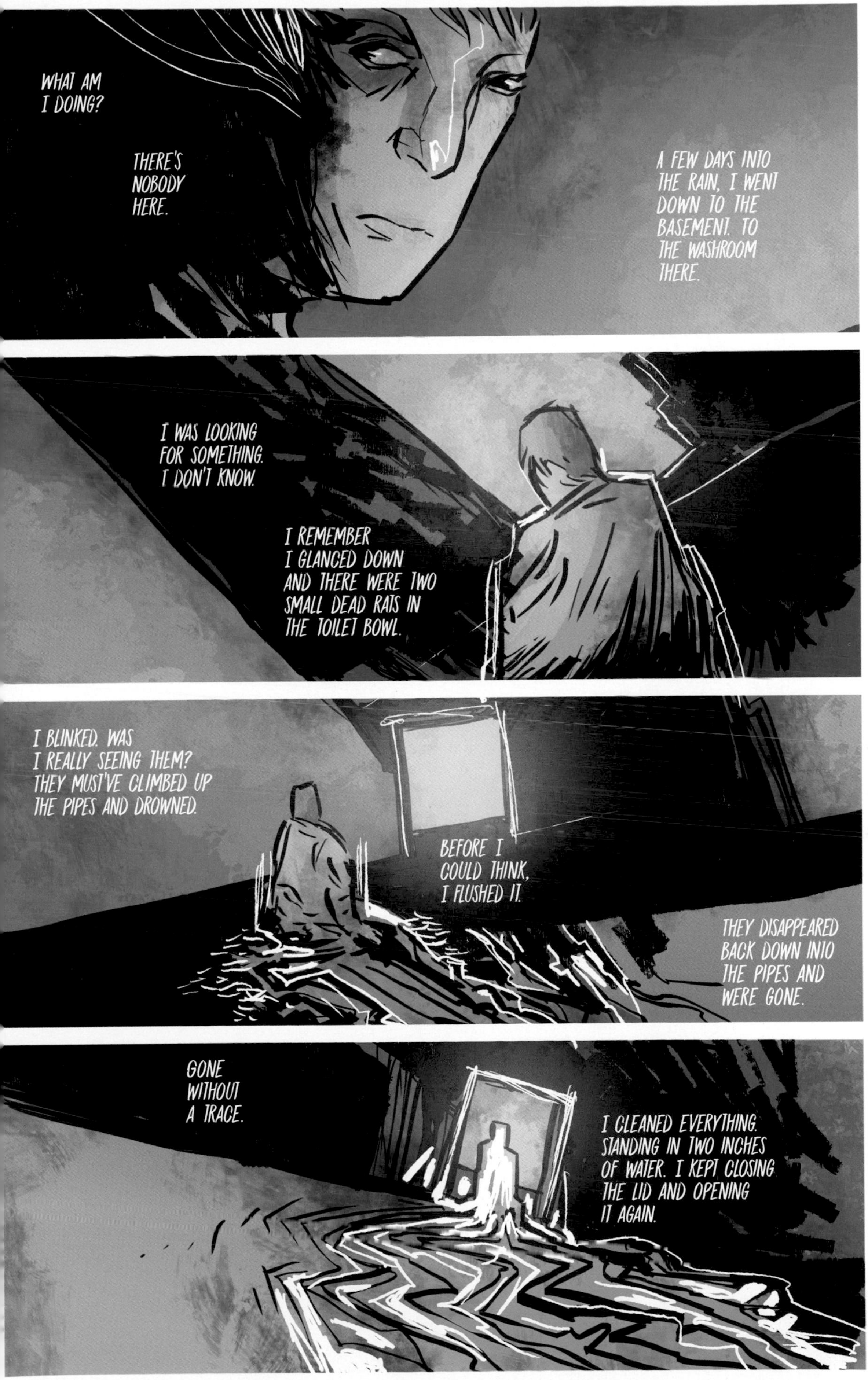
WHAT AM I DOING?
THERE'S NOBODY HERE.
A FEW DAYS INTO THE RAIN, I WENT DOWN TO THE BASEMENT. TO THE WASHROOM THERE.
I WAS LOOKING FOR SOMETHING. I DON'T KNOW.
I REMEMBER I GLANCED DOWN AND THERE WERE TWO SMALL DEAD RATS IN THE TOILET BOWL.
I BLINKED. WAS I REALLY SEEING THEM? THEY MUST'VE CLIMBED UP THE PIPES AND DROWNED.
BEFORE I COULD THINK, I FLUSHED IT.
THEY DISAPPEARED BACK DOWN INTO THE PIPES AND WERE GONE.
GONE WITHOUT A TRACE.
I CLEANED EVERYTHING. STANDING IN TWO INCHES OF WATER. I KEPT CLOSING THE LID AND OPENING IT AGAIN.

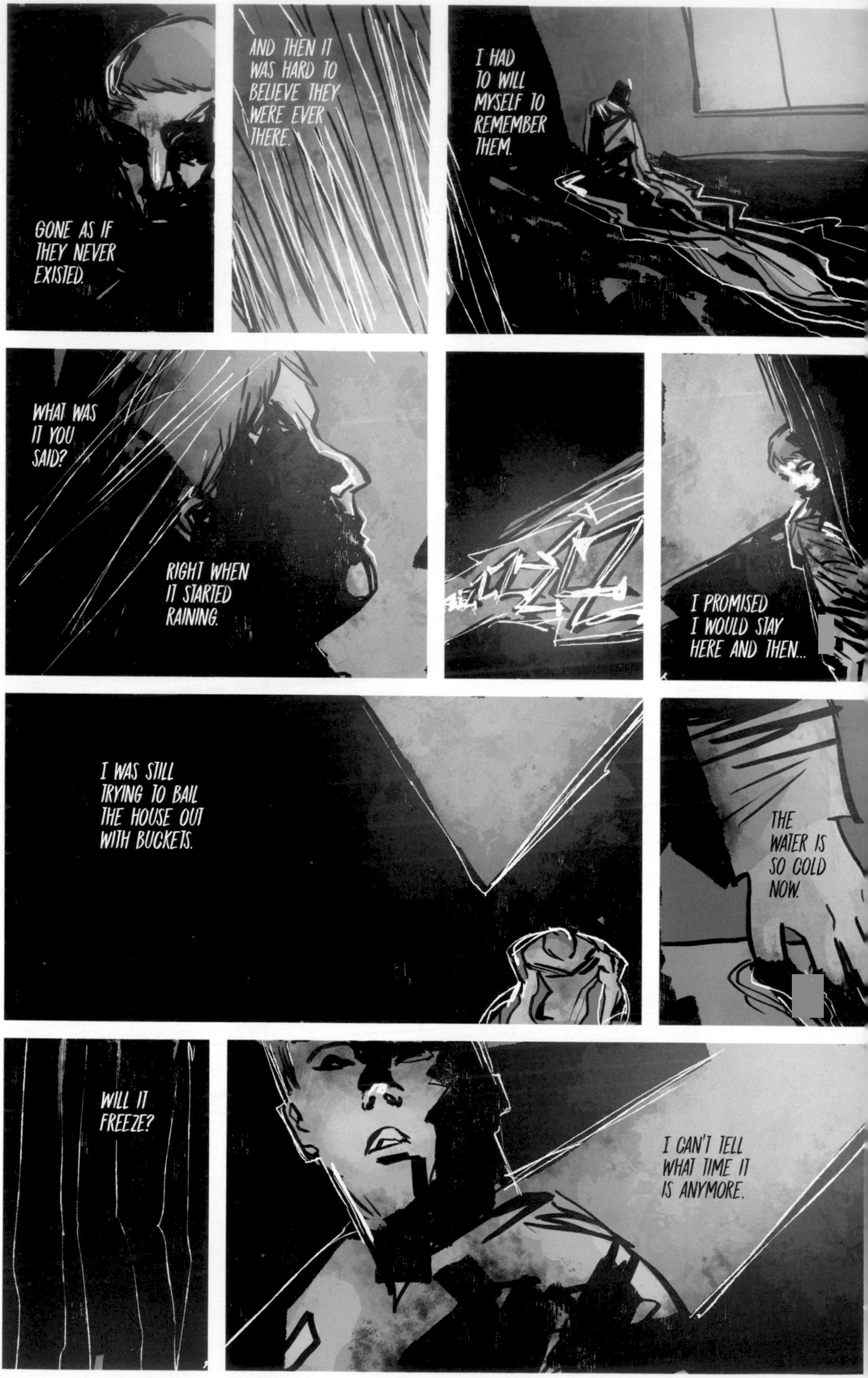
GONE AS IF THEY NEVER EXISTED.
AND THEN IT WAS HARD TO BELIEVE THEY WERE EVER THERE.
I HAD TO WILL MYSELF TO REMEMBER THEM.
WHAT WAS IT YOU SAID?
RIGHT WHEN IT STARTED RAINING.
I PROMISED I WOULD STAY HERE AND THEN...
I WAS STILL TRYING TO BAIL THE HOUSE OUT WITH BUCKETS.
THE WATER IS SO COLD NOW.
WILL IT FREEZE?
I CAN'T TELL WHAT TIME IT IS ANYMORE.

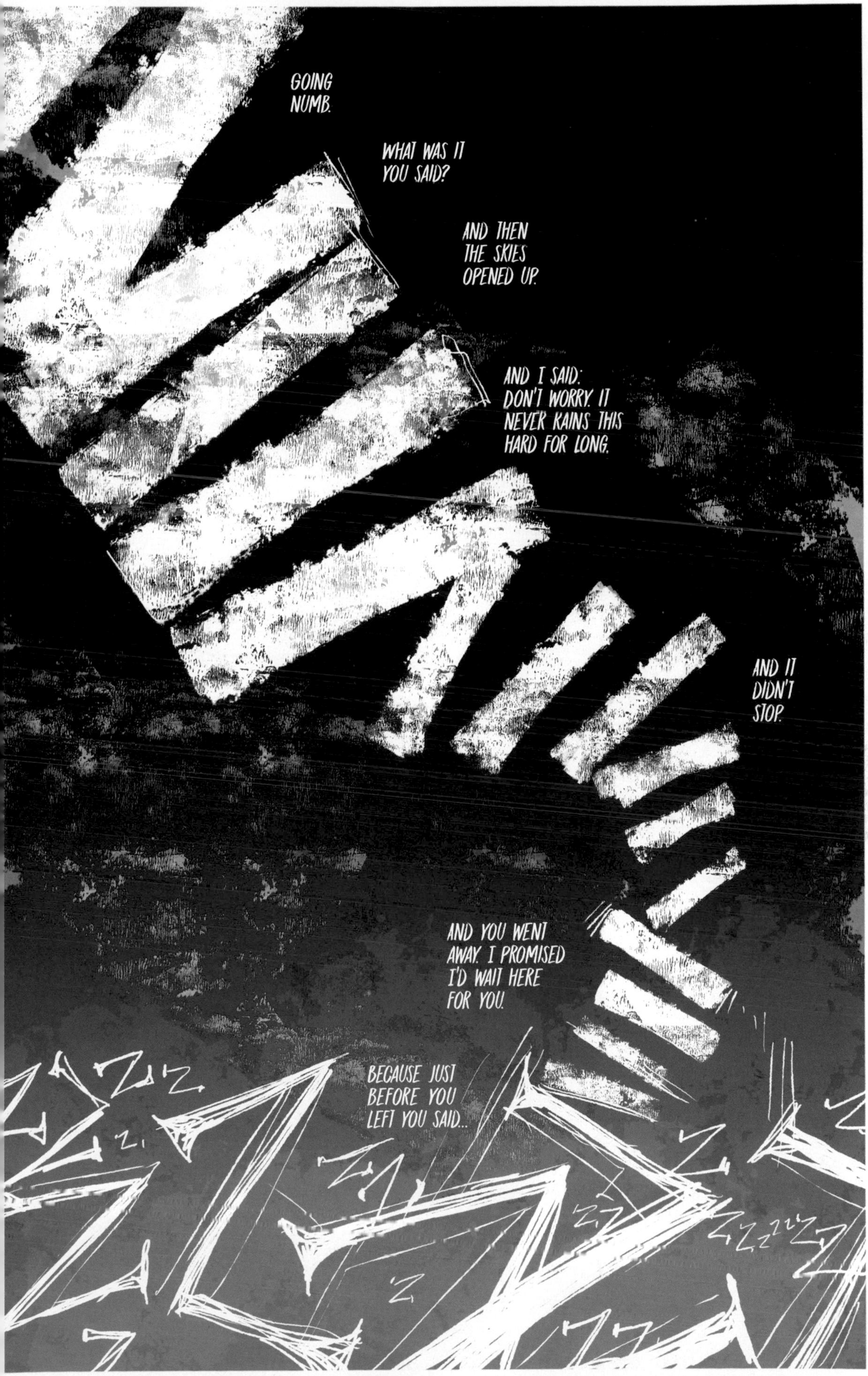
GOING NUMB.
WHAT WAS IT YOU SAID?
AND THEN THE SKIES OPENED UP.
AND I SAID: DON'T WORRY. IT NEVER RAINS THIS HARD FOR LONG.
AND IT DIDN'T STOP.
AND YOU WENT AWAY. I PROMISED I'D WAIT HERE FOR YOU.
BECAUSE JUST BEFORE YOU LEFT YOU SAID...

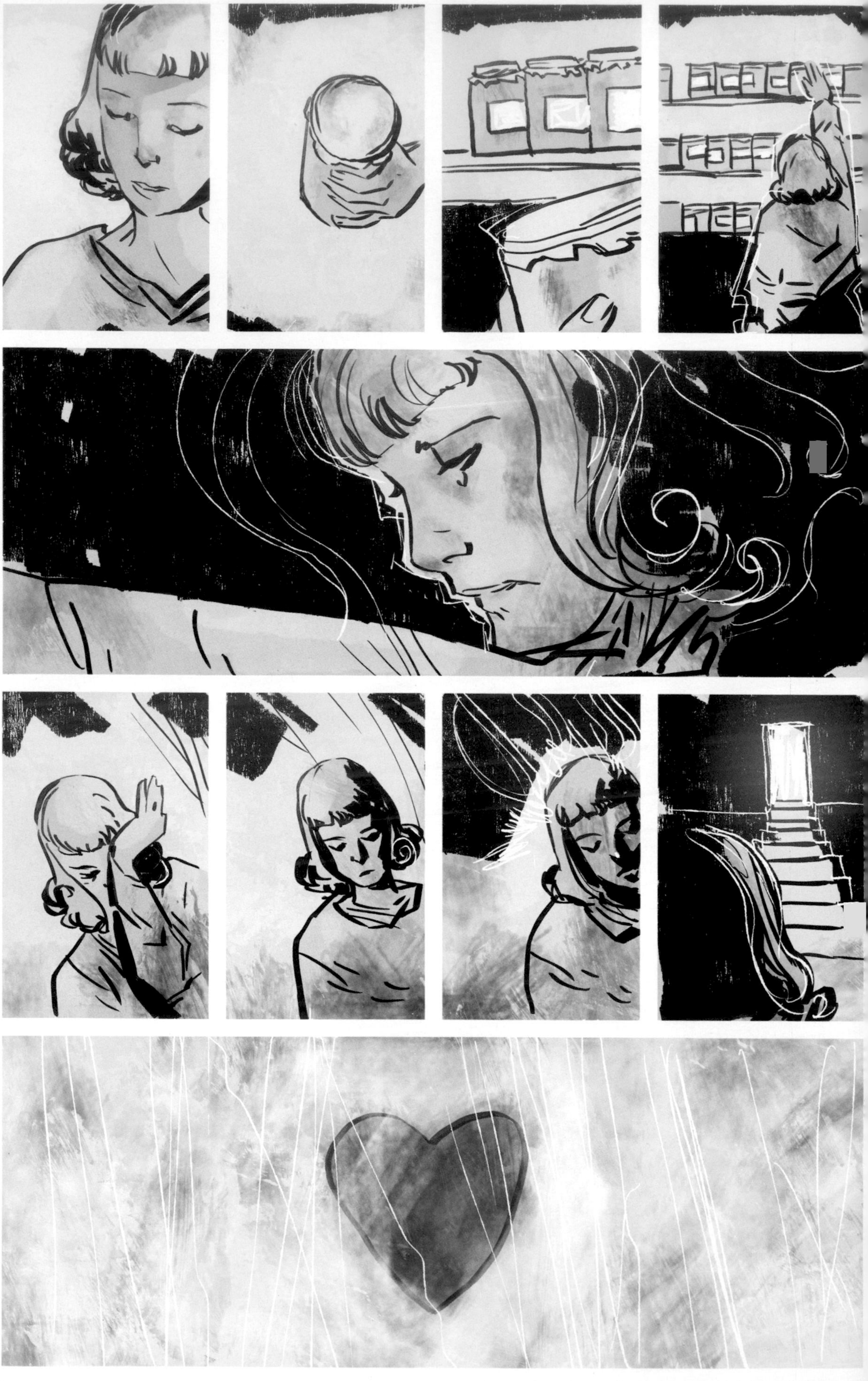

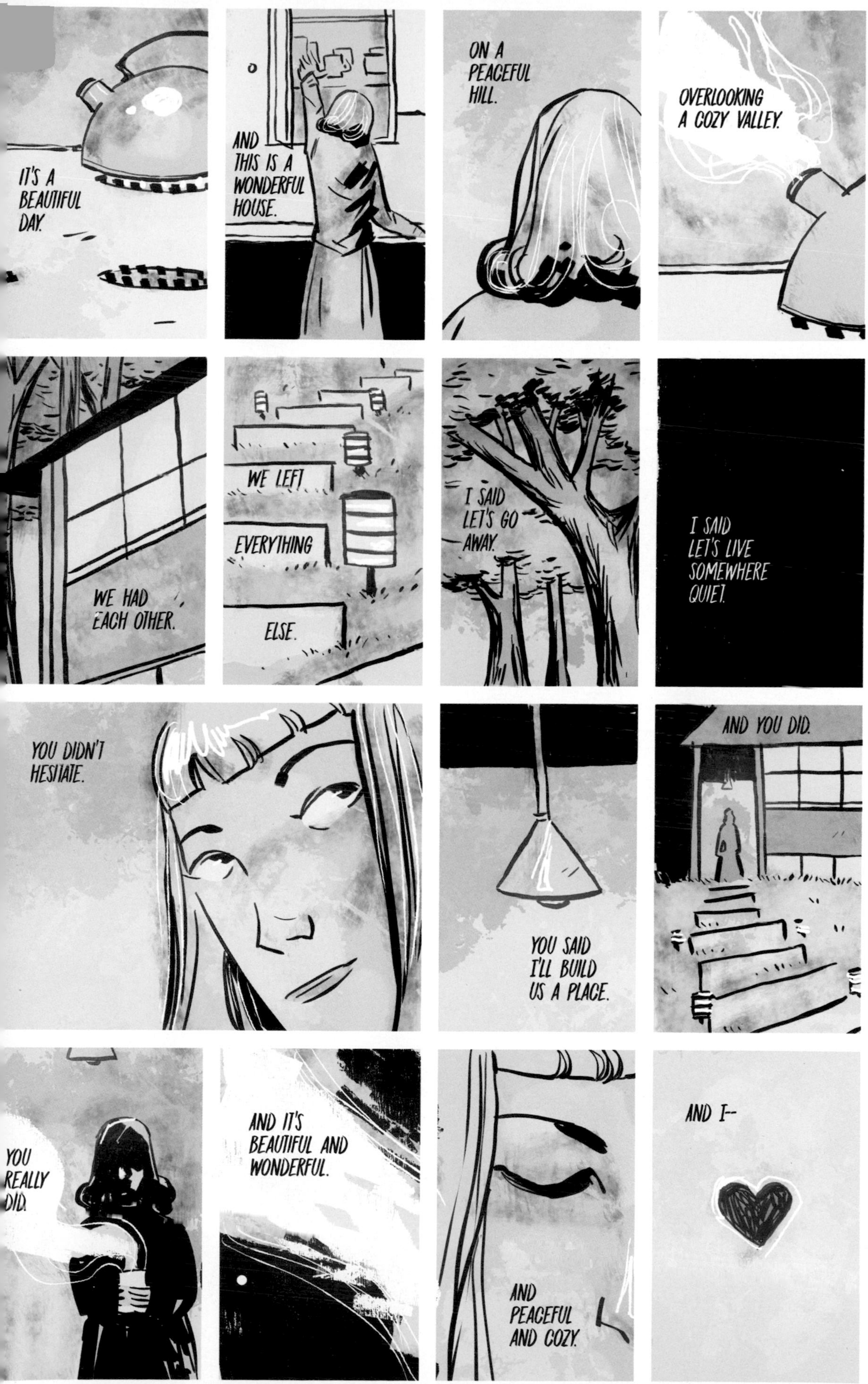
IT'S A BEAUTIFUL DAY.
AND THIS IS A WONDERFUL HOUSE.
ON A PEACEFUL HILL.
OVERLOOKING A COZY VALLEY.
WE HAD EACH OTHER.
WE LEFT
EVERYTHING
ELSE.
I SAID LET'S GO AWAY.
I SAID LET'S LIVE SOMEWHERE QUIET.
YOU DIDN'T HESITATE.
YOU SAID I'LL BUILD US A PLACE.
AND YOU DID.
YOU REALLY DID.
AND IT'S BEAUTIFUL AND WONDERFUL.
AND PEACEFUL AND COZY.
AND I--

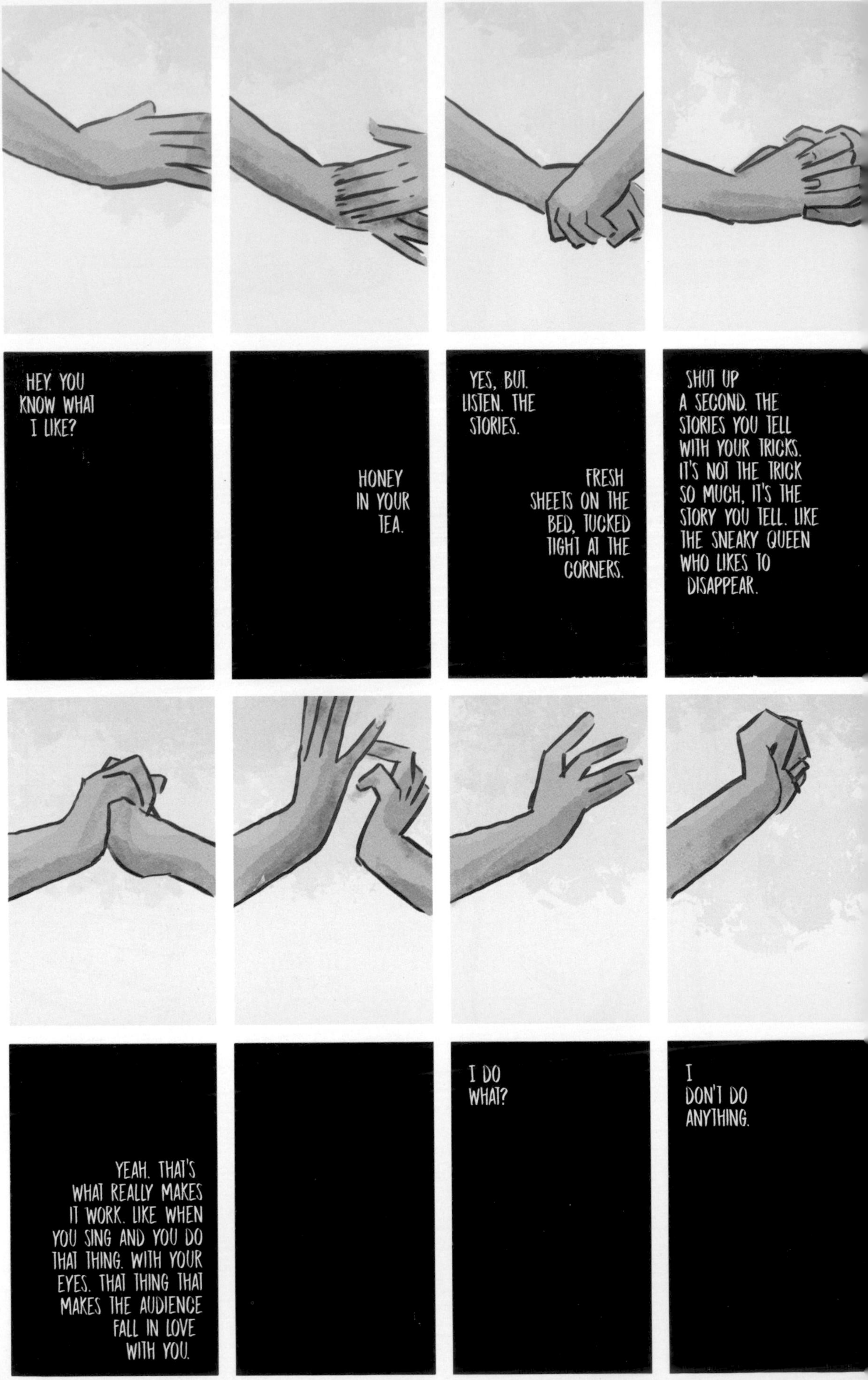
HEY. YOU KNOW WHAT I LIKE?
HONEY IN YOUR TEA.
YES, BUT. LISTEN. THE STORIES.
FRESH SHEETS ON THE BED, TUCKED TIGHT AT THE CORNERS.
SHUT UP A SECOND. THE STORIES YOU TELL WITH YOUR TRICKS. IT'S NOT THE TRICK SO MUCH, IT'S THE STORY YOU TELL. LIKE THE SNEAKY QUEEN WHO LIKES TO DISAPPEAR.
YEAH. THAT'S WHAT REALLY MAKES IT WORK. LIKE WHEN YOU SING AND YOU DO THAT THING. WITH YOUR EYES. THAT THING THAT MAKES THE AUDIENCE FALL IN LOVE WITH YOU.
I DO WHAT?
I DON'T DO ANYTHING.

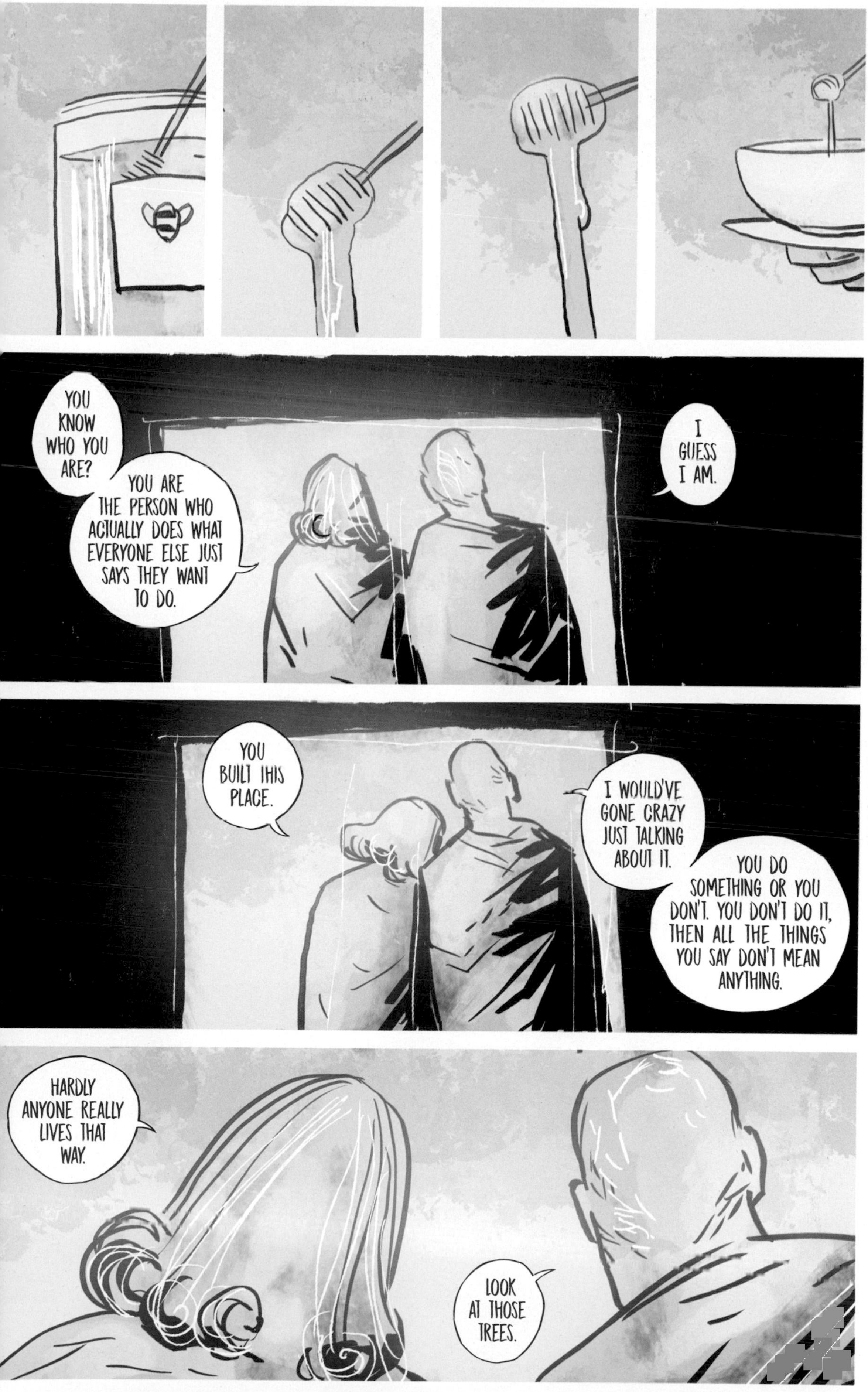
YOU KNOW WHO YOU ARE?
YOU ARE THE PERSON WHO ACTUALLY DOES WHAT EVERYONE ELSE JUST SAYS THEY WANT TO DO.
I GUESS I AM.
YOU BUILT THIS PLACE.
I WOULD'VE GONE CRAZY JUST TALKING ABOUT IT.
YOU DO SOMETHING OR YOU DON'T. YOU DON'T DO IT, THEN ALL THE THINGS YOU SAY DON'T MEAN ANYTHING.
HARDLY ANYONE REALLY LIVES THAT WAY.
LOOK AT THOSE TREES.

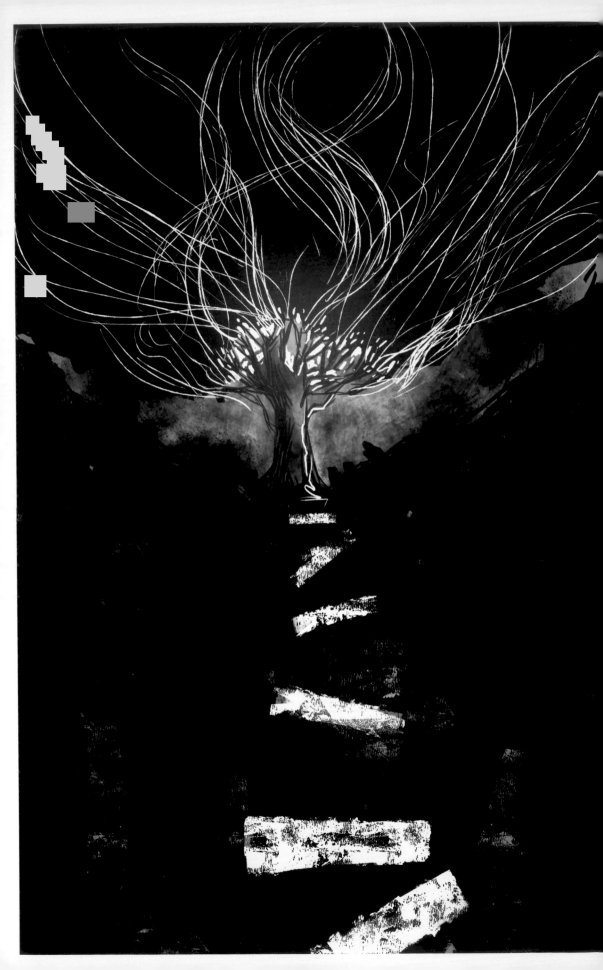

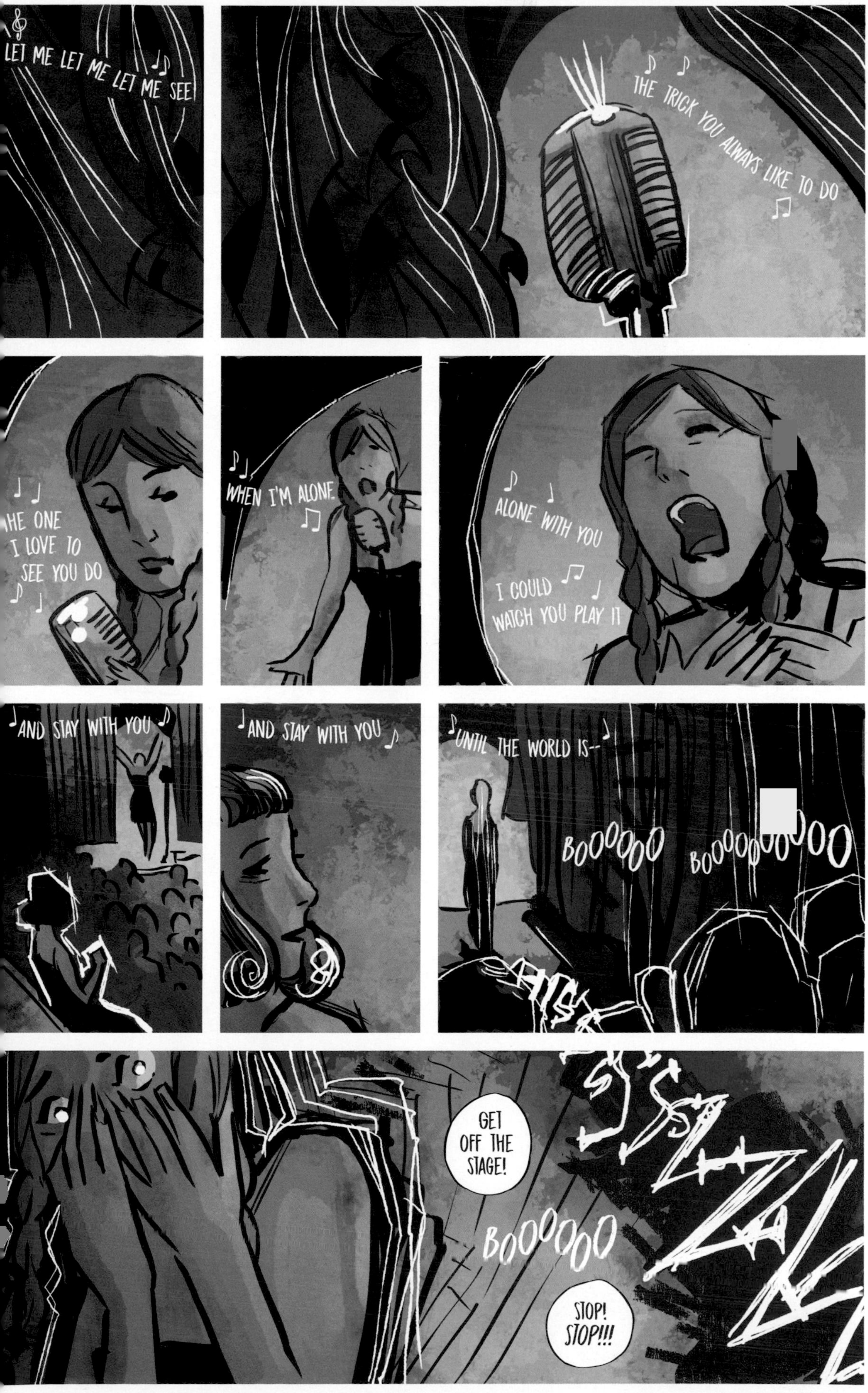
LET ME LET ME LET ME SEE
THE TRICK YOU ALWAYS LIKE TO DO
HE ONE I LOVE TO SEE YOU DO
WHEN I'M ALONE
ALONE WITH YOU
I COULD WATCH YOU PLAY IT
AND STAY WITH YOU
AND STAY WITH YOU
UNTIL THE WORLD IS--
BOOOOOO
BOOOOOOOOOO
GET OFF THE STAGE!
BOOOOOO
STOP! STOP!!!

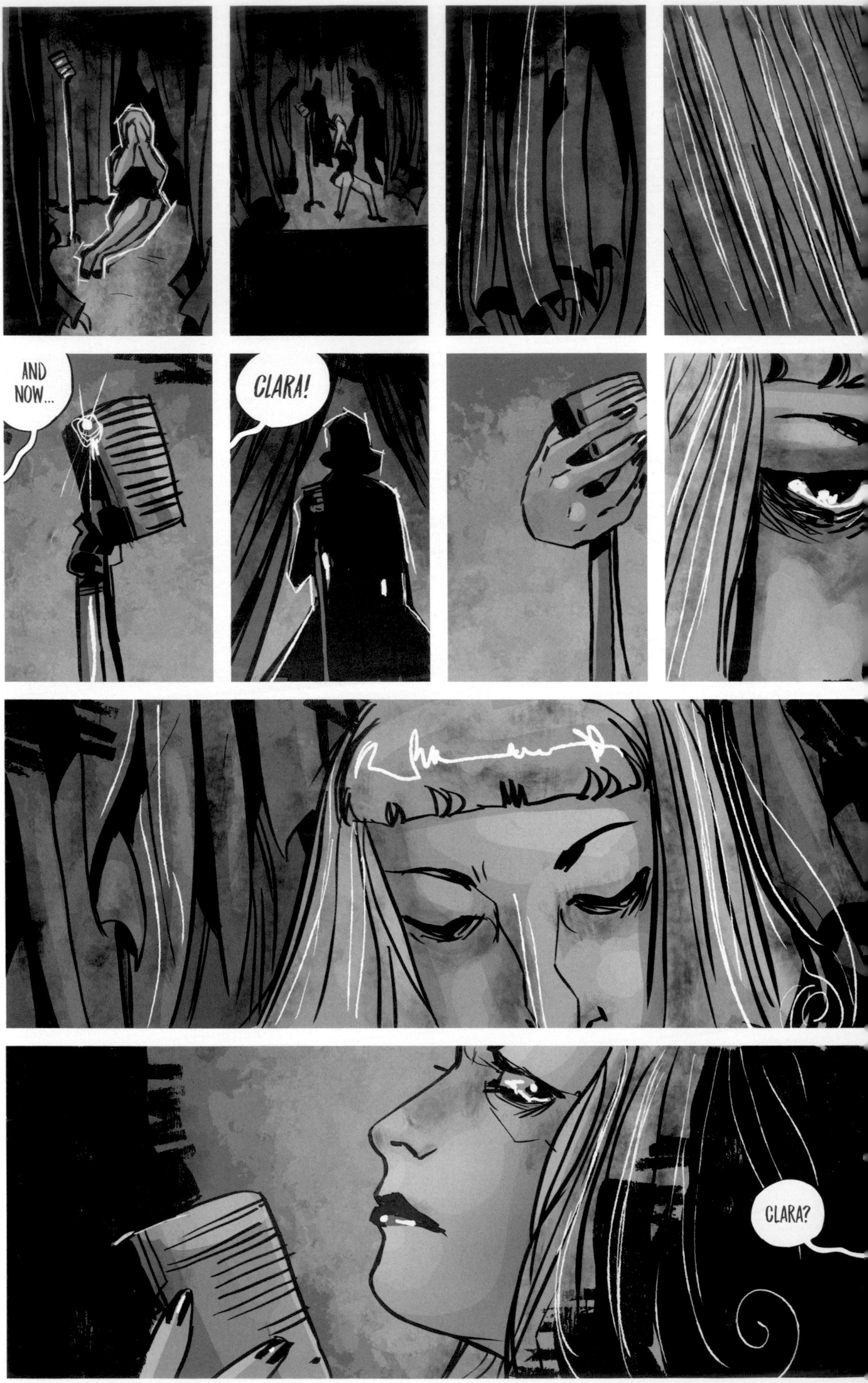
AND NOW...
CLARA!
CLARA?

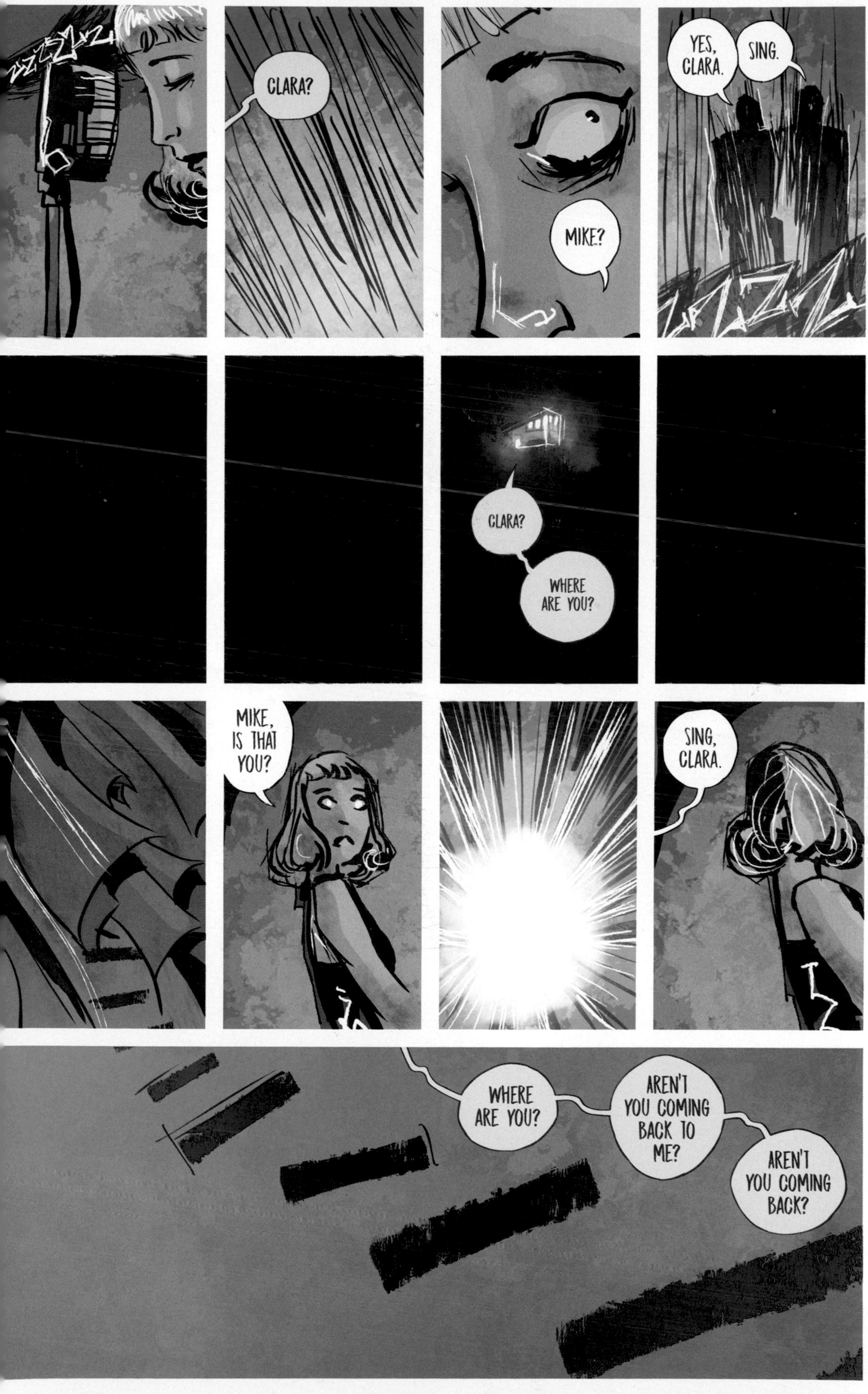
CLARA?
MIKE?
YES, CLARA.
SING.
CLARA?
WHERE ARE YOU?
MIKE, IS THAT YOU?
SING, CLARA.
WHERE ARE YOU?
AREN'T YOU COMING BACK TO ME?
AREN'T YOU COMING BACK?

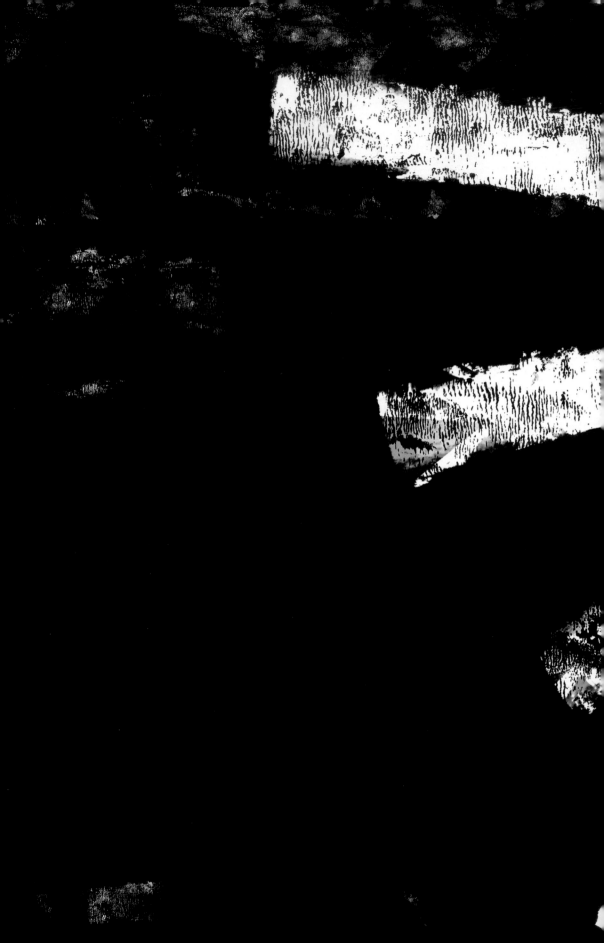

CHAPTER 4

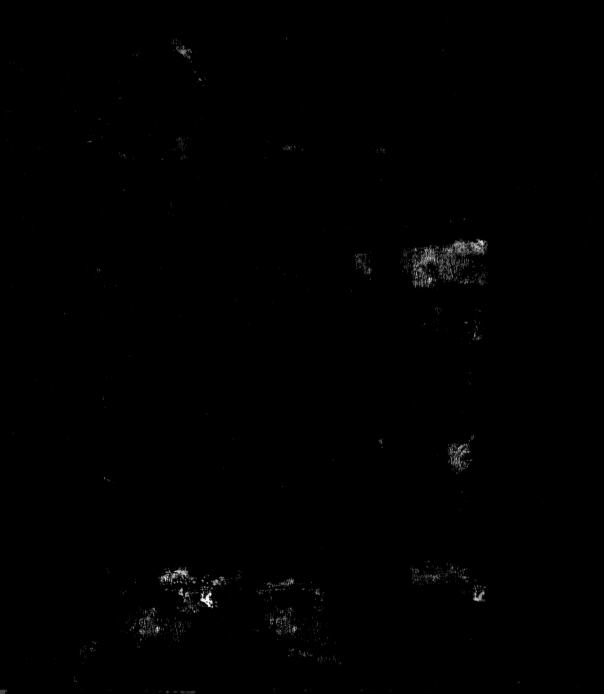

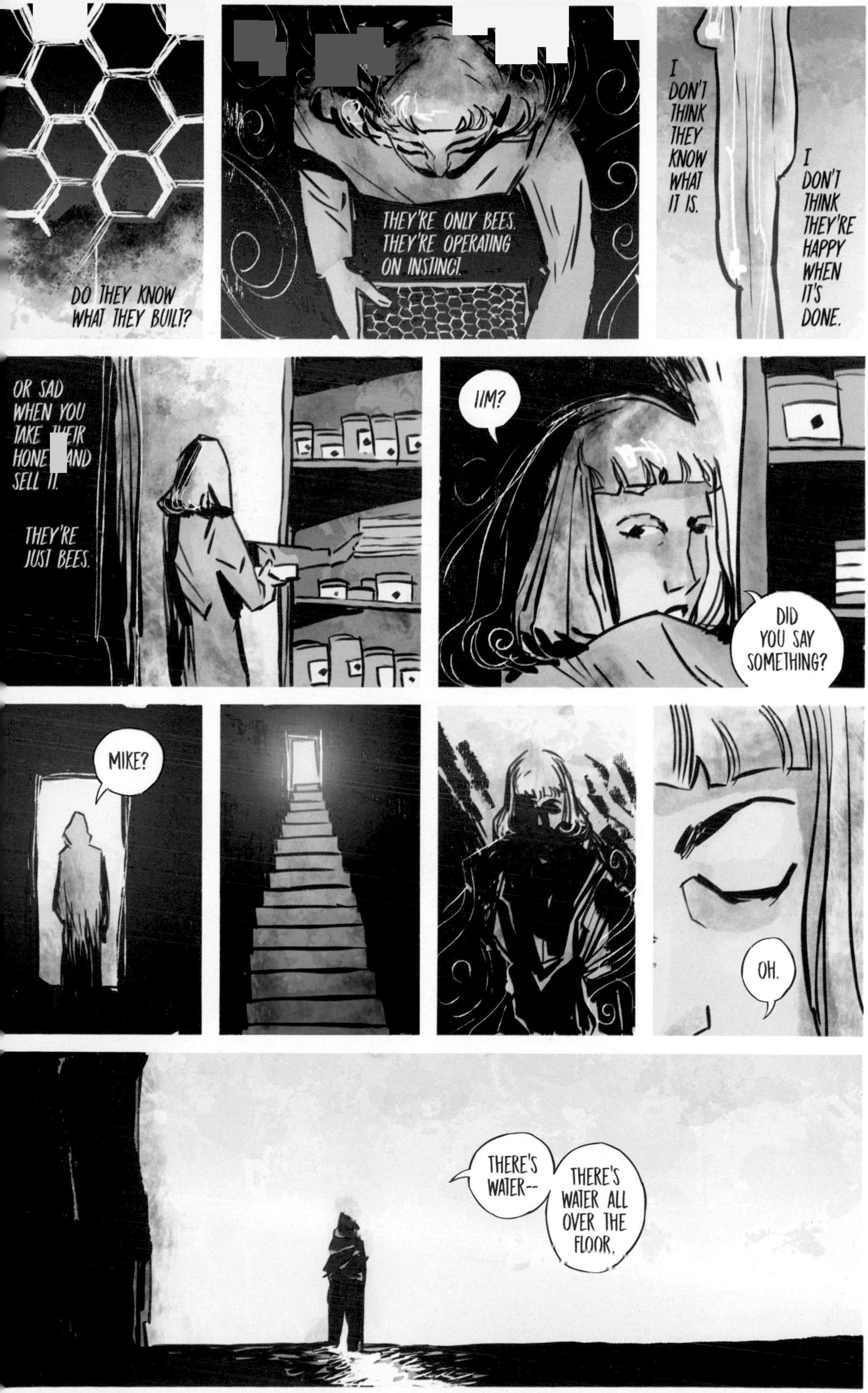
DO THEY KNOW WHAT THEY BUILT?
THEY'RE ONLY BEES. THEY'RE OPERATING ON INSTINCT.
I DON'T THINK THEY KNOW WHAT IT IS.
I DON'T THINK THEY'RE HAPPY WHEN IT'S DONE.
OR SAD WHEN YOU TAKE THEIR HONE AND SELL IT.
THEY'RE JUST BEES.
JIM?
DID YOU SAY SOMETHING?
MIKE?
OH.
THERE'S WATER--
THERE'S WATER ALL OVER THE FLOOR.

MIKE!

MIKE!!

THERE'S WATER
EVERYWHERE!

IS
IT STILL
RAINING?

IT'S
COMING IN
SOMEWHERE.

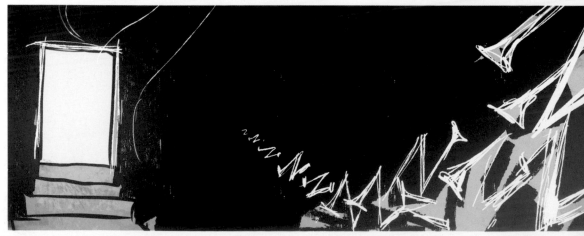

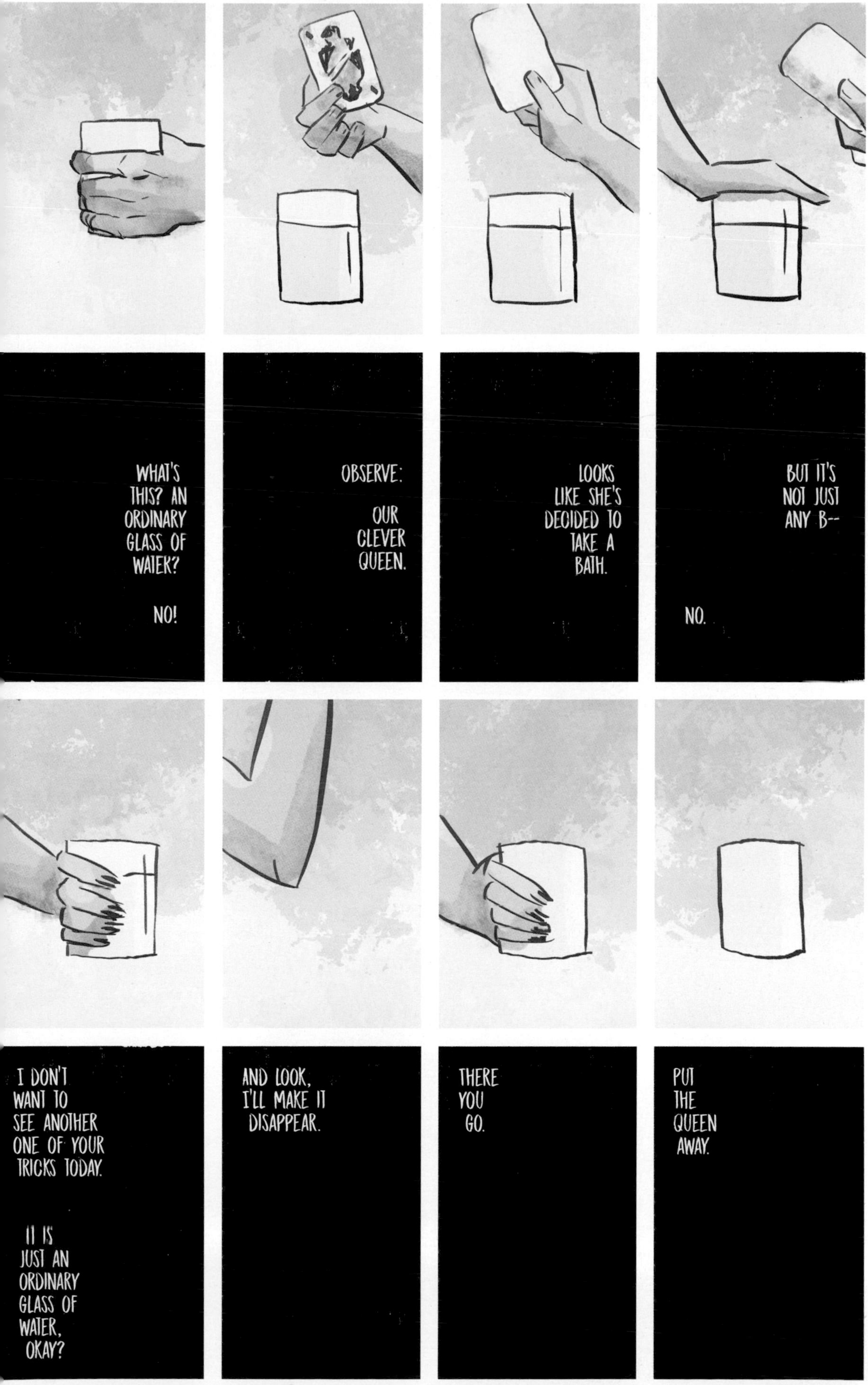
WHAT'S THIS? AN ORDINARY GLASS OF WATER?
NO!
OBSERVE:
OUR CLEVER QUEEN.
LOOKS LIKE SHE'S DECIDED TO TAKE A BATH.
BUT IT'S NOT JUST ANY B--
NO.
I DON'T WANT TO SEE ANOTHER ONE OF YOUR TRICKS TODAY.
IT IS JUST AN ORDINARY GLASS OF WATER, OKAY?
AND LOOK, I'LL MAKE IT DISAPPEAR.
THERE YOU GO.
PUT THE QUEEN AWAY.

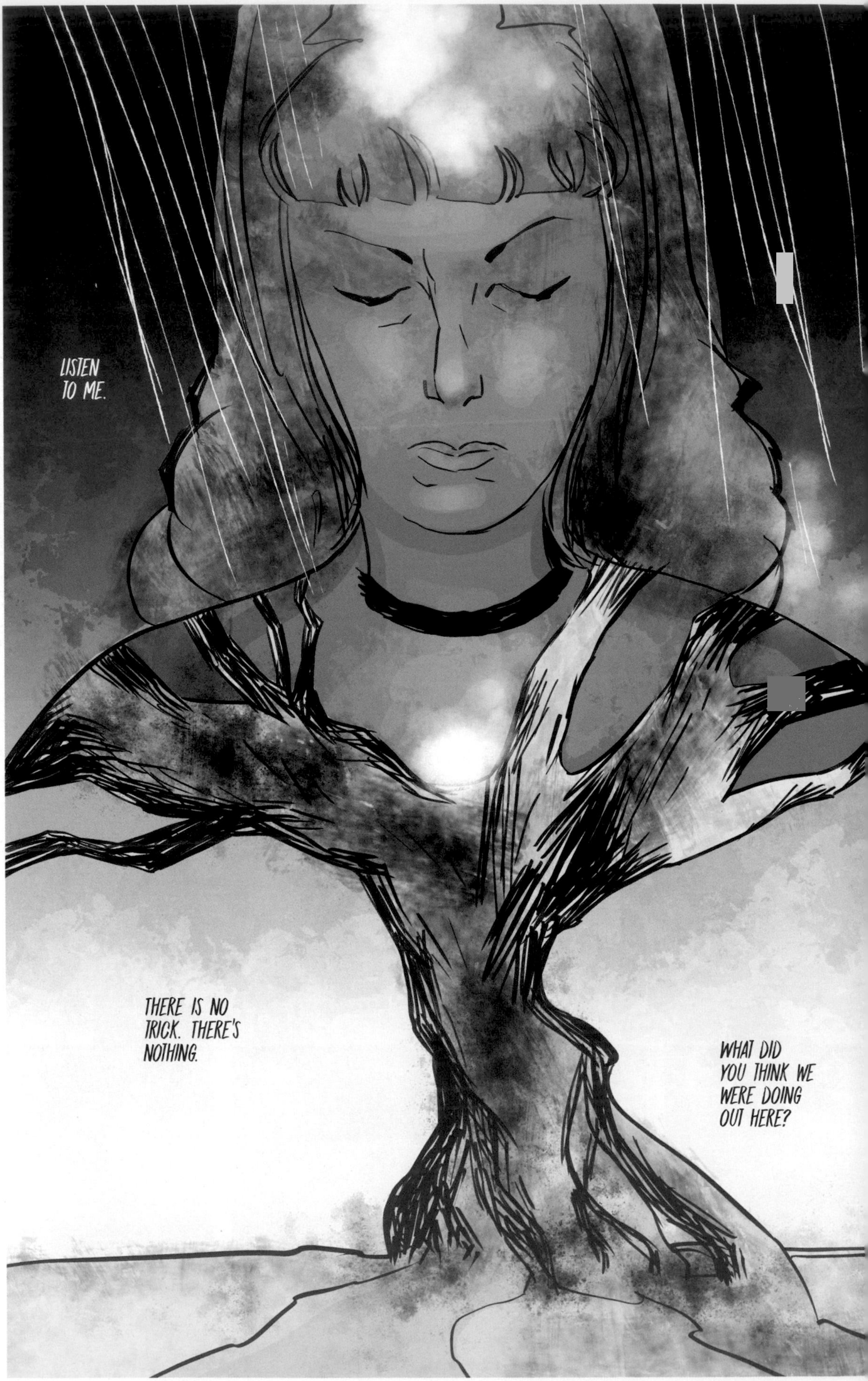
LISTEN TO ME.
THERE IS NO TRICK. THERE'S NOTHING.
WHAT DID YOU THINK WE WERE DOING OUT HERE?

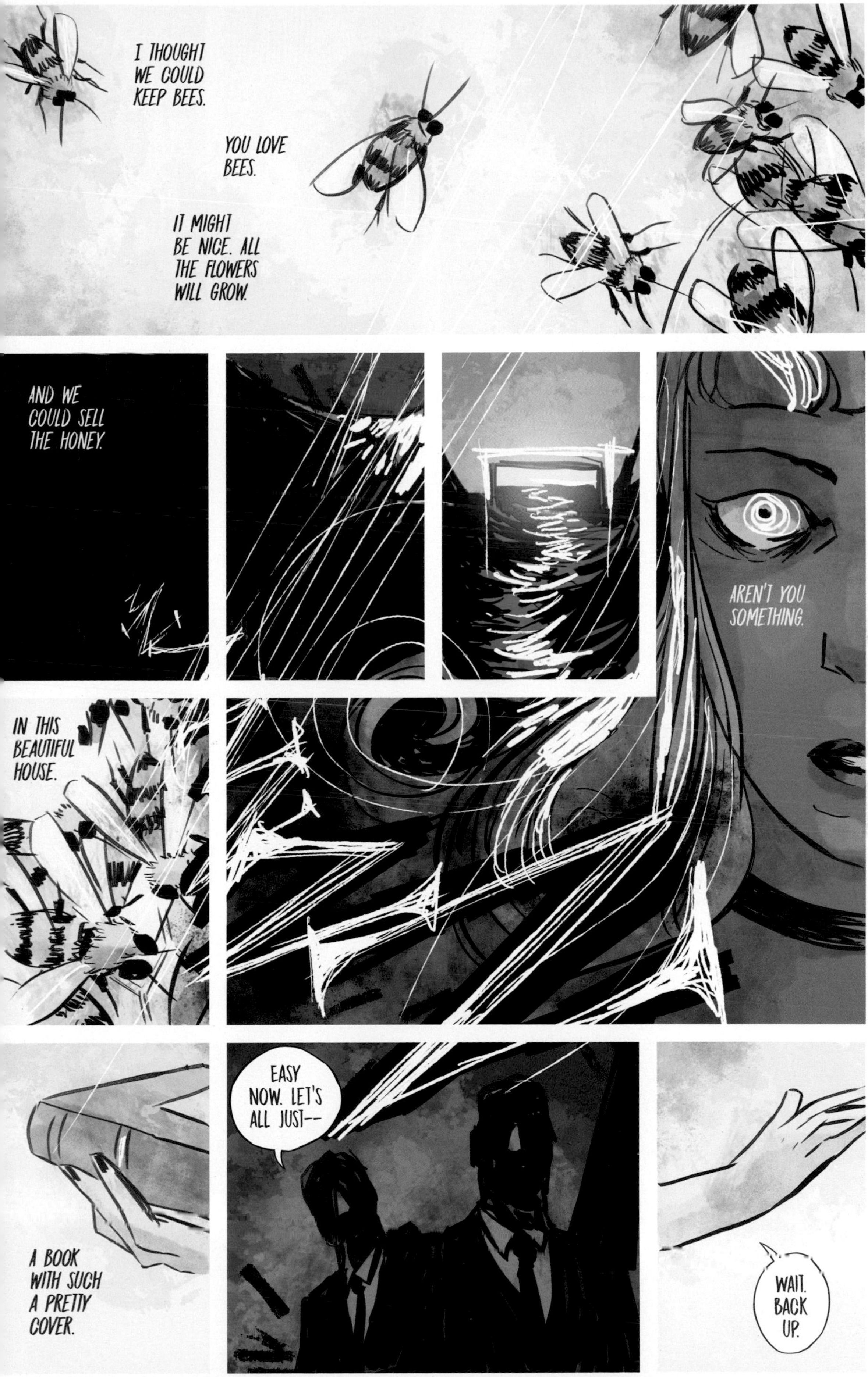
I THOUGHT WE COULD KEEP BEES.
YOU LOVE BEES.
IT MIGHT BE NICE. ALL THE FLOWERS WILL GROW.
AND WE COULD SELL THE HONEY.
AREN'T YOU SOMETHING.
IN THIS BEAUTIFUL HOUSE.
A BOOK WITH SUCH A PRETTY COVER.
EASY NOW. LET'S ALL JUST--
WAIT. BACK UP.

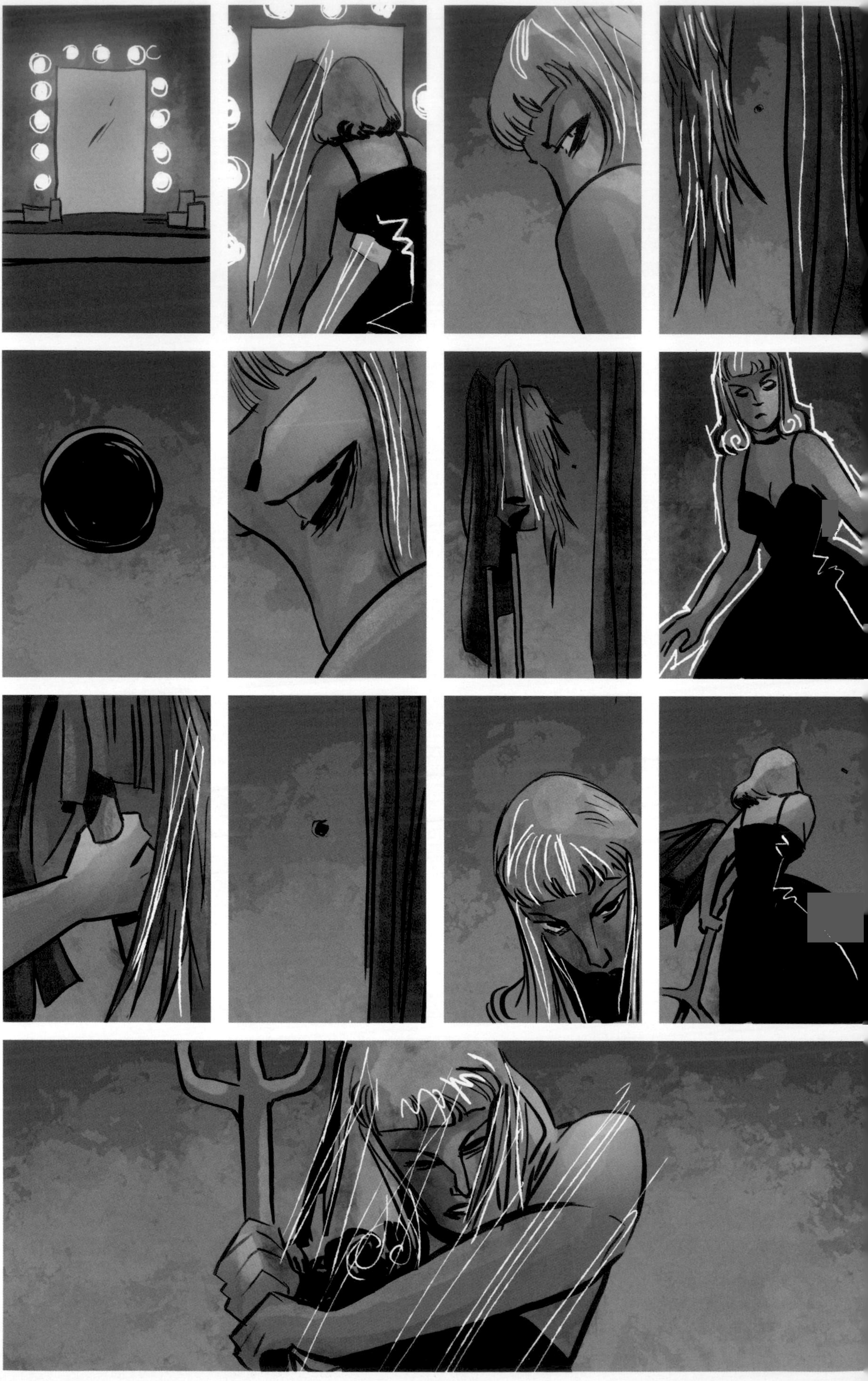

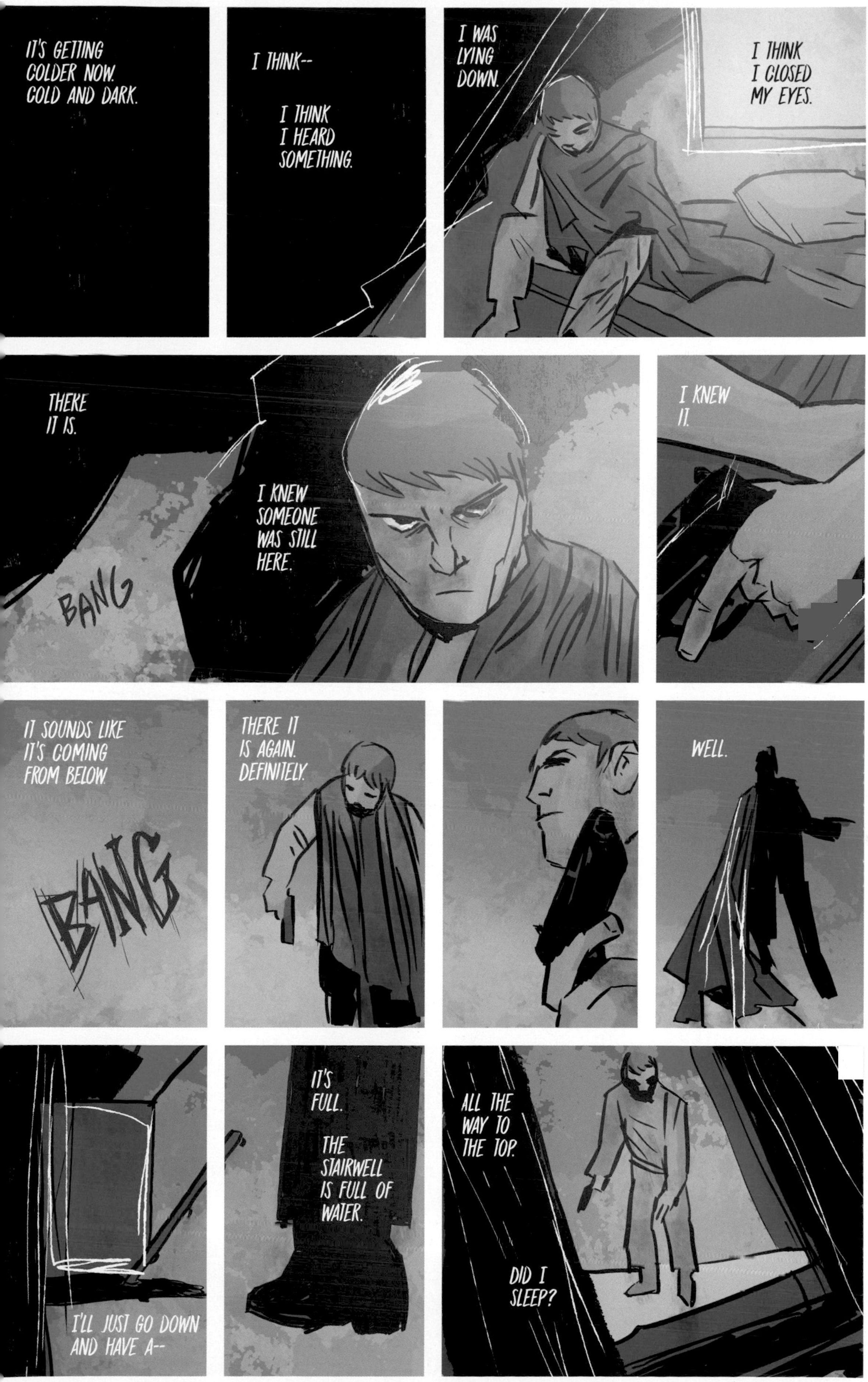
IT'S GETTING COLDER NOW. COLD AND DARK.
I THINK--
I THINK I HEARD SOMETHING.
I WAS LYING DOWN.
I THINK I CLOSED MY EYES.
THERE IT IS.
BANG
I KNEW SOMEONE WAS STILL HERE.
I KNEW IT.
IT SOUNDS LIKE IT'S COMING FROM BELOW.
BANG
THERE IT IS AGAIN. DEFINITELY.
WELL.
I'LL JUST GO DOWN AND HAVE A--
IT'S FULL.
THE STAIRWELL IS FULL OF WATER.
ALL THE WAY TO THE TOP.
DID I SLEEP?

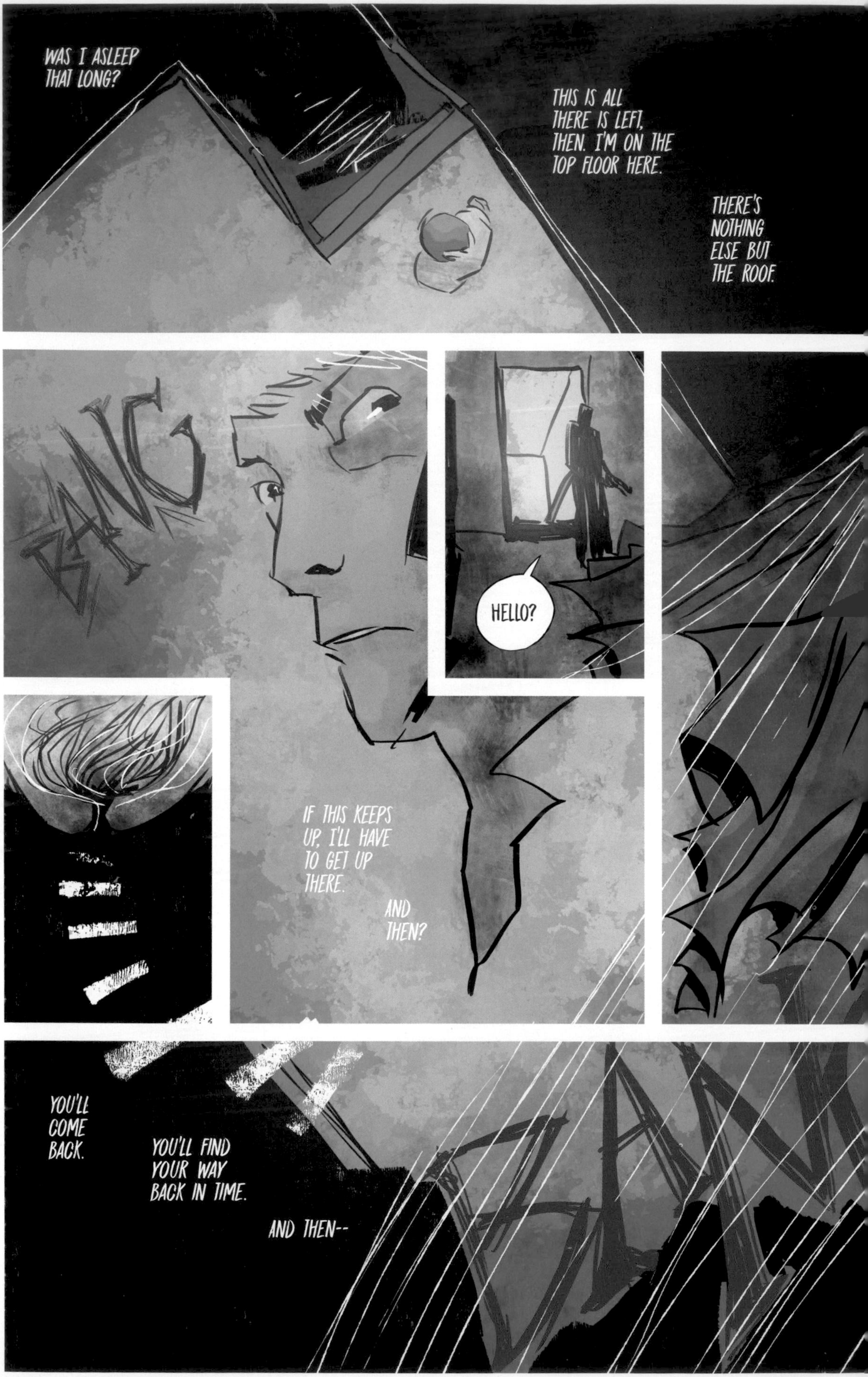
WAS I ASLEEP THAT LONG?
THIS IS ALL THERE IS LEFT, THEN. I'M ON THE TOP FLOOR HERE.
THERE'S NOTHING ELSE BUT THE ROOF.
BANG
HELLO?
IF THIS KEEPS UP, I'LL HAVE TO GET UP THERE.
AND THEN?
YOU'LL COME BACK.
YOU'LL FIND YOUR WAY BACK IN TIME.
AND THEN--

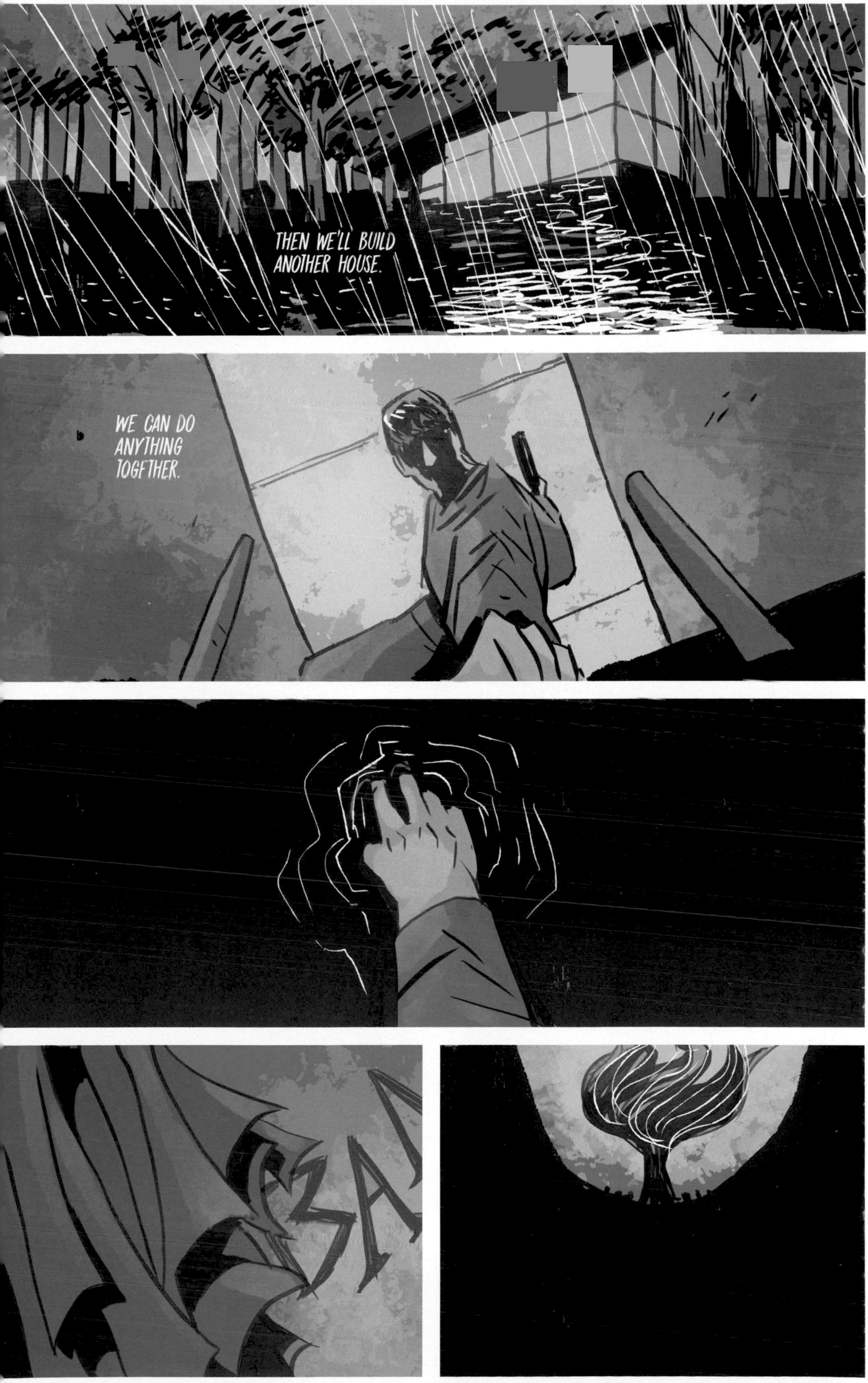

THEN WE'LL BUILD ANOTHER HOUSE.
WE CAN DO ANYTHING TOGETHER.

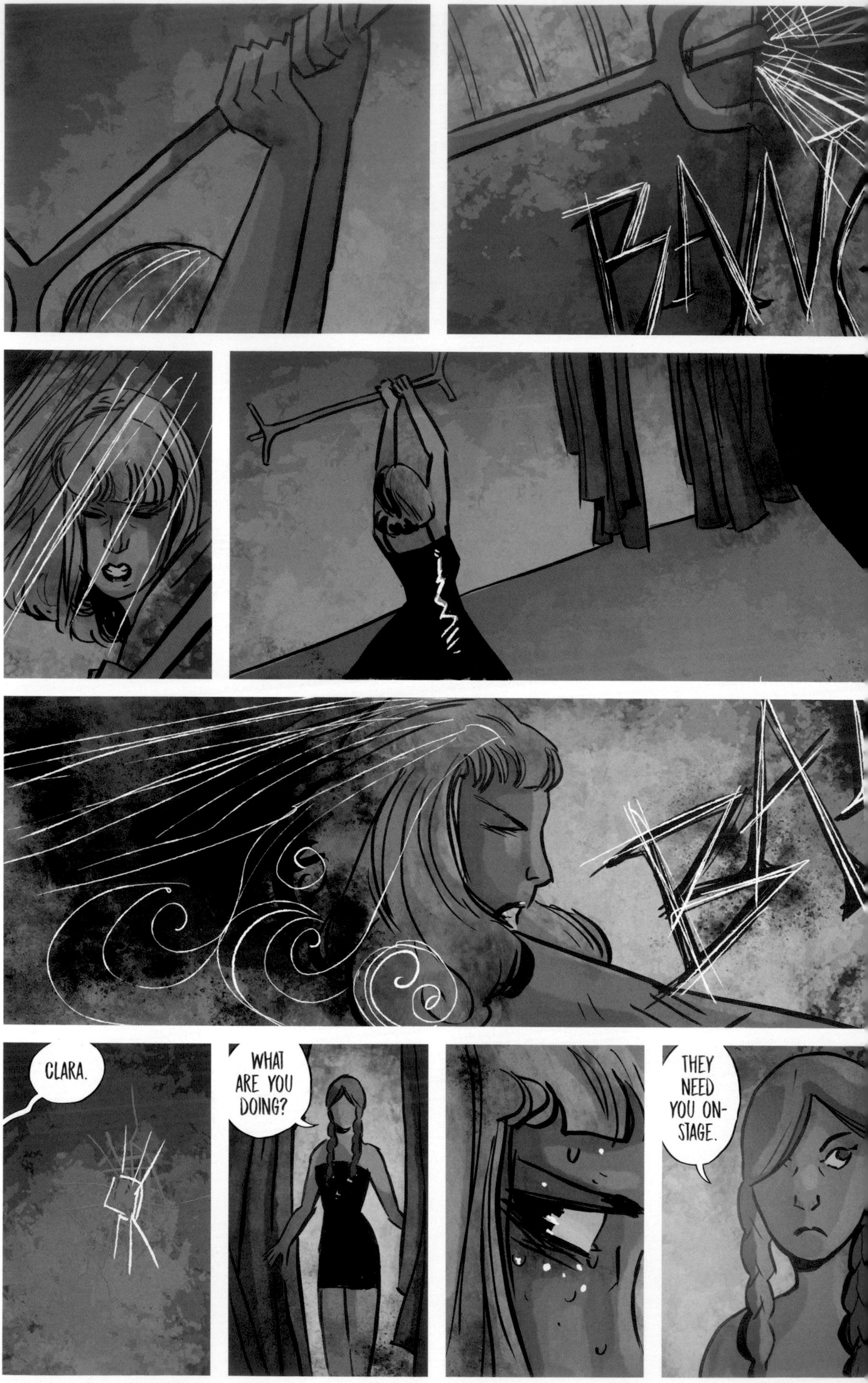
BANG
BANG
CLARA.
WHAT ARE YOU DOING?
THEY NEED YOU ON-STAGE.

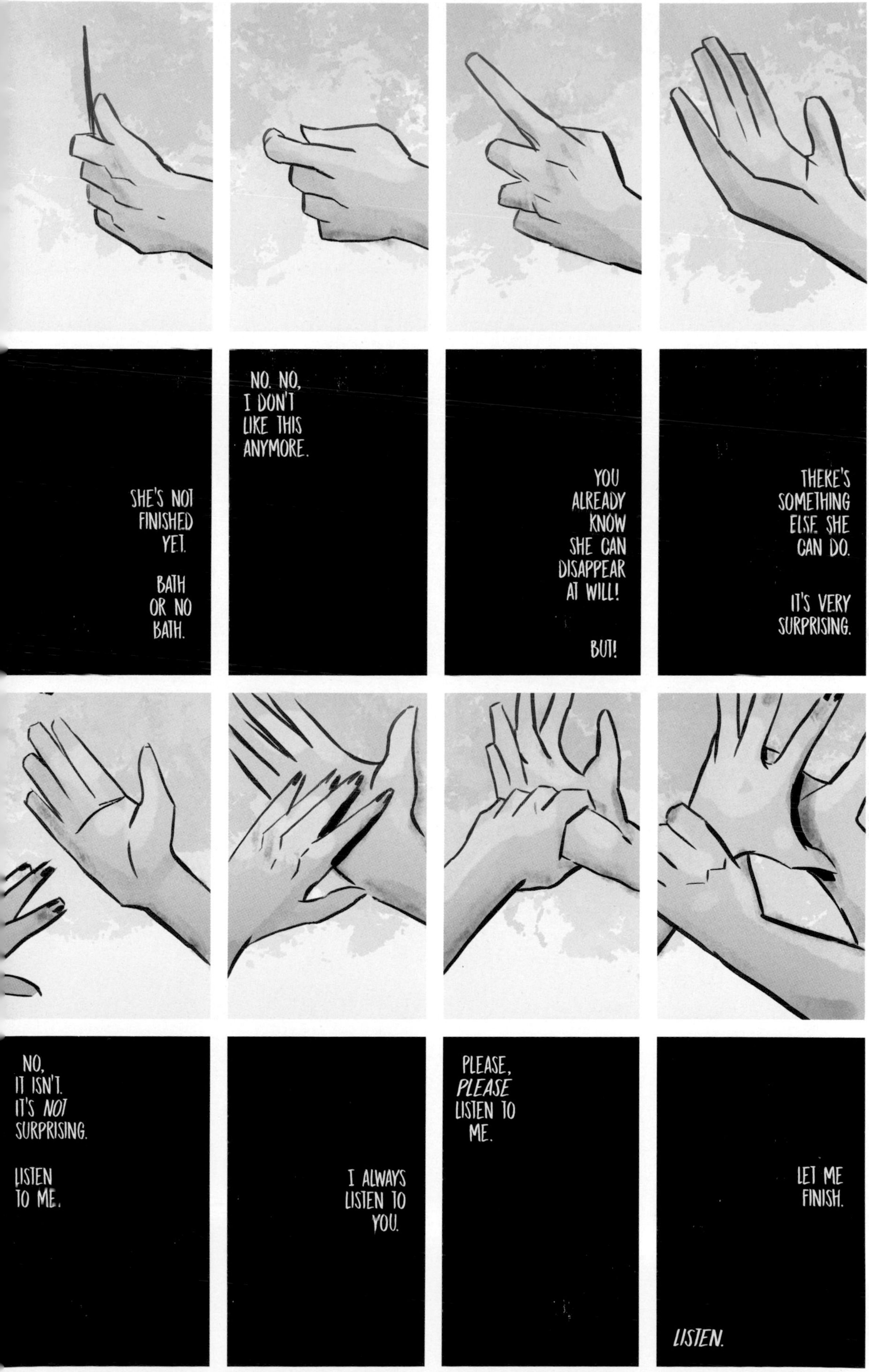
SHE'S NOT FINISHED YET.
BATH OR NO BATH.
NO. NO, I DON'T LIKE THIS ANYMORE.
YOU ALREADY KNOW SHE CAN DISAPPEAR AT WILL!
BUT!
THERE'S SOMETHING ELSE SHE CAN DO.
IT'S VERY SURPRISING.
NO, IT ISN'T. IT'S *NOT* SURPRISING.
LISTEN TO ME.
I ALWAYS LISTEN TO YOU.
PLEASE, *PLEASE* LISTEN TO ME.
LET ME FINISH.
LISTEN.

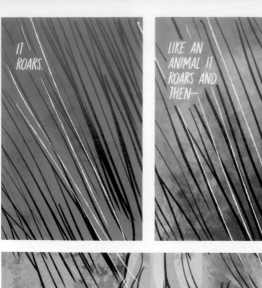

IT ROARS.

LIKE AN ANIMAL IT ROARS AND THEN--

--IT HISSES.

HISSES AND SNAPS.

WHAT'S WRONG WITH YOU?

THEY'RE WAITING.

EVERYBODY'S WAITING.

IS THERE SOMETHING WRONG?

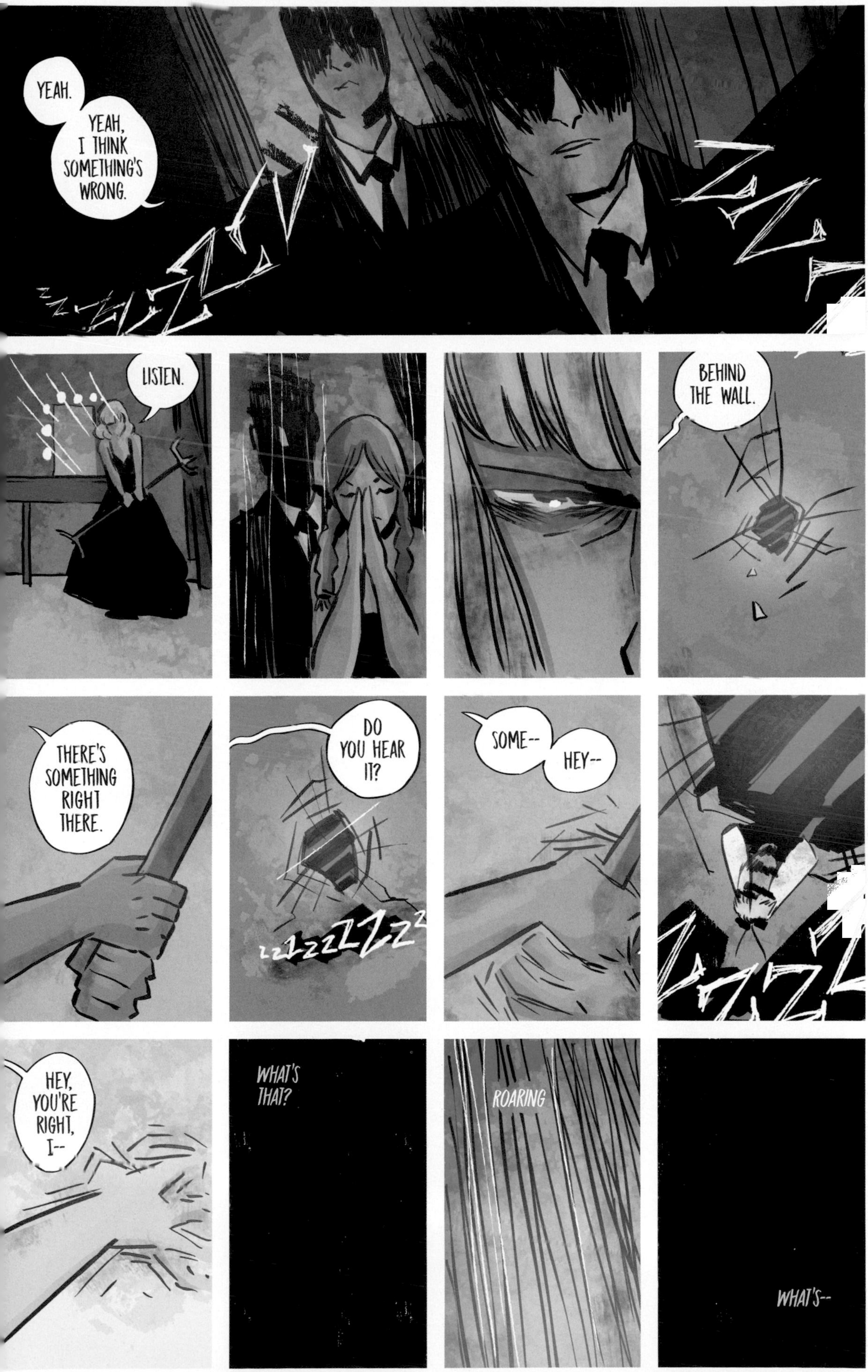
YEAH.
YEAH, I THINK SOMETHING'S WRONG.
LISTEN.
BEHIND THE WALL.
THERE'S SOMETHING RIGHT THERE.
DO YOU HEAR IT?
SOME--
HEY--
HEY, YOU'RE RIGHT, I--
WHAT'S THAT?
ROARING
WHAT'S--

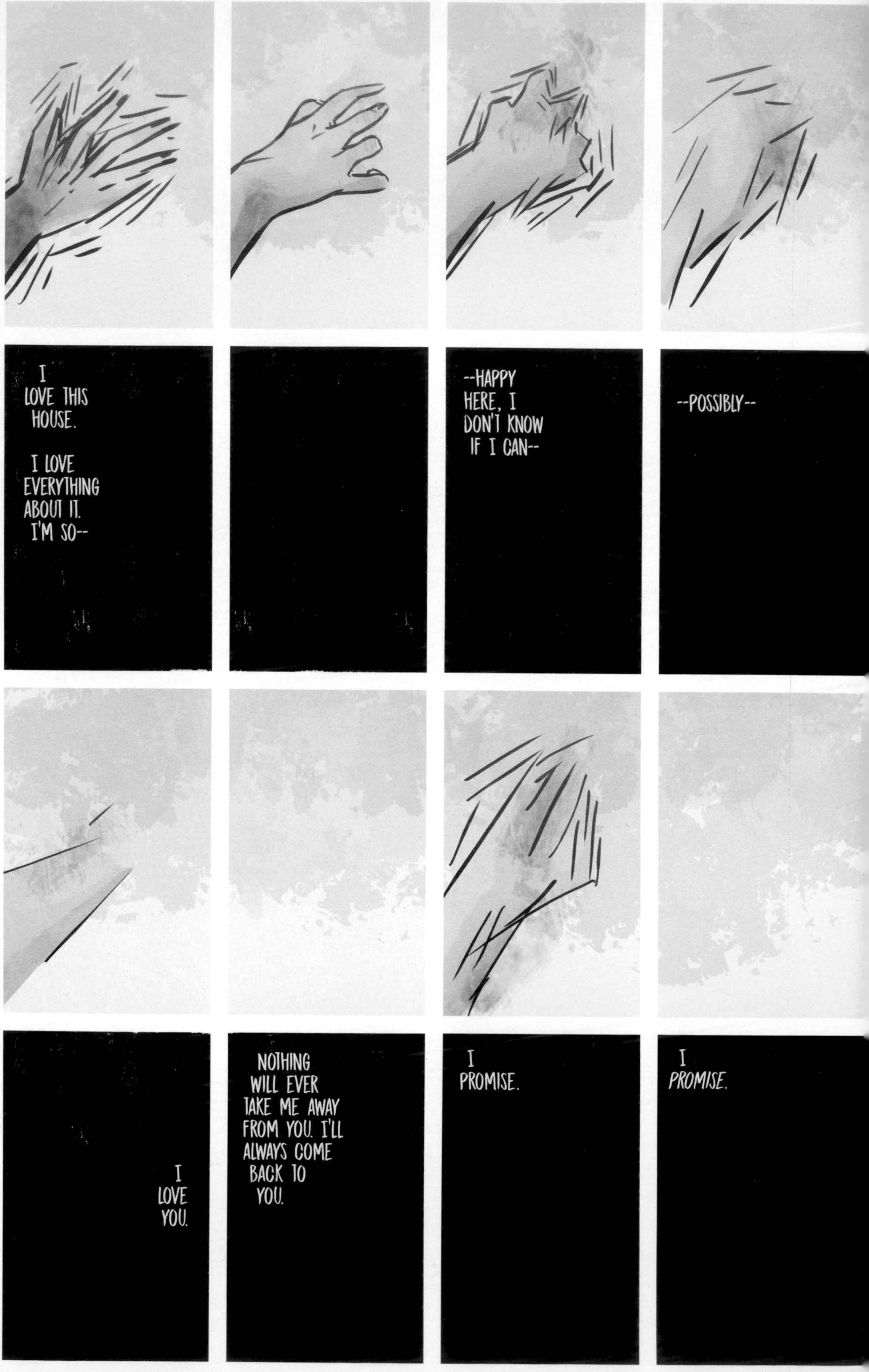
I LOVE THIS HOUSE.
I LOVE EVERYTHING ABOUT IT. I'M SO--
--HAPPY HERE, I DON'T KNOW IF I CAN--
--POSSIBLY--
I LOVE YOU.
NOTHING WILL EVER TAKE ME AWAY FROM YOU. I'LL ALWAYS COME BACK TO YOU.
I PROMISE.
I *PROMISE.*

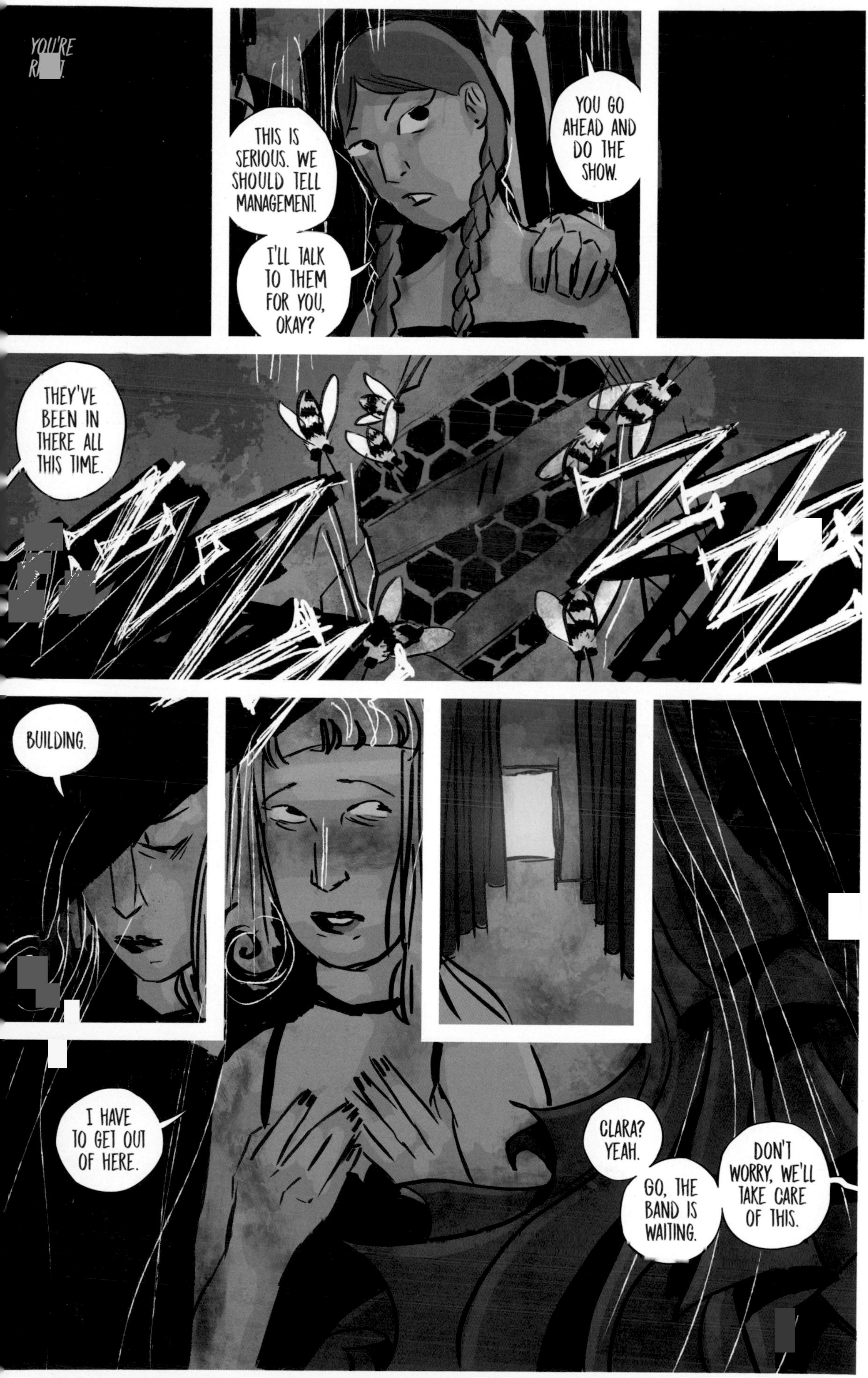
YOU'RE
THIS IS SERIOUS. WE SHOULD TELL MANAGEMENT.
I'LL TALK TO THEM FOR YOU, OKAY?
YOU GO AHEAD AND DO THE SHOW.
THEY'VE BEEN IN THERE ALL THIS TIME.
BUILDING.
I HAVE TO GET OUT OF HERE.
CLARA? YEAH.
GO, THE BAND IS WAITING.
DON'T WORRY, WE'LL TAKE CARE OF THIS.

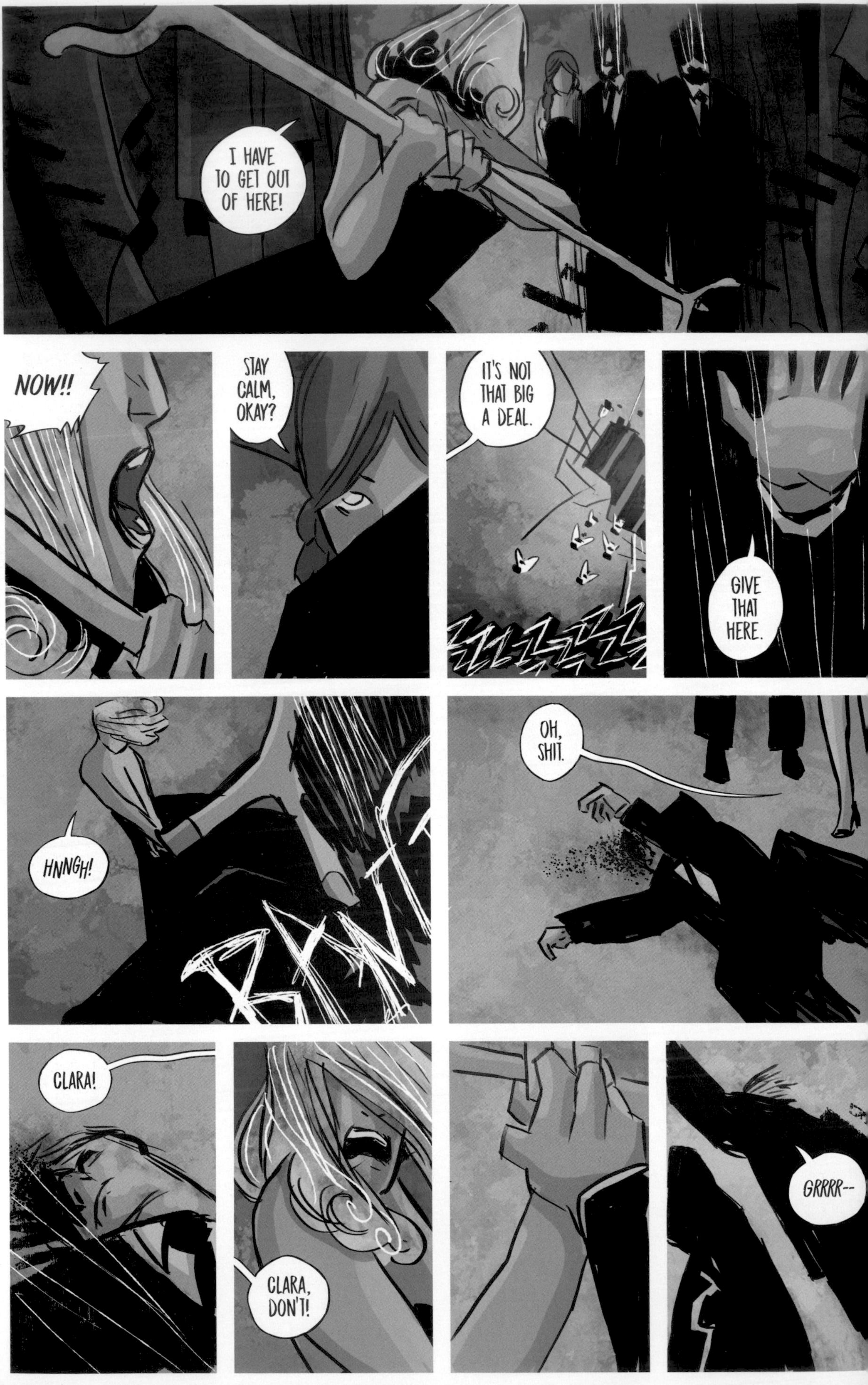
I HAVE TO GET OUT OF HERE!
NOW!!
STAY CALM, OKAY?
IT'S NOT THAT BIG A DEAL.
GIVE THAT HERE.
HNNGH!
OH, SHIT.
CLARA!
CLARA, DON'T!
GRRRR--

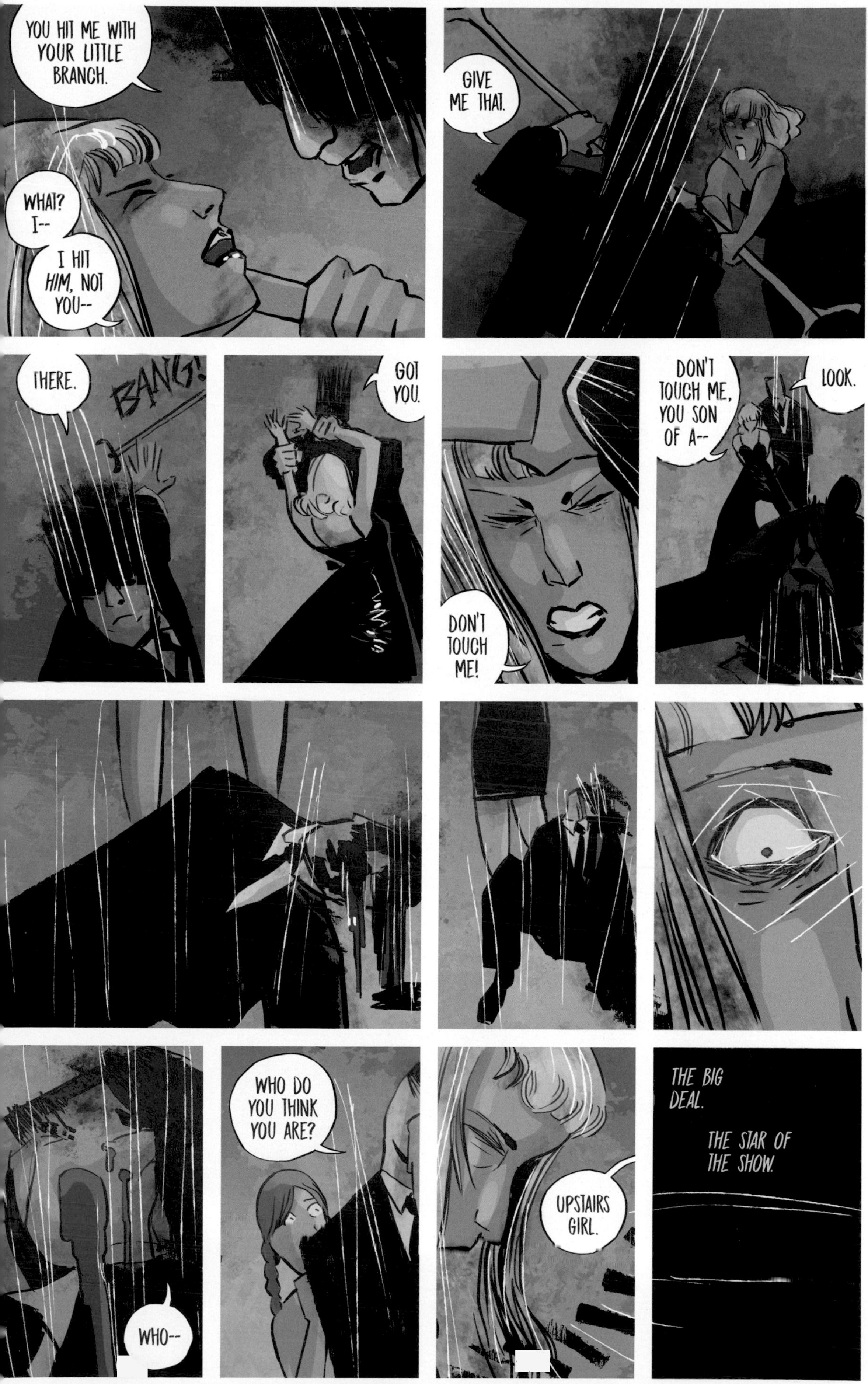
YOU HIT ME WITH YOUR LITTLE BRANCH.
WHAT? I--
I HIT *HIM*, NOT YOU--
GIVE ME THAT.
THERE.
BANG!
GOT YOU.
DON'T TOUCH ME!
DON'T TOUCH ME, YOU SON OF A--
LOOK.
WHO--
WHO DO YOU THINK YOU ARE?
UPSTAIRS GIRL.
THE BIG DEAL.
THE STAR OF THE SHOW.

THERE IS NO DOWNSTAIRS ANYMORE.

IT'S GONE.

IF IT'S LIKE THIS HERE NOW--

WHAT'S IT LIKE EVERYWHERE ELSE?

CITIES UNDER WATER.

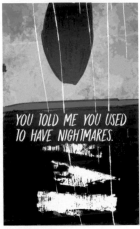

YOU TOLD ME YOU USED TO HAVE NIGHTMARES.

BEFORE WE CAME HERE.

I PICKED THIS PLACE FOR US.

HIGH ON A--

THERE IS SOMETHING DOWN THERE.

IN THE WATER.

I SAW IT MOVE.

I SAW IT.

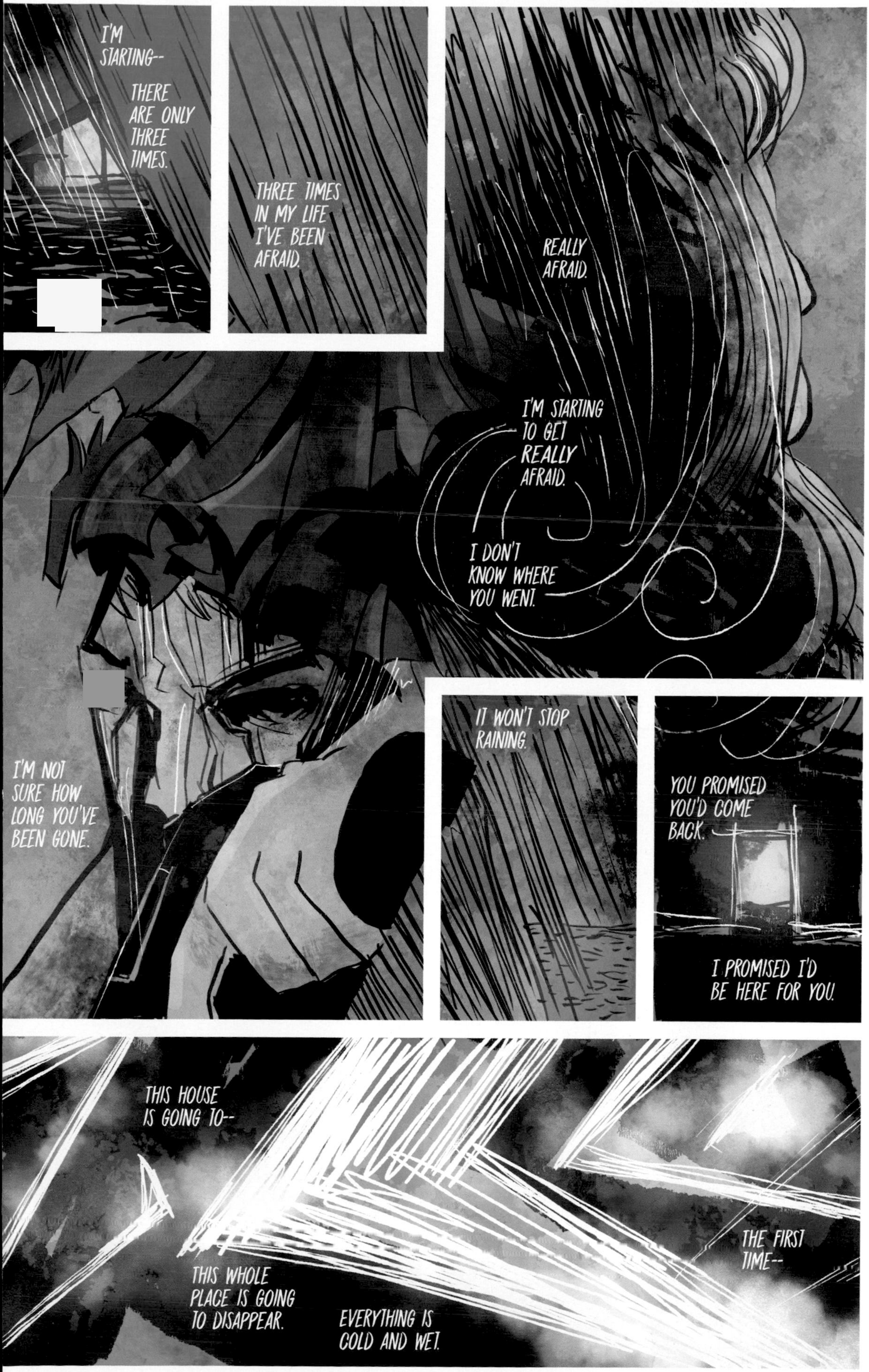
I'M STARTING--
THERE ARE ONLY THREE TIMES.
THREE TIMES IN MY LIFE I'VE BEEN AFRAID.
REALLY AFRAID.
I'M STARTING TO GET REALLY AFRAID.
I DON'T KNOW WHERE YOU WENT.
I'M NOT SURE HOW LONG YOU'VE BEEN GONE.
IT WON'T STOP RAINING.
YOU PROMISED YOU'D COME BACK.
I PROMISED I'D BE HERE FOR YOU.
THIS HOUSE IS GOING TO--
THIS WHOLE PLACE IS GOING TO DISAPPEAR.
EVERYTHING IS COLD AND WET.
THE FIRST TIME--

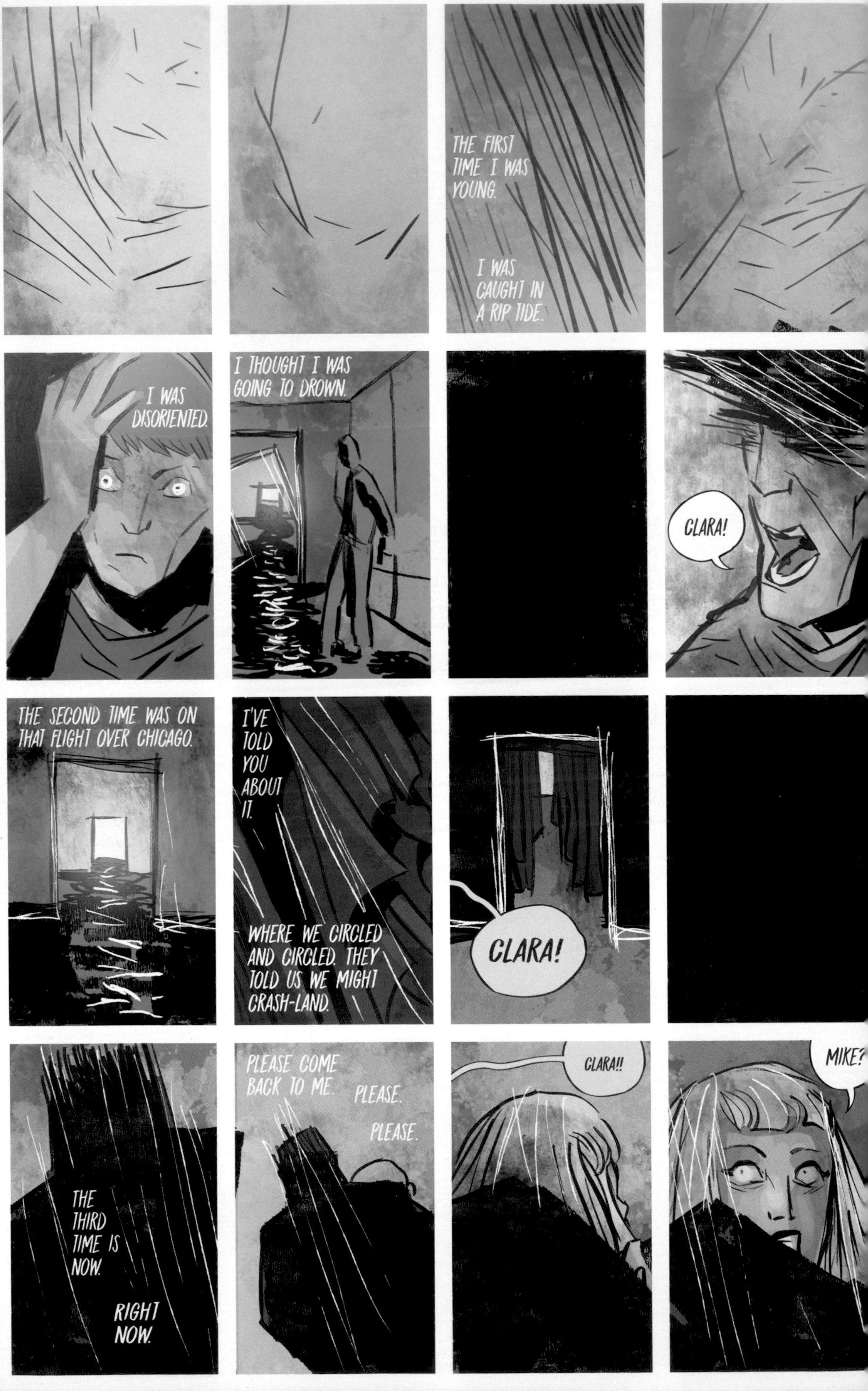
THE FIRST TIME I WAS YOUNG.
I WAS CAUGHT IN A RIP TIDE.
I WAS DISORIENTED.
I THOUGHT I WAS GOING TO DROWN.
CLARA!
THE SECOND TIME WAS ON THAT FLIGHT OVER CHICAGO.
I'VE TOLD YOU ABOUT IT.
WHERE WE CIRCLED AND CIRCLED. THEY TOLD US WE MIGHT CRASH-LAND.
CLARA!
THE THIRD TIME IS NOW.
RIGHT NOW.
PLEASE COME BACK TO ME.
PLEASE.
PLEASE.
CLARA!!
MIKE?

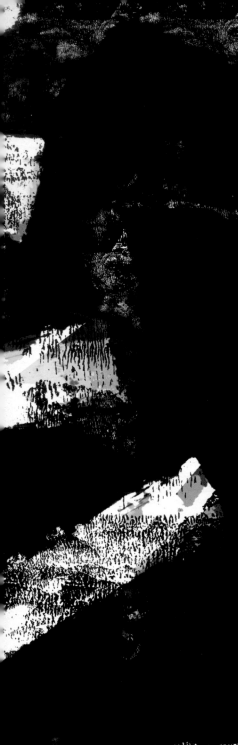

CHAPTER 5

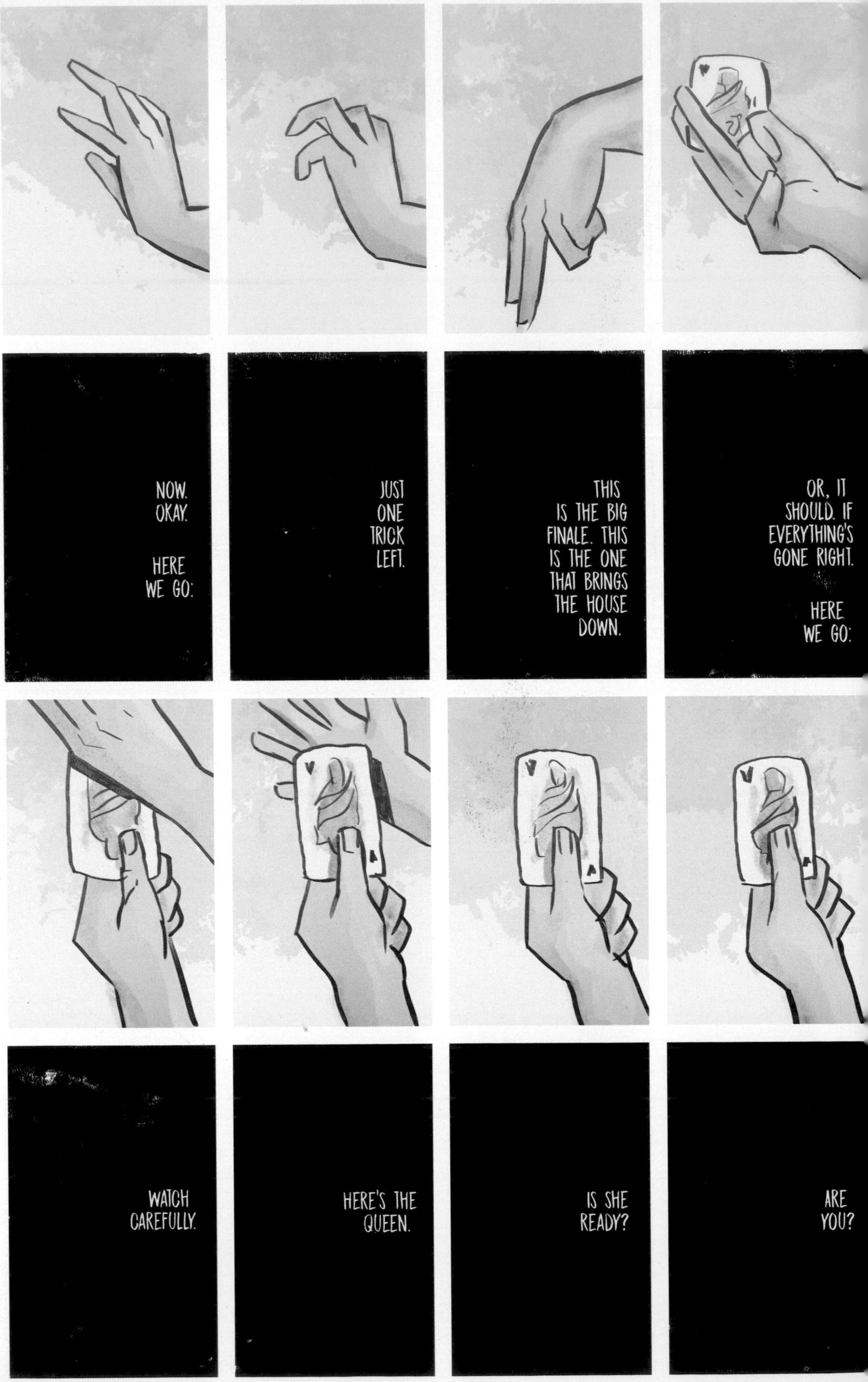
NOW. OKAY.
HERE WE GO:
JUST ONE TRICK LEFT.
THIS IS THE BIG FINALE. THIS IS THE ONE THAT BRINGS THE HOUSE DOWN.
OR, IT SHOULD. IF EVERYTHING'S GONE RIGHT.
HERE WE GO:
WATCH CAREFULLY.
HERE'S THE QUEEN.
IS SHE READY?
ARE YOU?

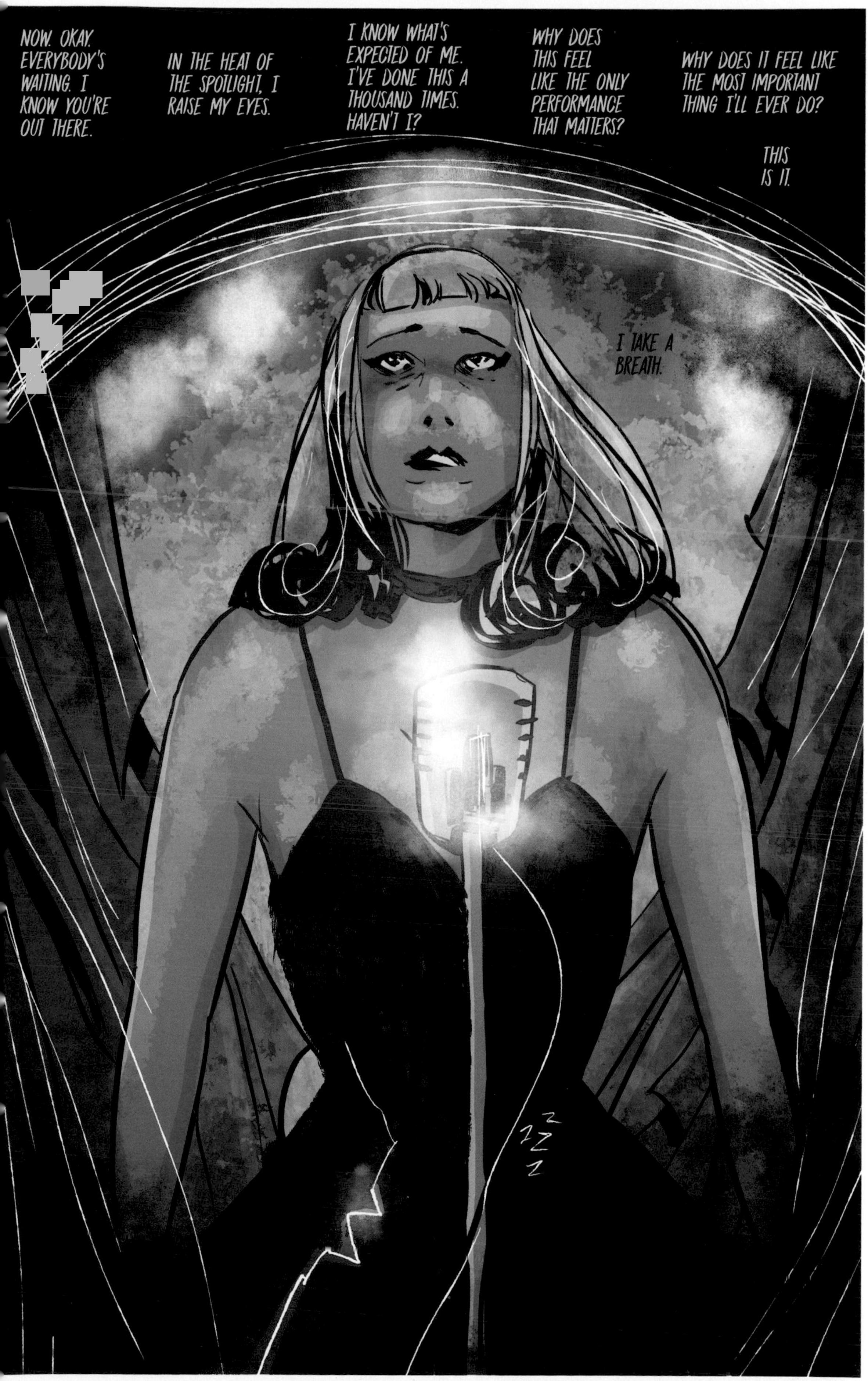
NOW. OKAY. EVERYBODY'S WAITING. I KNOW YOU'RE OUT THERE.
IN THE HEAT OF THE SPOTLIGHT, I RAISE MY EYES.
I KNOW WHAT'S EXPECTED OF ME. I'VE DONE THIS A THOUSAND TIMES. HAVEN'T I?
WHY DOES THIS FEEL LIKE THE ONLY PERFORMANCE THAT MATTERS?
WHY DOES IT FEEL LIKE THE MOST IMPORTANT THING I'LL EVER DO?
THIS IS IT.
I TAKE A BREATH.
ZZZZ

THIS IS IT.

IT'S COMING UP FASTER THAN EVER.

HOW--

INK BLACK AND COLD AS ICE.

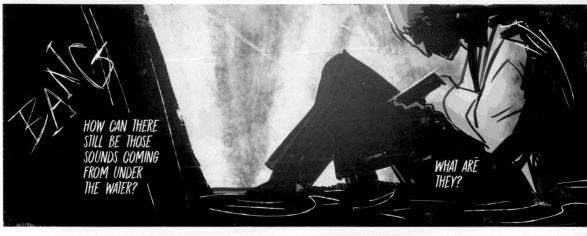

BANG

HOW CAN THERE STILL BE THOSE SOUNDS COMING FROM UNDER THE WATER?

WHAT ARE THEY?

SO COLD.

WHAT DO I DO?

BANG

WHAT DO I DO NOW?

BANG

I KNOW.

THERE'S A SKYLIGHT IN THE BATHROOM UP HERE. THE ONE OFF CLARA'S WORKSHOP.

COLD AND--

I KNOW WHAT THAT SOUND IS.

IT'S THE HOUSE.

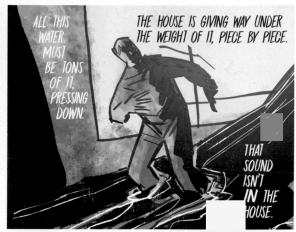

ALL THIS WATER. MUST BE TONS OF IT, PRESSING DOWN.

THE HOUSE IS GIVING WAY UNDER THE WEIGHT OF IT, PIECE BY PIECE.

THAT SOUND ISN'T IN THE HOUSE.

IT IS THE HOUSE.

I CAN STILL GET TO THE—

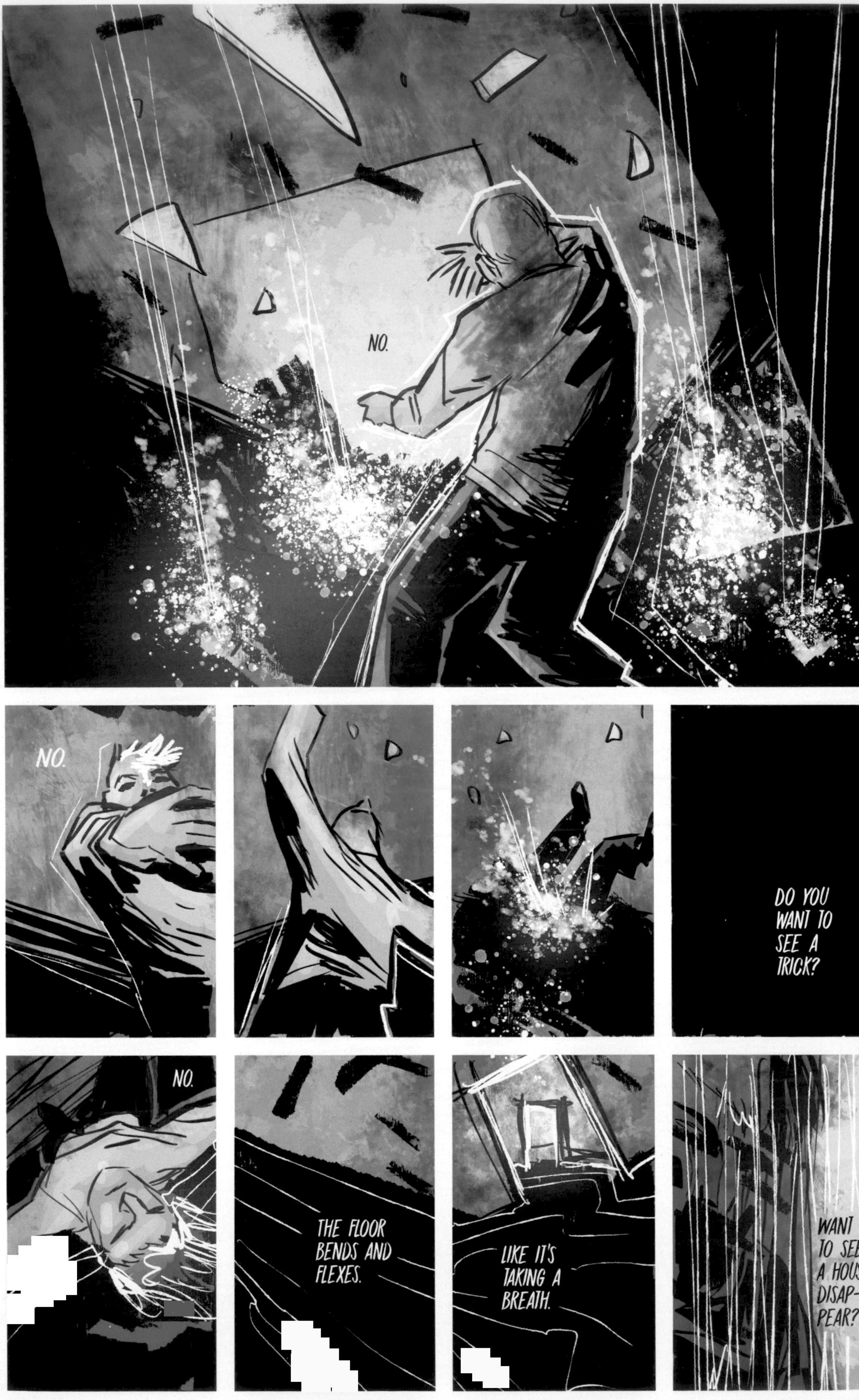
NO.
NO.
DO YOU WANT TO SEE A TRICK?
NO.
THE FLOOR BENDS AND FLEXES.
LIKE IT'S TAKING A BREATH.
WANT TO SEE A HOUSE DISAP- PEAR?

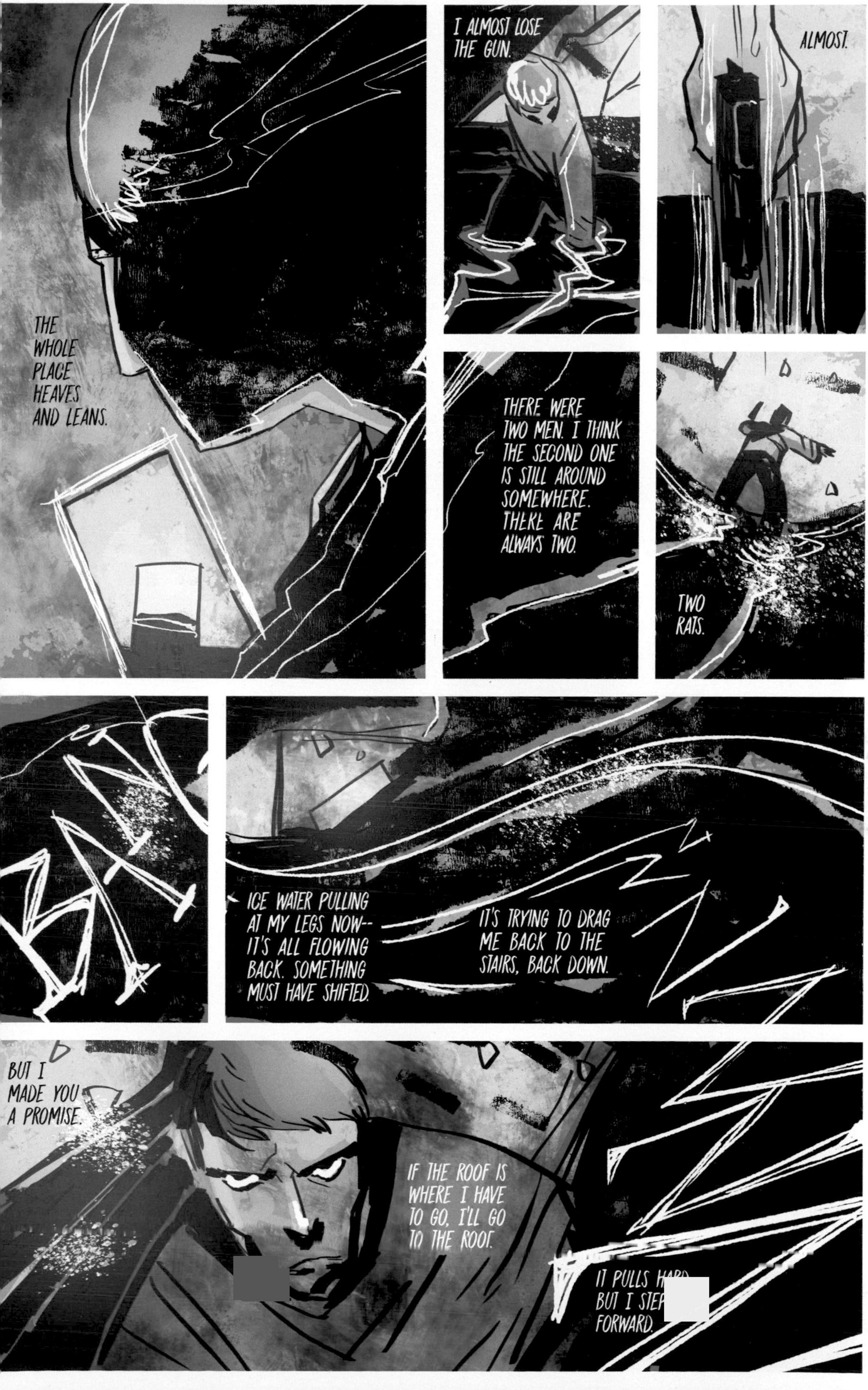
THE WHOLE PLACE HEAVES AND LEANS.
I ALMOST LOSE THE GUN.
ALMOST.
THERE WERE TWO MEN. I THINK THE SECOND ONE IS STILL AROUND SOMEWHERE. THERE ARE ALWAYS TWO.
TWO RATS.
ICE WATER PULLING AT MY LEGS NOW-- IT'S ALL FLOWING BACK. SOMETHING MUST HAVE SHIFTED.
IT'S TRYING TO DRAG ME BACK TO THE STAIRS, BACK DOWN.
BUT I MADE YOU A PROMISE.
IF THE ROOF IS WHERE I HAVE TO GO, I'LL GO TO THE ROOF.
IT PULLS HA
BUT I STE
FORWARD.

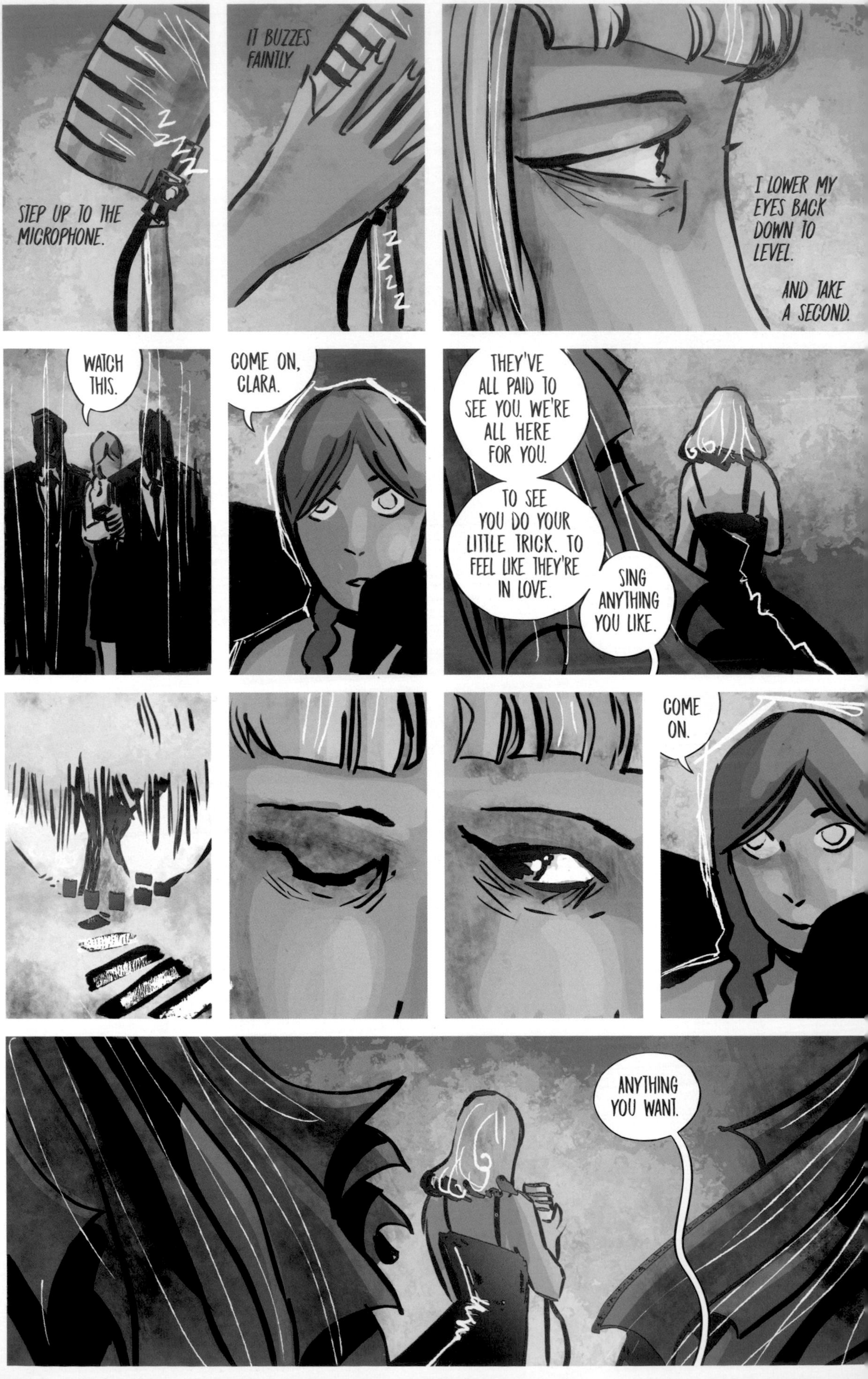
STEP UP TO THE MICROPHONE.
IT BUZZES FAINTLY.
I LOWER MY EYES BACK DOWN TO LEVEL.
AND TAKE A SECOND.
WATCH THIS.
COME ON, CLARA.
THEY'VE ALL PAID TO SEE YOU. WE'RE ALL HERE FOR YOU.
TO SEE YOU DO YOUR LITTLE TRICK. TO FEEL LIKE THEY'RE IN LOVE.
SING ANYTHING YOU LIKE.
COME ON.
ANYTHING YOU WANT.

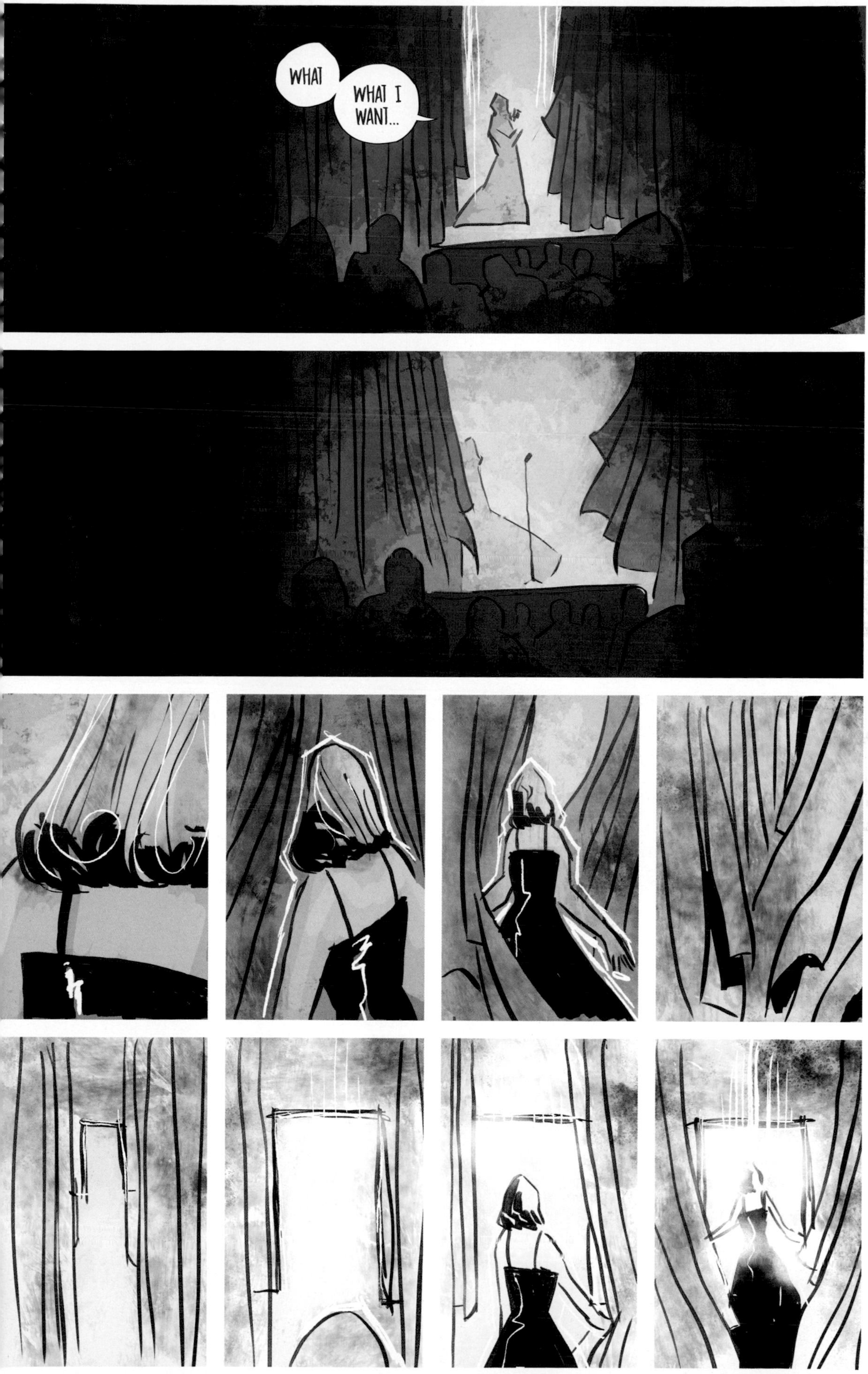
WHAT
WHAT I WANT...

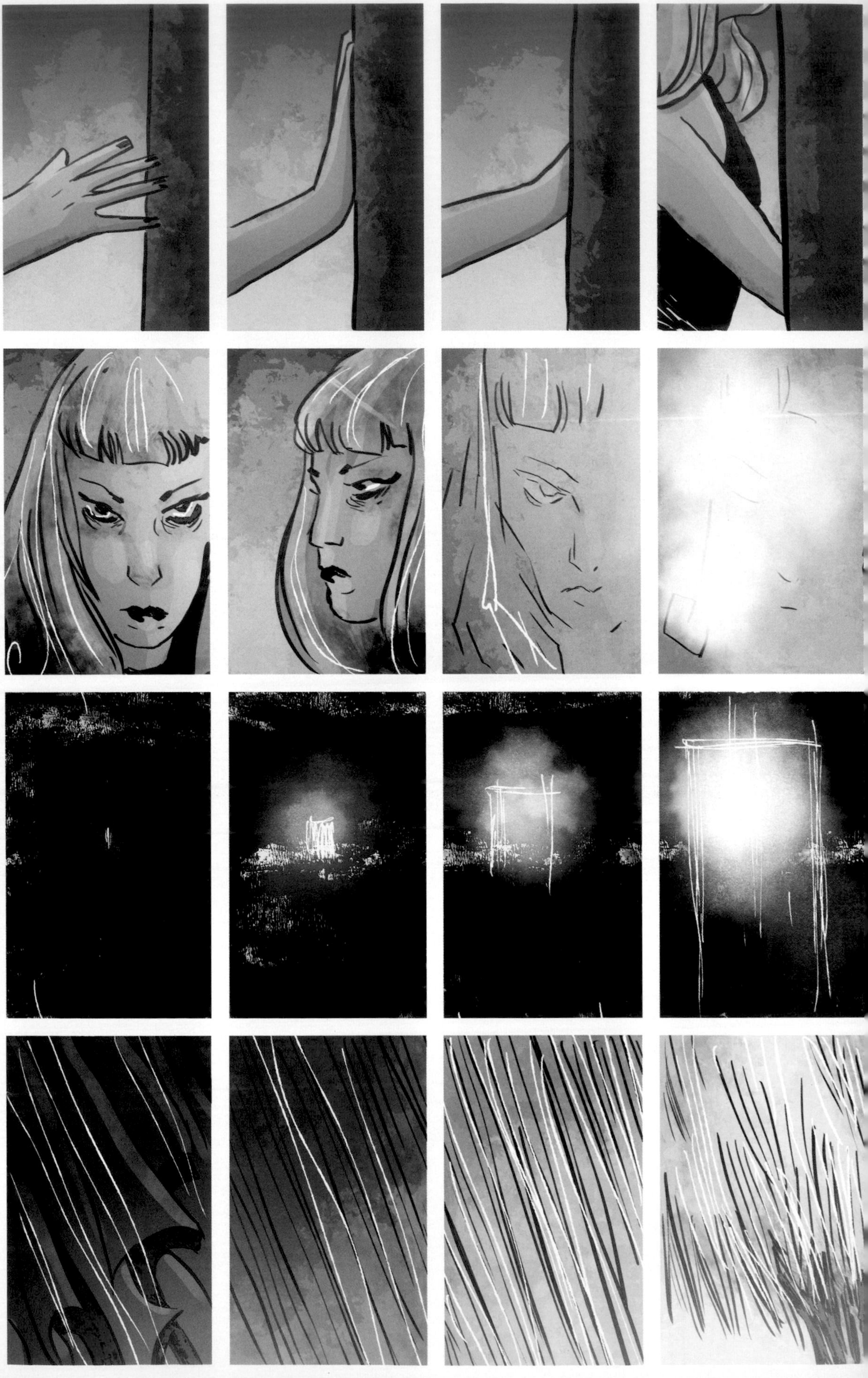

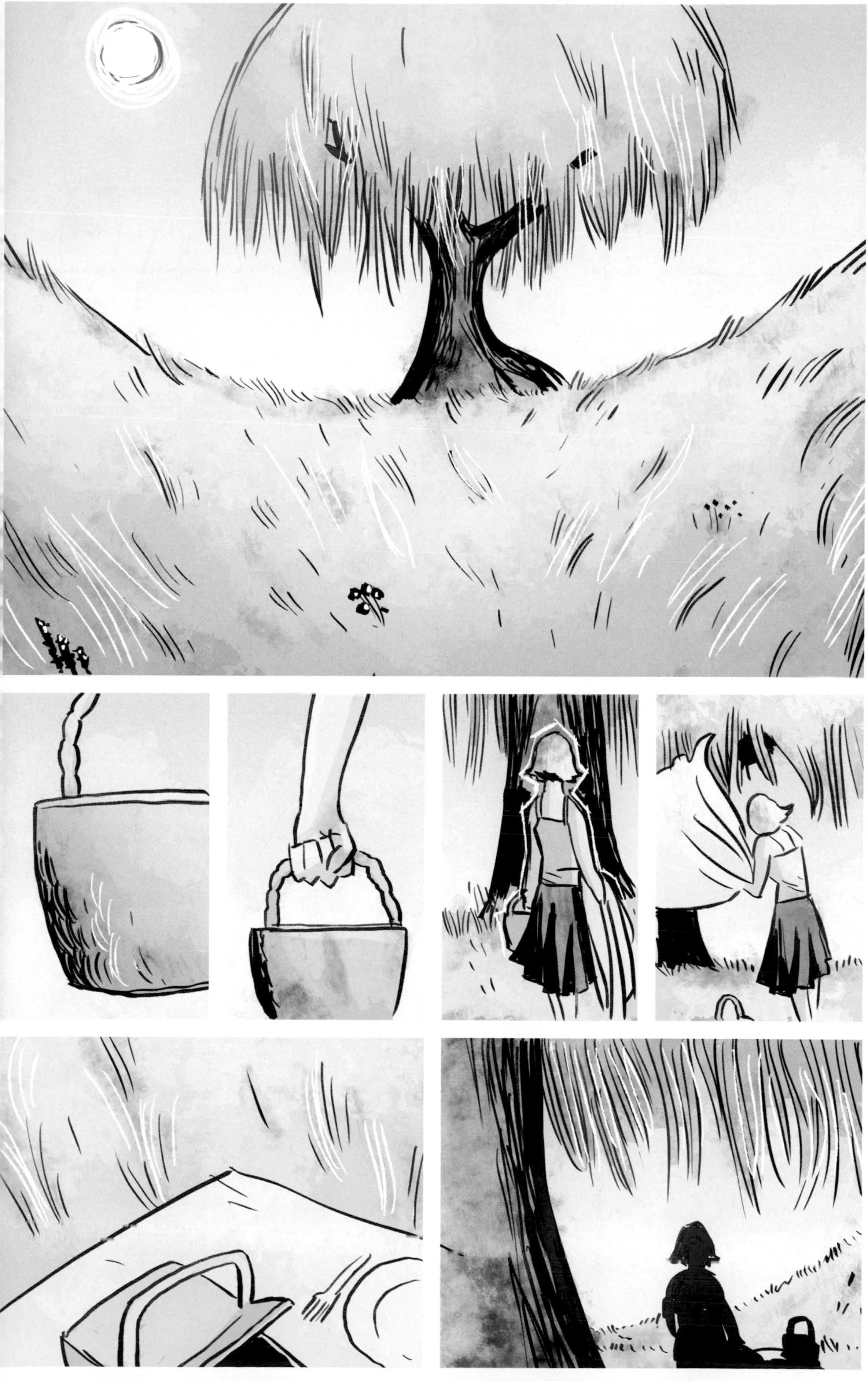

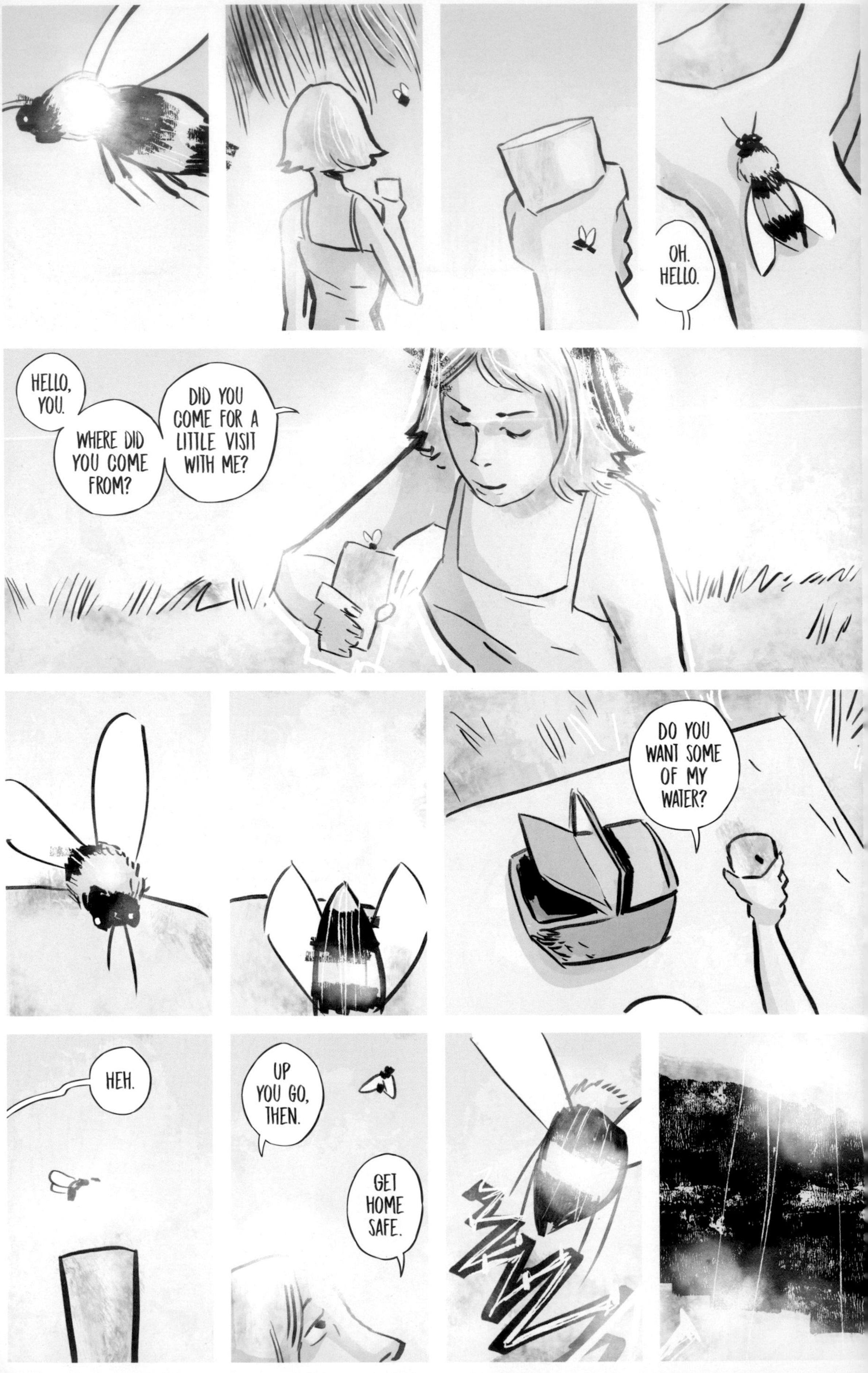
OH.
HELLO.
HELLO,
YOU.
WHERE DID
YOU COME
FROM?
DID YOU
COME FOR A
LITTLE VISIT
WITH ME?
DO YOU
WANT SOME
OF MY
WATER?
HEH.
UP
YOU GO,
THEN.
GET
HOME
SAFE.

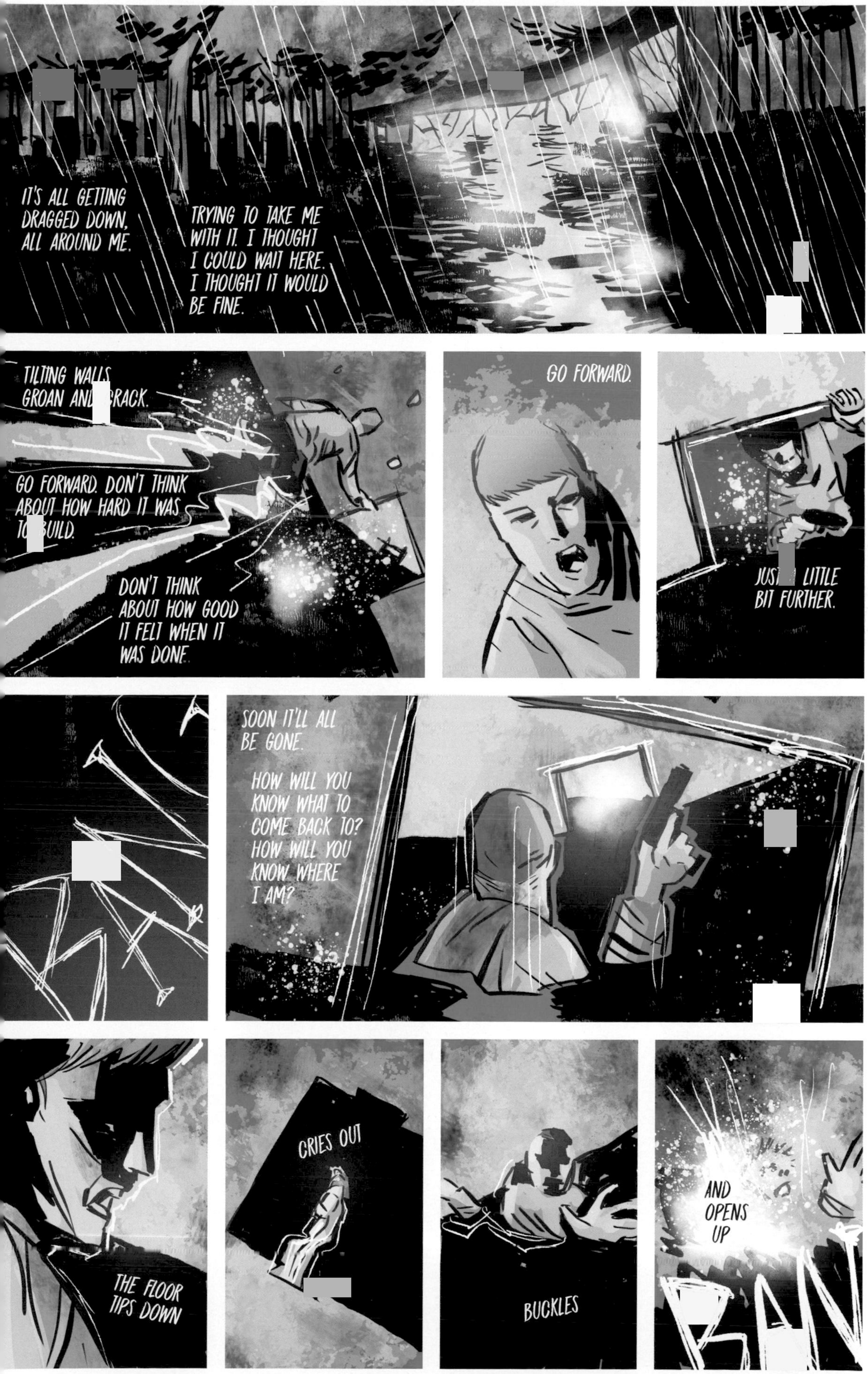

IT'S ALL GETTING DRAGGED DOWN, ALL AROUND ME.
TRYING TO TAKE ME WITH IT. I THOUGHT I COULD WAIT HERE. I THOUGHT IT WOULD BE FINE.
TILTING WALLS GROAN AND CRACK.
GO FORWARD. DON'T THINK ABOUT HOW HARD IT WAS TO BUILD.
DON'T THINK ABOUT HOW GOOD IT FELT WHEN IT WAS DONE.
GO FORWARD.
JUST A LITTLE BIT FURTHER.
SOON IT'LL ALL BE GONE.
HOW WILL YOU KNOW WHAT TO COME BACK TO? HOW WILL YOU KNOW WHERE I AM?
THE FLOOR TIPS DOWN
CRIES OUT
BUCKLES
AND OPENS UP

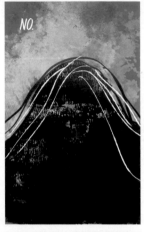

NO.

NO!

I WON'T LET IT DISAPPEAR.

I'LL BE HERE.

ON THE ROOF IF I HAVE TO.

IN THE TREETOPS IF I HAVE TO.

I'M RIGHT HERE. DON'T WORRY.

ONE STEP AT A TIME.

FIND THE BOAT THOSE TWO MEN CAME IN IF I HAVE TO.

I MADE IT TO THE SKYLIGHT. CLARA, I MADE IT.

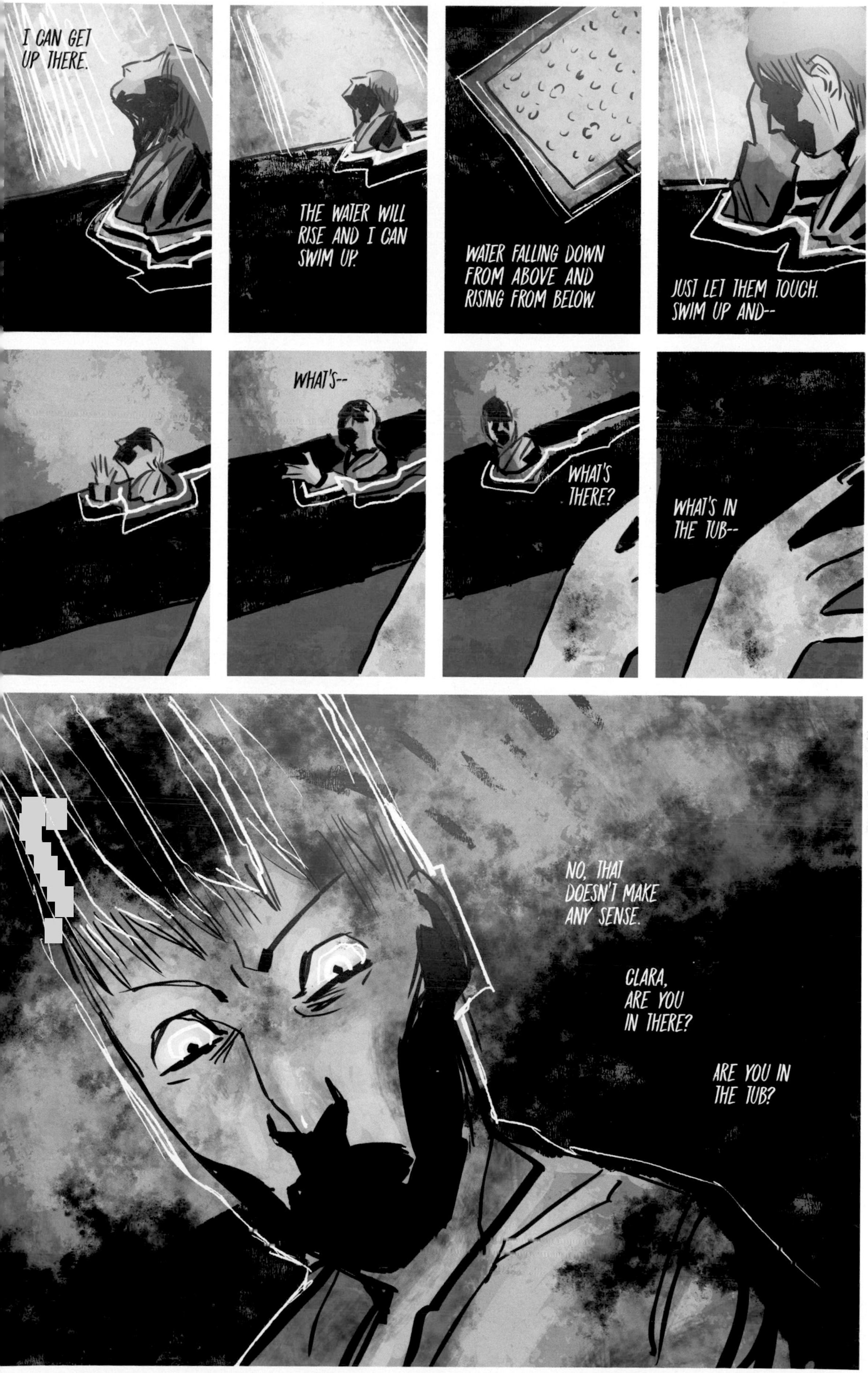
I CAN GET UP THERE.
THE WATER WILL RISE AND I CAN SWIM UP.
WATER FALLING DOWN FROM ABOVE AND RISING FROM BELOW.
JUST LET THEM TOUCH. SWIM UP AND--
WHAT'S--
WHAT'S THERE?
WHAT'S IN THE TUB--
NO, THAT DOESN'T MAKE ANY SENSE.
CLARA, ARE YOU IN THERE?
ARE YOU IN THE TUB?

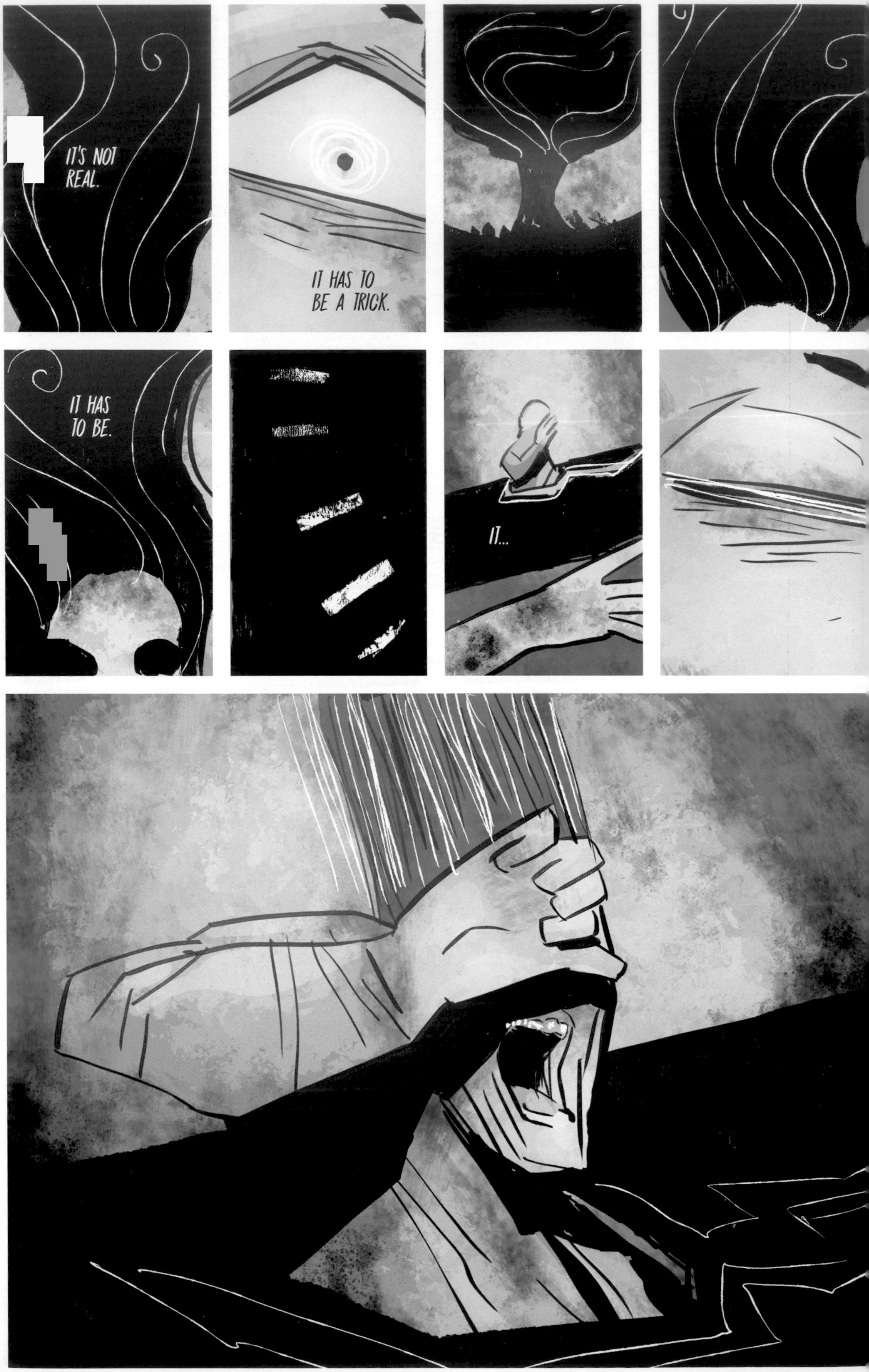
IT'S NOT REAL.
IT HAS TO BE A TRICK.
IT HAS TO BE.
IT...

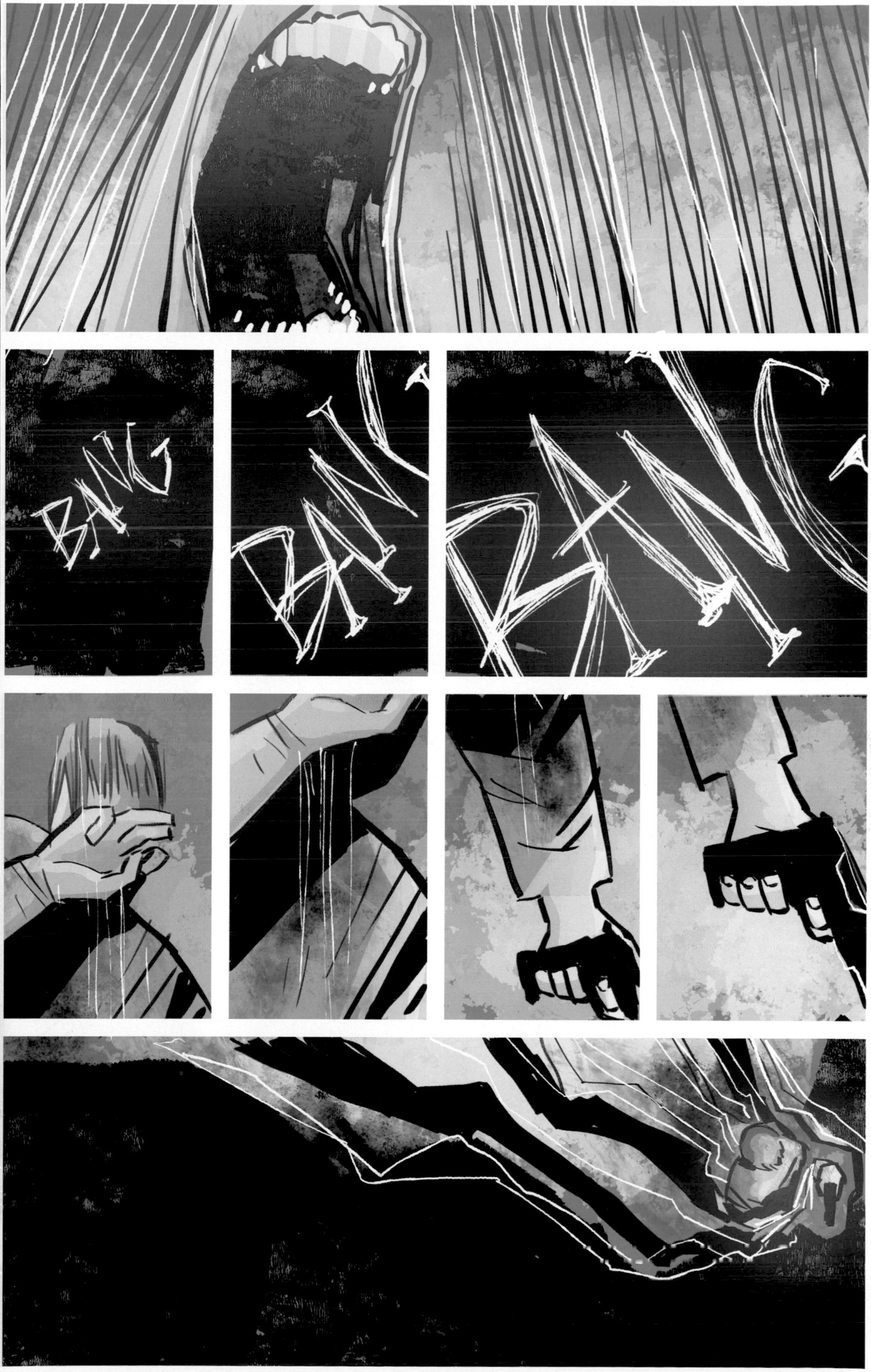
BANG
BAN
BANG

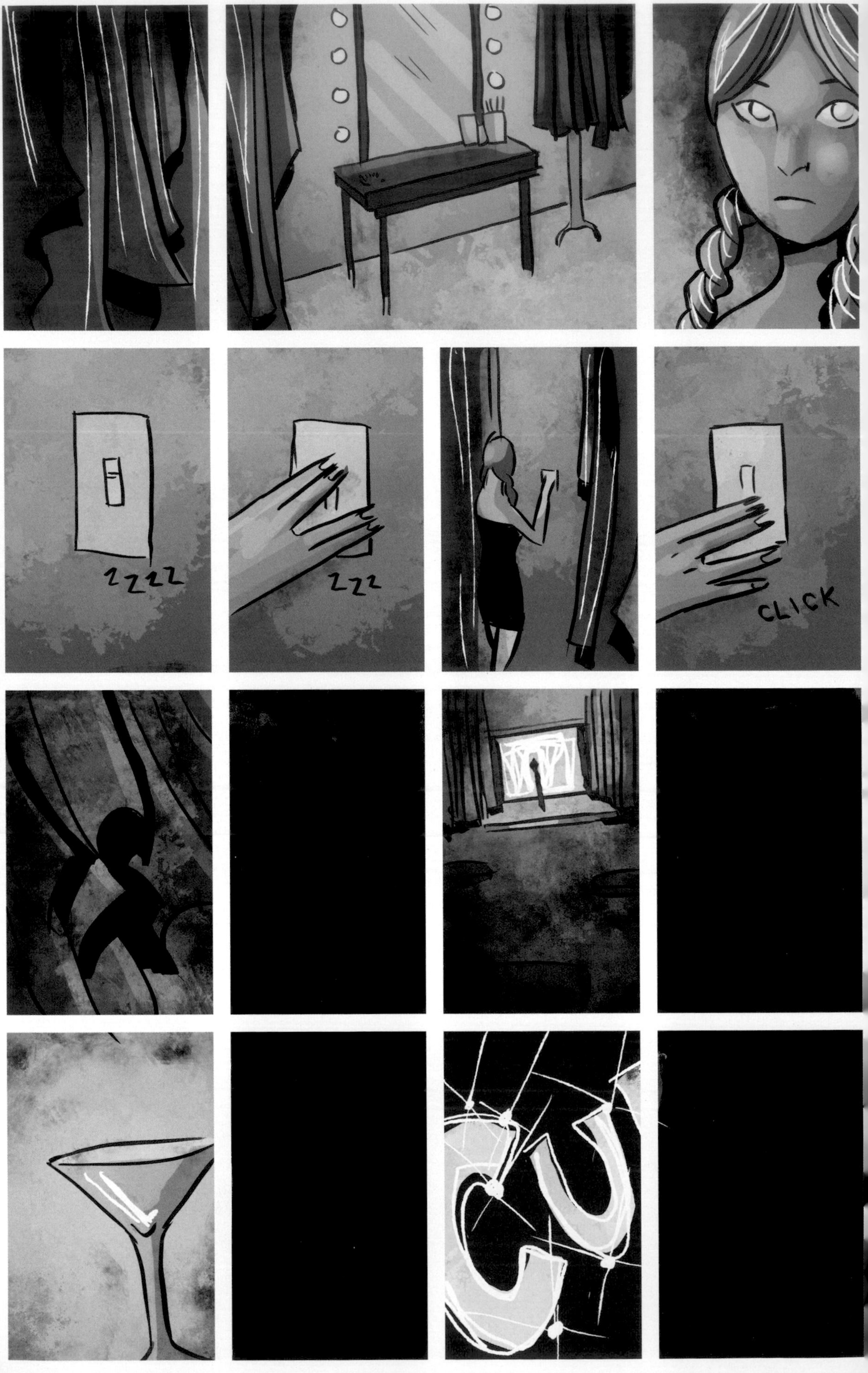
ZZZZ
ZZZ
CLICK

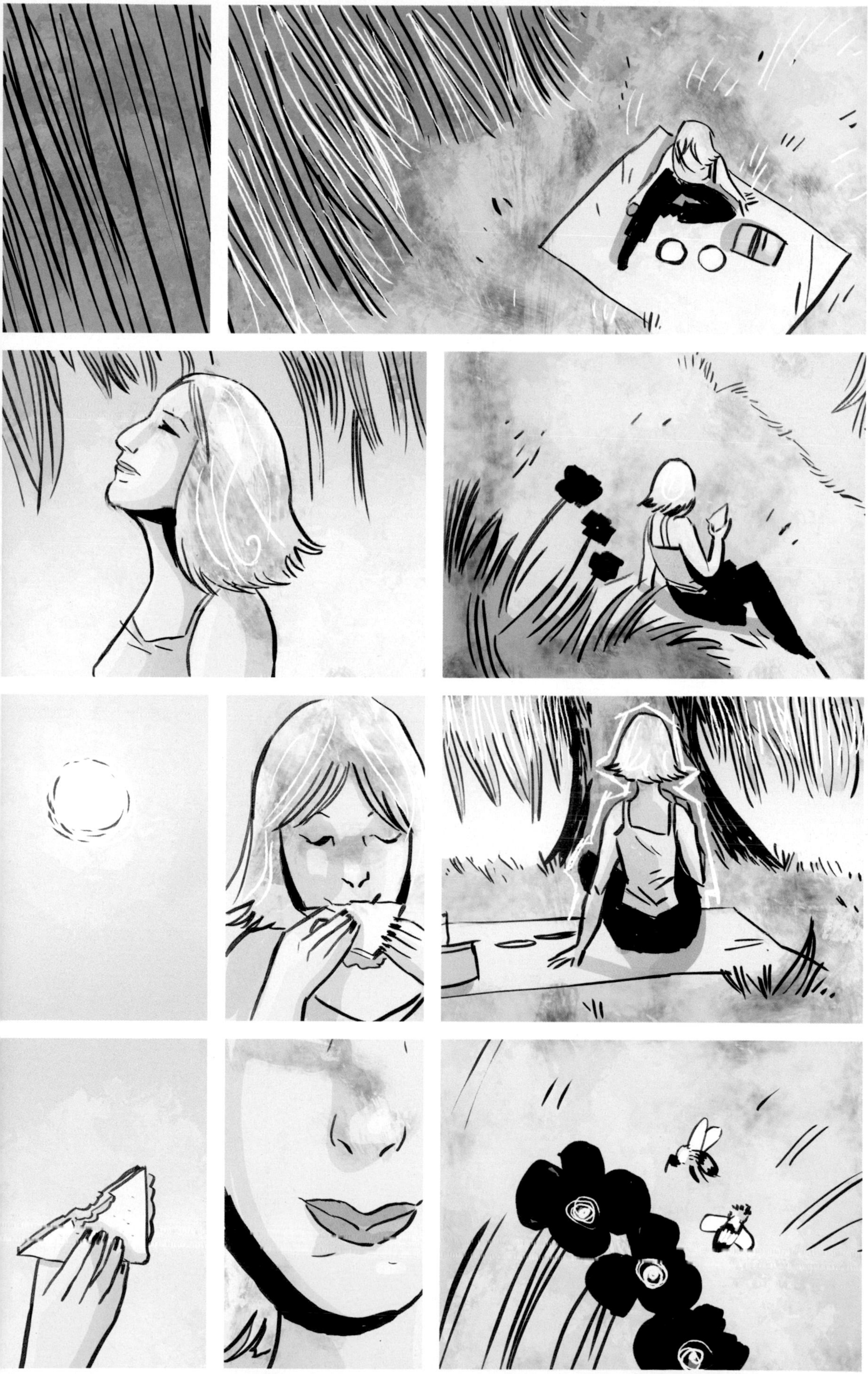

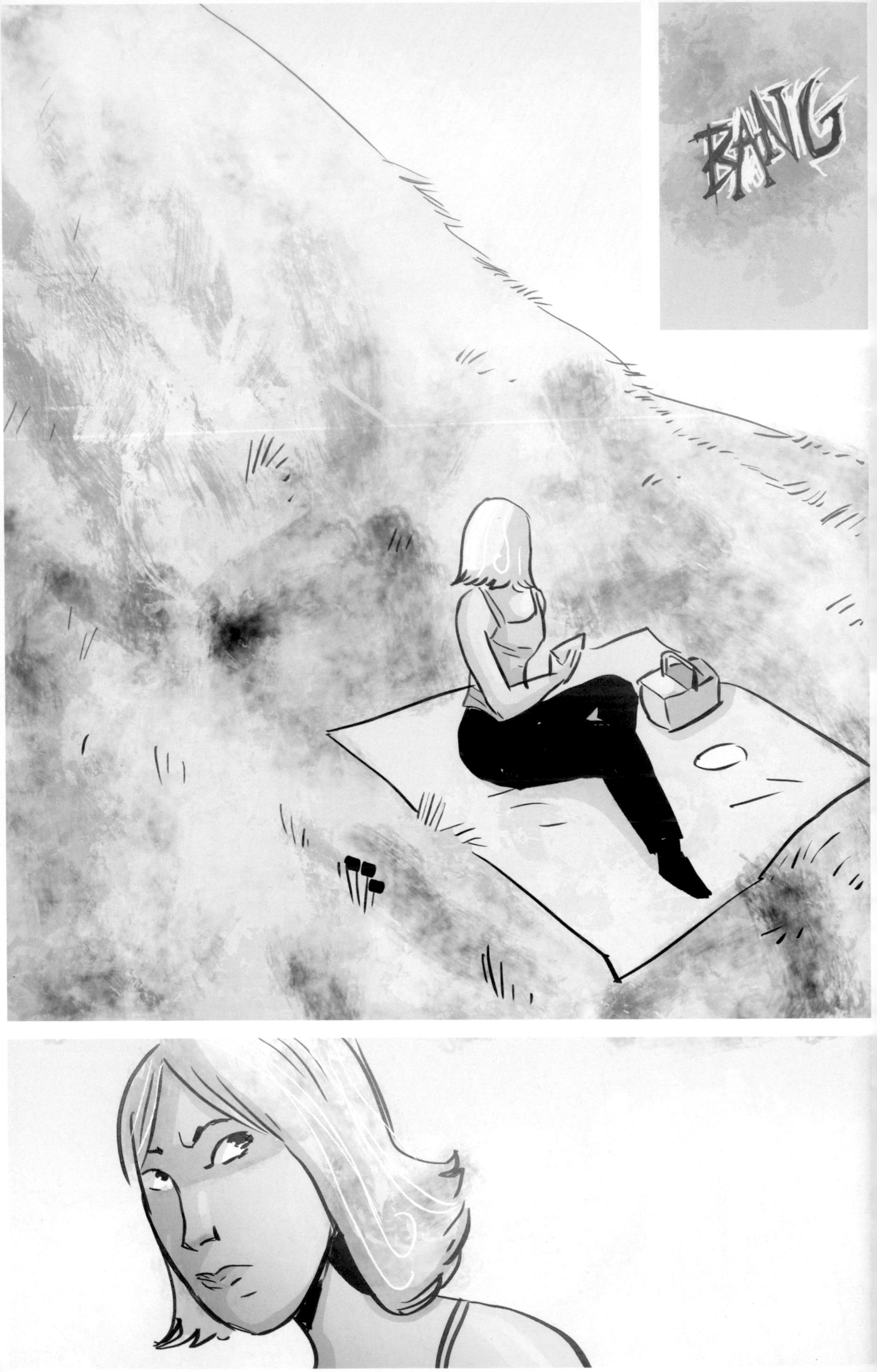
BANG

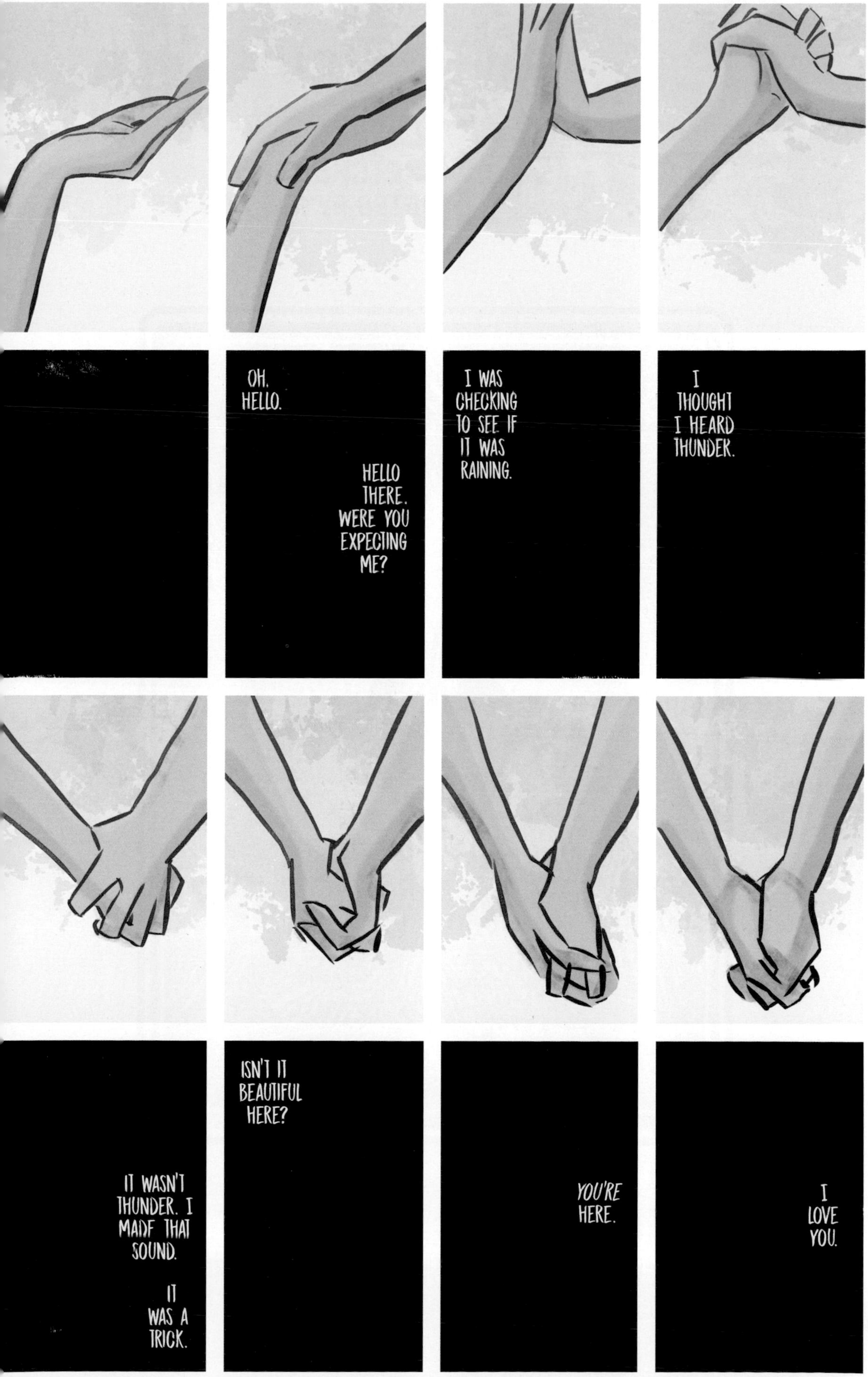
OH. HELLO.
HELLO THERE. WERE YOU EXPECTING ME?
I WAS CHECKING TO SEE IF IT WAS RAINING.
I THOUGHT I HEARD THUNDER.
IT WASN'T THUNDER. I MADE THAT SOUND.
IT WAS A TRICK.
ISN'T IT BEAUTIFUL HERE?
YOU'RE HERE.
I LOVE YOU.

IN THE FLOOD

SKETCHBOOK
NOTES BY RAY FAWKES

This was an early mood piece for the project—just a sketch as I worked up the idea for the book, focused on the submerged tree, mirroring it to represent the worlds of the story. Though I ended up abandoning it, the icon of the mirrored tree stuck with me for a while, and I kept this sketch on the wall over the drawing table while I worked.

The first drawing I did of the tree—in fact, I think it was the first drawing I did for this project.

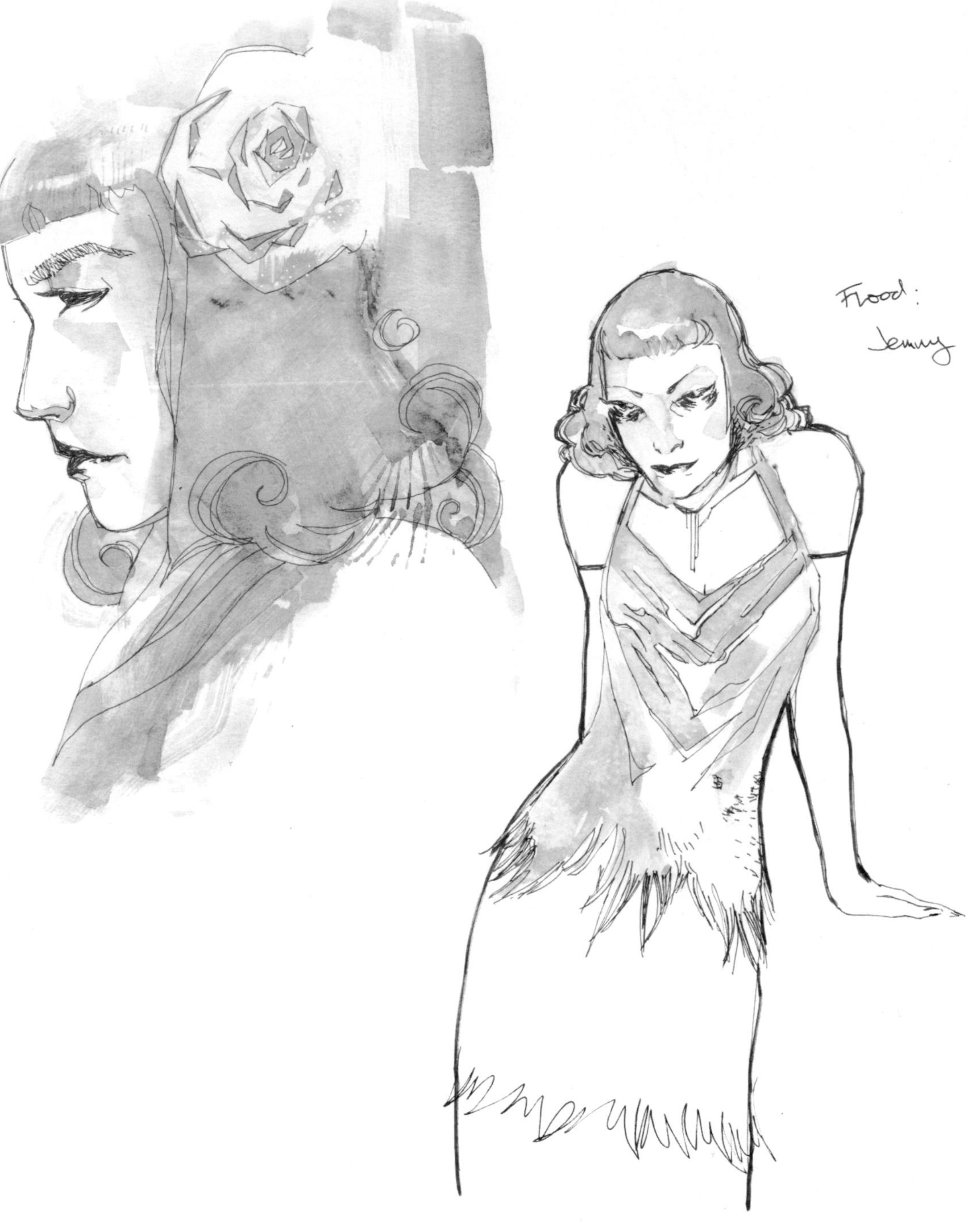
Flood:
Jenny

While the design for Mike seemed to come easily (maybe because he spends so much time in deep shadows), I had to get the ideas to gel more in order to pull Clara together. I wanted her to be glamorous, but subdued—as if the world is working to dim her light. Her hair changed length, her makeup and accessories became more ornate and then less again, and eventually I was happy.

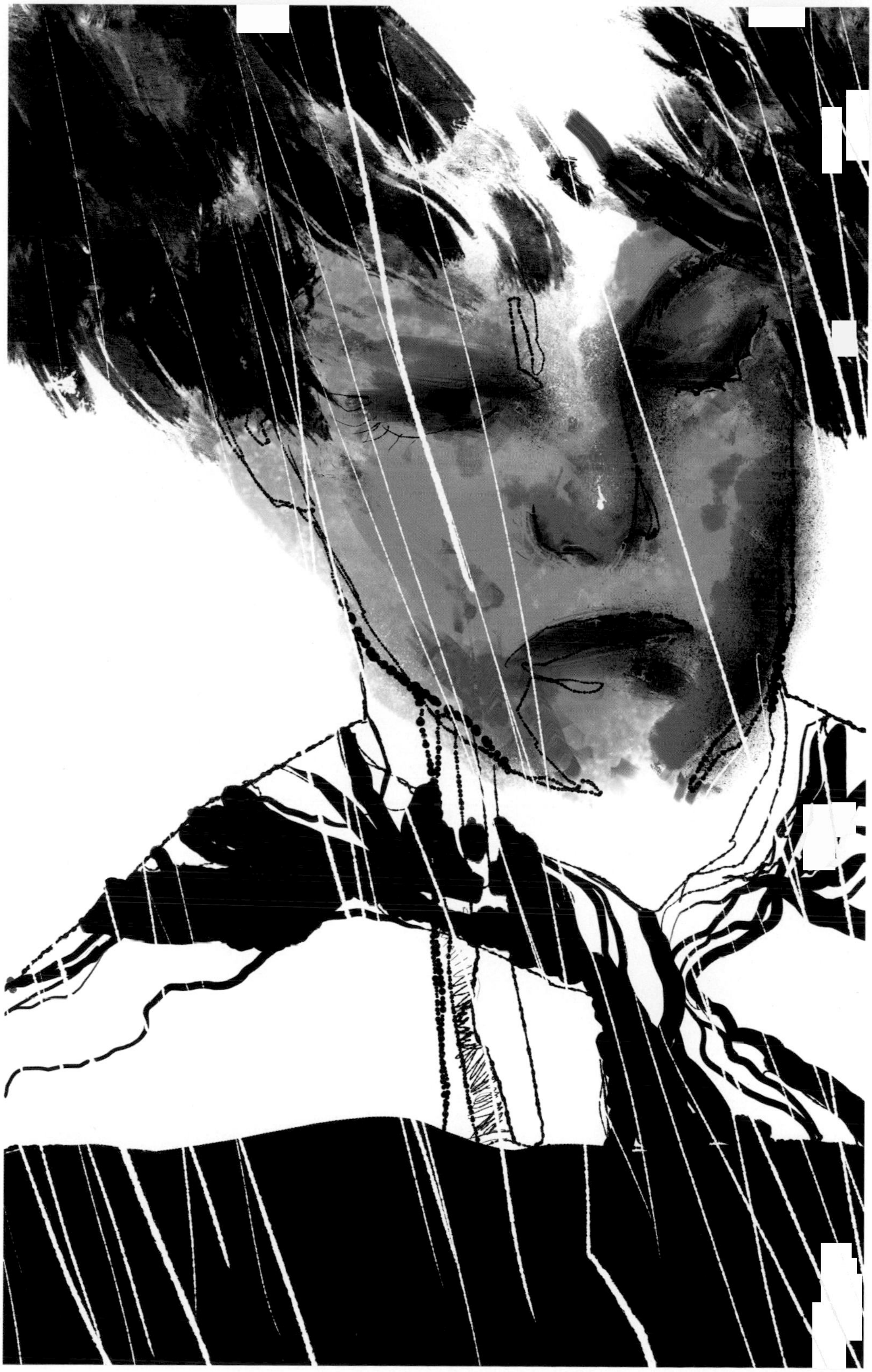

When I began drawing the actual pages of the book, I went for a more rendered, painterly style—as this original version of page 1 demonstrates. But I felt that the rendering was actually deadening the feel I was going for a bit—and I left this look behind and went for a flatter, heavier ink-brayer-and-pen feel.

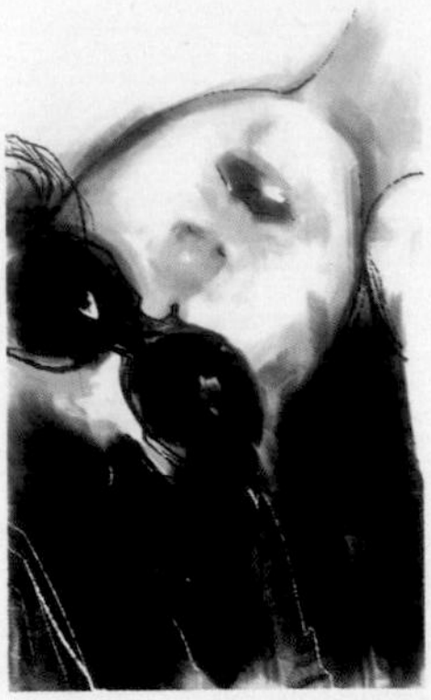

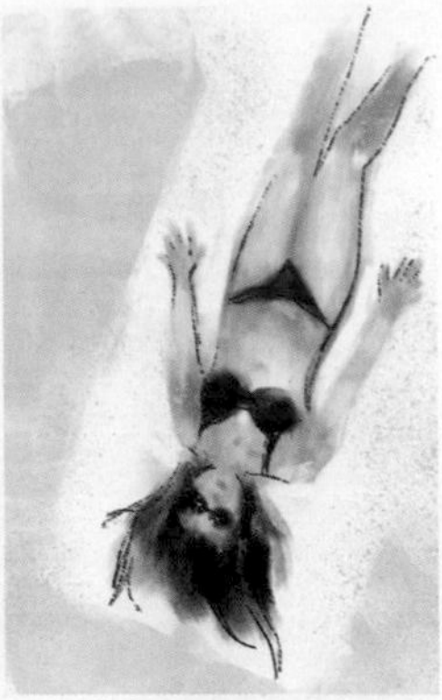

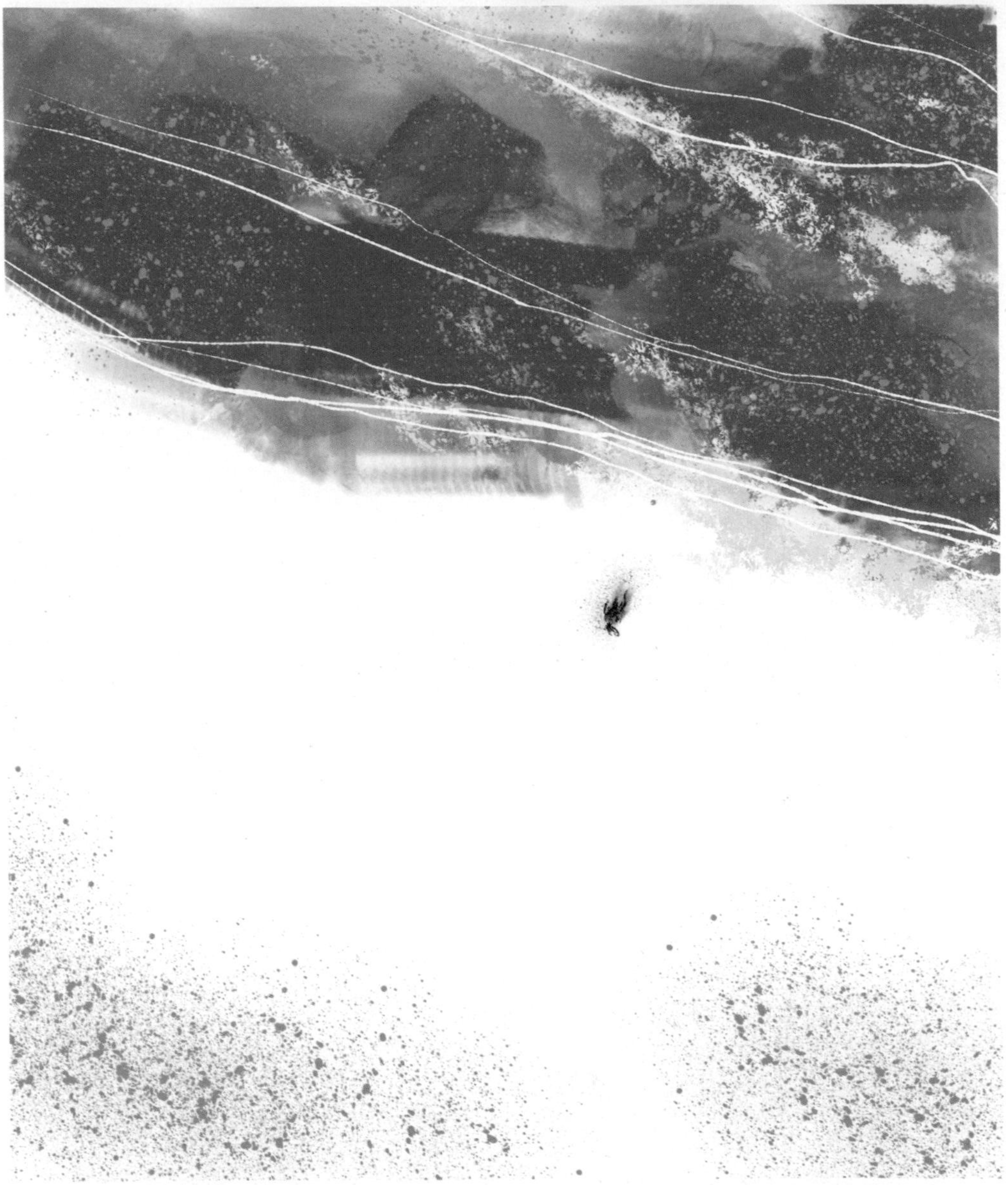

Back when I was working in the more painterly style, the script had Clara on a beach instead of inside a nightclub. That was quickly scrapped when I started drawing the pages and realized that I wanted to do a lot with the light and dark that a beach setting didn't provide (without some contortions that I didn't feel like adding to the script). Of course, once I shifted the setting, a lot of things ended up changing anyway and it was just as much work. So it goes!

ABOUT THE AUTHORS

RAY FAWKES IS THE TORONTO-BASED AUTHOR OF MANY COMICS AND GRAPHIC NOVELS, INCLUDING **ONE SOUL, UNDERWINTER,** AND **GOTHAM BY MIDNIGHT.** HE IS AN EISNER, HARVEY, AND SHUSTER AWARD NOMINEE AND A YALSA AWARD WINNER. HE'S BEEN MAKING COMICS FOR OVER 20 YEARS, STARTING WITH AND CONTINUING THE TRADITION OF INDEPENDENT DIY FICTION AS WELL AS WORKING FOR MANY MAJOR COMICS PUBLISHERS IN THE U.S. AND CANADA.

LEE LOUGHRIDGE IS A DEVILISHLY HANDSOME MAN, DESPITE HIS EVER DEPLETING TESTOSTERONE, WHO HAS BEEN WORKING PRIMARILY IN THE COMICS INDUSTRY FOR WELL OVER 20 YEARS. HE HAS WORKED ON HUNDREDS OF TITLES FOR VIRTUALLY EVERY COMPANY IN THE BUSINESS.

THOMAS MAUER HAS LENT HIS LETTERING AND DESIGN TALENT TO NUMEROUS CRITICALLY ACCLAIMED AND AWARD-WINNING PROJECTS. AMONG HIS RECENT WORK ARE COMIXOLOGY ORIGINALS' **THE DARK,** AFTERSHOCK COMICS' **DEAD KINGS,** AND IMAGE COMICS' **CRUDE, HARDCORE, THE BEAUTY,** AND **THE REALM.**

COMIXOLOGY COMES TO DARK HORSE BOOKS!

JASON LOO
CHIP ZDARSKY
PARIS ALLEYNE ADITYA BIDIKAR ALLISON O'TOOLE
AFTERLIFT

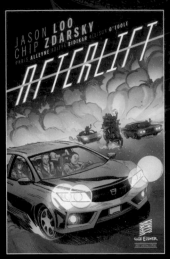

ISBN 978-1-50672-440-9 / $19.99

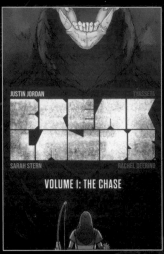

JUSTIN JORDAN
TYASSETA
BREAK
LANDS
SARAH STERN
RACHEL DEERING
VOLUME I: THE CHASE

ISBN 978-1-50672-441-6 / $19.99

curt pires
alex diotto
dee cunniffe
micah myers
Youth
"Bold, genre-defying and heartfelt. Youth hits a reader like the meteor in its own pages: an angry, wondrous and transformative book." —Scott Snyder (Batman, Justice League)

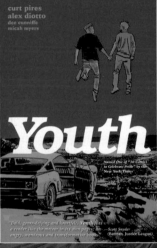

ISBN 978-1-50672-461-4 / $19.99

GHOST
HARD REVOLUTION

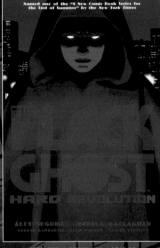

ISBN 978-1-50672-446-1 / $19.99

THE
PRIDE
OMNIBUS

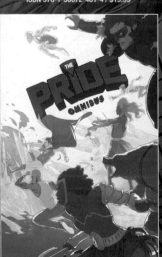

ISBN 978-1-50672-447-8 / $29.99

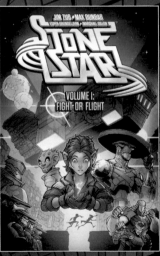

JIM ZUB MAX DUNBAR
STONE
STAR
VOLUME I:
FIGHT OR FLIGHT

ISBN 978-1-50672-458-4 / $19.99

AFTERLIFT

Written by Chip Zdarsky, art by Jason Loo

This Eisner Award–winning series from Chip Zdarsky (*Sex Criminals*, Daredevil) and Jason Loo (*The Pitiful Human-Lizard*) features car chases, demon bounty hunters, and figuring out your place in this world and the next.

BREAKLANDS

Written by Justin Jordan, art by Tyasseta and Sarah Stern

Generations after the end of the civilization, everyone has powers; you need them just to survive in the new age. Everyone except Kasa Fain. Unfortunately, her little brother, who has the potential to reshape the world, is kidnapped by people who intend to do just that. *Mad Max* meets *Akira* in a genre-mashing, expectation-smashing new hit series from Justin Jordan, creator of *Luther Strode*, *Spread*, and *Reaver*!

YOUTH

Written by Curt Pires, art by Alex Diotto and Dee Cunniffe

A coming of age story of two queer teenagers who run away from their lives in a bigoted small town, and attempt to make their way to California. Along the way their car breaks down and they join a group of fellow misfits on the road. travelling the country together in a van, they party and attempt to find themselves. And then . . . something happens. The story combines the violence of coming of age with the violence of the superhero narrative—as well as the beauty.

THE BLACK GHOST SEASON ONE: HARD REVOLUTION

Written by Alex Segura and Monica Gallagher, art by George Kambadais

Meet Lara Dominguez—a troubled Creighton cops reporter obsessed with the city's debonair vigilante the Black Ghost. With the help of a mysterious cyberinformant named LONE, Lara's inched closer to uncovering the Ghost's identity. But as she searches for the breakthrough story she desperately needs, Lara will have to navigate the corruption of her city, the uncertainties of virtues, and her own personal demons. Will she have the strength to be part of the solution—or will she become the problem?

THE PRIDE OMNIBUS

Joseph Glass, Gavin Mitchell and Cem Iroz

FabMan is sick of being seen as a joke. Tired of the LGBTQ+ community being seen as inferior to straight heroes, he thinks it's about damn time he did something about it. Bringing together some of the world's greatest LGBTQ+ superheroes, the Pride is born to protect the world and fight prejudice, misrepresentation and injustice—not to mention a pesky supervillain or two.

STONE STAR

Jim Zub and Max Zunbar

The brand-new space-fantasy saga that takes flight on comiXology Originals from fan-favorite creators Jim Zub (*Avengers*, *Samurai Jack*) and Max Dunbar (*Champions*, *Dungeons & Dragons*)! The nomadic space station called Stone Star brings gladiatorial entertainment to ports across the galaxy. Inside this gargantuan vessel of tournaments and temptations, foragers and fighters struggle to survive. A young thief named Dail discovers a dark secret in the depths of Stone Star and must decide his destiny—staying hidden in the shadows or standing tall in the searing spotlight of the arena. Either way, his life and the cosmos itself, will never be the same!

AVAILABLE AT YOUR LOCAL COMICS SHOP OR BOOKSTORE / To find a comics shop near you, visit comicshoplocator.com / For more information or to order direct, visit darkhorse.com

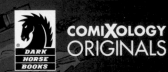

DARK HORSE BOOKS

COMIXOLOGY ORIGINALS